The Way to Hudson Bay

THORKILD HANSEN

The Way to Hudson Bay

The Life and Times of Jens Munk

Translated by
James McFarlane and John Lynch

Published in Great Britain under the title
North West to Hudson Bay

A Helen and Kurt Wolff Book
Harcourt, Brace & World, Inc.
NEW YORK

The English translation is a somewhat abridged version of the
Danish original, Jens Munk

First American edition

Library of Congress Catalog Card Number: 76-95854

Printed in the United States of America

Contents

1 The Journal 9
2 Three Cocks' Gules upon a Field Azure 20
3 Dreams of the New World 37
4 Can We See by Night? 47
5 Larder and Cellar 56
6 Hafnia Metropolis et Portus Celeberrimus
  Daniae 62
7 "What care I for the moon, while the sun is
  shining?" 68
8 A Certain Christian Frederiksen 85
9 The Ships in Krabbeløkke Bay 109
10 Captain in the Royal Navy 120
11 The Storming of Elfsborg 132
12 The Neighbor's Daughter 145
13 The First Retort 164
14 Ove Giedde 180
15 Almighty God in Heaven 196
16 The Wintry Road 220
17 Munk Haven 249
18 The Days Grow Longer 268
19 The Lamprey 284
20 The Captain and the King 312

INDEX 345

List of Illustrations and Maps

Jens Munk's testament   13
The frigate *Norwegian Lion*   17
Erik Munk's coat of arms   27
Map of Scandinavia, 1567   30
Ships off Kronborg   41
Map of the bay of Bahia   53
Dragsholm from the west   58
Dutch man-of-war   59
Hafnia Metropolis Celeberrima, the inner harbor   65
Willem Barents's ships   79
Pink ice-bound off Novaya Zemlya   83
Christian Frederiksen   89
A Russian lodie, 1595   95
Polar-bear hunt on the Barents Sea. Winter   97
Polar-bear hunt on the Barents Sea. Summer   99
The Kildin harbor with ships, huts, and stockfish   107
A launching on Bremerholm   111
Bremerholm   113
A man-of-war on the open sea   116
Life on the gun deck   122
The siege of Elfsborg   139
Elfsborg after its reconstruction   141
Basque whalers   183
Whalers off Spitsbergen   185
Hessel Gerritszoon's chart of the North
    Atlantic and Hudson Bay   200

Ships in Tøjhushavnen   215
Modern map of the Northwest Passage   223
Pink in trouble in the pack ice   233
The *Unicorn* and the *Lamprey* in Reindeer Sound   239
The Cape of Good Hope   242
The *Unicorn* and the *Lamprey* in Munk Haven   253
Old map of Ceylon   283
Christian IV's handwriting   286
Jens Munk's map of Hudson Bay   297
Seaman making his way out along the bowsprit
    in rough seas   306
The harbor at Bergen and Bergenhus   309
Christian IV sending Jens Munk back to
    Hudson Bay   315
Last meeting between the King and the captain   329

1

The Journal

On Whitsunday, June 4th, in the Year of our Redemption 1620, the white snow field extended unbroken toward the northern horizon. No rifts, no patch of blue water anywhere to glitter in the light. Hudson Bay was a flat and desolate dance floor where here and there the wind danced with a ghost.

Within the river mouth two Danish ships were caught fast in the ice. The smaller of them, the sloop *Lamprey*, was moored inshore, while the frigate *Unicorn* lay listing a hundred and twenty fathoms from land. Around its tar-daubed sides the pack ice gathered like a ruff; from the quarter-deck an incessant pounding resounded.

Ashore, the snow lay deep among the wooden huts. The gray goose had begun migrating north; great flocks of birds flew unmolested overhead. No man raised his musket in the hope of a tasty morsel, only the dead were there. Fifty wooden crosses stood planted in the snow. And stretched out on the ice between the larger ship and the shore lay the men without a cross. Some were half covered by snowdrifts. They looked as though, lacking a proper grave, they had tried to draw a white eiderdown over them against the cold. Still, as Movritz Stygge had already observed on a cold April day as he stood, left almost alone, with his ravaged hands on the rail, looking out over the crosses: "The dead don't feel the cold. On

9

the contrary. There's probably more than one poor devil among them who wishes it wasn't quite so hot where he is now."

This was spoken on April 7, 1620. Five days later three new wooden crosses were prepared on board, one of them for Herr Movritz.

That had been some time ago. Now it was quite still here in Hudson Bay. The only sound heard on that long Whitsunday was a regular knocking from the larger ship where a piece of rigging had come loose and a tackle clattered against the side of the sterncastle at short intervals. Nearby lay three black figures. None of them asked what it was that drummed unceasingly above their heads. They lay with outstretched arms, their faces to the deck, as though even in death they meant to cling to the tilting ship.

Down in the cabin at the stern, the fire in the bronze brazier had gone out. Through the curved window the Pentecostal sun fell into the room, revealing a bundle of ropes, brushing over a pewter tankard, and sketching the outline of three dark figures. Down here lay three men. The captain was in a bunk near the table; he looked old and wasted, prematurely gray. On the plank bed to the left lay the sailmaker. And on the floor before the captain's bunk the cook's boy was stretched, his head buried in his devastated hands. The sunlight kindled a glow in the chart lantern, hanging from the deck beam over the table and indicating the ship's list in the ice. Gradually, as the day began to wane, the streak of light deserted the shining brass and wandered over the three men, moving from one to the other. Two of them remained motionless. The third stirred. It was the captain. He was still alive.

Outside, the usual evening scene began: the pack ice was broken up into gold and dark purple surfaces. The snow turned blue. Winter still held sway. As time passed, spring seemed to be a whole season late; but in these latitudes it always arrives abruptly, as William Gordon, first mate on the *Unicorn*, observed. He knew what he was talking about; he had sailed earlier to Cherry Island, Pechora, Greenland, Svalbard, and Pustozersk on the Barents Sea. But he got no chance to repeat the experience at Hudson Bay. William Gordon died on April 8th.

Down in the aft cabin the captain tried to push aside his bearskin and sit up; the breath from his lips formed small clouds of vapor in the dank room. At last he succeeded in swinging his legs out of the bunk, but for a time he had to sit with his hands braced on the table, fighting against vertigo. The cabin rolled from side to side. It was as if the ship had suddenly torn itself loose from the ice; but then it once more reached calmer water and gradually assumed the same list as before. The captain raised his head from his hands; his face was broad, heavy, and compact, with clear, piercing eyes. He looked around the room: the sailmaker was asleep; the cabin boy was dead. He cautiously pushed off his mittens and stared a little at his ravaged hands, as if he had difficulty in believing that they belonged to him.

The light fell almost horizontally into the cabin. In a little while it would be dark. Fumblingly, he drew out a copybook on the table in front of him, the soft parchment cover spotted with blood, a few sentences scrawled on the first page. *Emtrar sempre deue de comesar Vida Noua Vida*. This Portuguese dictum declares that right from the beginning of this brief life we should endeavor to enter the new life. Next to these words, a column of figures. Calculations. A total of 1105 marks, 5 skillings, and 8 pennings.

There was no oil left in the lantern. If he waited any longer it would be dark. Cautiously he inserted his hand into an inner pocket, where he kept his phial of India ink to protect it from the frost. Then he found the goose quill on the table, elbowed some of the jumble to one side, opened the book, and turned over the pages till he came to the place where the last entry was made, halfway down on the right-hand page. He sat over the paper thinking a little. His face was burned red as a brick; a squat figure below massive shoulders. The sailmaker breathed in his sleep; the loose tackle knocked against the side of the cabin. The captain dipped the quill into the ink, leaned back far-sightedly, and, forming every syllable with his lips, began to put down these last words:

June 4, 1620

Since I no longer have any hopes of living, I can only pray to God that we may be found by some good Christians and that for God's sake they will cause my poor corpse together with the others to be buried in the earth, receiving their reward from God in Heaven, and that this my account be given unto my Gracious Lord and King (for every word herein is altogether true), so that some good may arise unto my poor wife and children out of my great hardship and sorry departure. Herewith, I say good-bye to the world and give my soul into God's keeping.

JENS MUNK

2

With these words from Hudson Bay one of the last great hopes held out to Denmark was snuffed. It was 1620, midway between the triumphs of Kalmar and the disastrous battle at Lutter am Barenberge. Behind lay the union of the Scandinavian countries; ahead lay the Peace of Roskilde, when the land was divided. The period of triumph had passed, and the future was to bring no one capable of turning the tide. To the eyes of posterity, ever wise after the event, it appeared as though the country's history during these years had reached a watershed, beyond which all endeavor was simply to fall away into defeat.

Jens Munk's testament marks the first in this long series of defeats. It requires courage to go to one's death with open eyes. And yet, anticipating the events that followed, the chronicler asks himself whether death is not sometimes the simplest

Jens Munk's testament. From the original manuscript of *Navigatio Septentrionalis*. (The Royal Library) solution. The dead do not feel the cold, as Movritz Stygge said. That is true, replies the chronicler, it is the living who feel the cold. Death keeps open house. It asks neither age nor rank, it welcomes one and all. Life is different; it is reserved for the few.

Unfortunately, it is necessary even at this starting point to look ahead into the gloom. For if things had gone according to Jens Munk's expectations on June 4, 1620, we would know but little of him today. It is improbable that the diary of his expedition, the main source of our knowledge, would have been preserved. Many years were to pass before the next Christians again happened to come this way. The *Unicorn* disappeared almost without trace; the ice bore down upon the ship, splintering its twelve-inch oaken timbers like matchsticks, flattening the carpenter's wooden huts, and removing the flimsy wooden crosses on the beach. But the diary in the parchment cover survived. More than three hundred years after these fateful events, it is still preserved in the Royal Library in Copenhagen, catalogued as Additamenta No. 184. Here, far removed from the snowstorms of the polar night, one may undo two tapes, open up a little package, and find that very book which Jens Munk in his utter isolation took out and opened on Whitsun evening in the ice of Hudson Bay.

Additamenta No. 184 is a manuscript in quarto; it measures about 7¾″ in height by 6¾″ across and contains fifty pages of handmade sized paper. The binding is of plain parchment, fashioned like a cover and cut to match the size of the book; the back is provided with a folded inner flap. The cover and the individual leaves are fastened together with thin twine of the variety marketed as "lightly tarred marline." The parchment is the skin of newborn kid and of the best quality, still supple and intact except for a slight rent on the front, apparently made by the point of a knife. Just above this rent there is a dark stain, probably blood. The stain covers part of the

14

title of the volume, which is written in a beautiful embellished hand and reads: "Captain Jens Munk's Account of the Voyage, 1619." In the top right-hand corner some lines are written in the same hand as the rest of the book; but these four lines are only partially readable, either because the ink did not adhere to the parchment or because the writing has gradually been worn off at this exposed position.

The inside of the parchment cover also has writing. The greater part of the space is taken by some verses from the 91st Psalm:

Thou shalt not be afraid for the terror by night,
Nor for the arrow that flieth by day;
For the pestilence that walketh in darkness,
Nor for the destruction that wasteth at noonday. . . .

After the psalm comes the title page with the ship's prayer, followed by the words in Portuguese and by the calculations.

The narrative itself begins on the fourth page of the book. The handwriting is firm and regular, with gently rising lines. There are practically no corrections. The paragraphs begin with a date and vary in length from a few lines to several pages. Here and there space has been left for later additions, presumably drawings. In other places there are diagrams, some of which are of the mock-sun phenomenon well known in arctic regions, others of an eclipse of the moon. A margin of about an inch and a half has been spared on the left. Starting from and including February 20, 1620, a number of notations occur in this margin at regular intervals. Thus, against the appropriate date there is written: 21 corpses. Five days later appears: 22 corpses. Against March 9th appears: 26 corpses. Against April 1st: 34 dead. Against April 16th: 47 dead. Against May 6th: 53 dead. Against May 19th: 57 dead. And finally against June 4th, the date of the testament: 61 dead.

Thanks to this book we can follow the course of the tragedy

in all its details even today. We know why Jens Munk sailed from Copenhagen with the *Unicorn* and the *Lamprey*. We have the names of nearly all the participants in that fateful expedition; we know when they died, and the cause of their deaths. Indirectly, we also gain a picture of the captain who led them. It is incomplete and reveals only glimpses of him: a taciturn and aloof man, gentle of manner but straight to the point, clearsighted, resolute, and yet with an enigmatic split in his nature, a flaw somewhere in that strong will.

As to the man himself, his antecedents and history, the journal is silent. The fullest account of his life available hitherto is only some fifty pages long. For reasons at present obscure, his death brought forth no funeral oration—often an important source of biographical information. Not one letter from his hand has survived. Not one portrait, nor even so much as a gravestone with the barest details. His name is missing among the sarcophagi and banners in Holmen Church. True, in Osterbo, in Copenhagen, there is a tiny street called Jens Munk Gade; but Munk's Cape and Munk's Haven and all those other distant regions he discovered and gave his name to have long borne the names of others who arrived long after him. Yet somewhere among the ice and snow at the eastern outlet of the Fury and Hecla Strait there is a barren rocky island the maps call Jens Munk's Island. He was in fact never within several hundred miles of this island; it bears his name simply as a compliment paid to him by a later Danish explorer.

The story of Jens Munk, the chronicler reports, is the story of a man who began at the bottom. Three times he made a bid for fame. Twice Fate cast him down, and it was many difficult years before he stood on his feet again. But then a great monarch began to take an interest in him. Two ships and sixty-six of the navy's best men were placed at his disposal. He tried again, and took the book with the parchment cover along with him. Six months later Fate once more cast

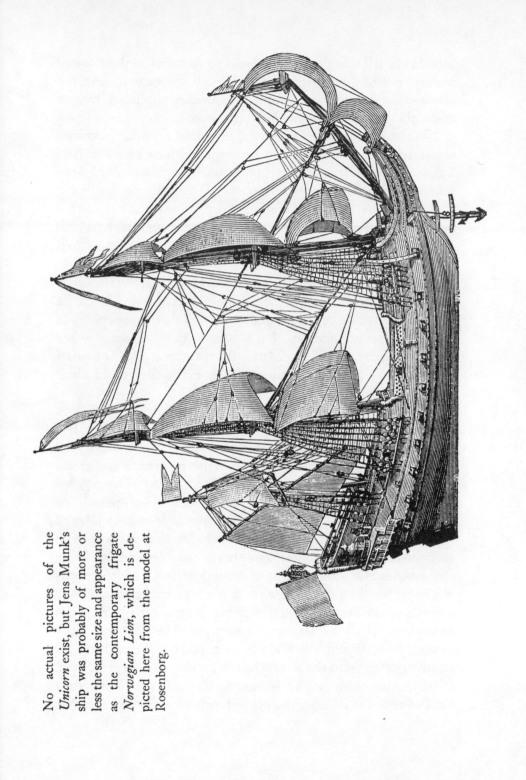

No actual pictures of the *Unicorn* exist, but Jens Munk's ship was probably of more or less the same size and appearance as the contemporary frigate *Norwegian Lion*, which is depicted here from the model at Rosenborg.

him down. All that remains of him is a footnote in the book of history, one of those names known to all and to none. An unremarkable street trodden by an incurious public. A remote and uninhabited island in the arctic seas.

Nevertheless it is wrong to suppose that nothing is known about Jens Munk apart from his expedition to Hudson Bay. True, the material is sparse, but it can be supplemented from sources that earlier went unregarded. The main source is the abstract of his logbooks compiled by an anonymous author and printed under the title "A Description of the Life and Works of Captain Jens Munk/Extracted for the greater part from his personal Journals/the remainder from other reliable Papers." Further information can be gleaned from the Norwegian National Archives, the Zealand Directory and Records, and the financial records of Bremerholm. The reminiscences of an Icelandic contemporary, Jon Olafsson, have cast unexpected light on the drama of Jens Munk from a new angle; and other scholars have further illuminated the expedition to Hudson Bay.

Finally, the man I have called "the chronicler" falls in a separate category. His real identity will become obvious. For the present it is sufficient to say that his account is not distinguished by perfect accuracy; it is by no means impartial. This is not to imply that the chronicler fabricates events that never took place, or introduces people who never existed, or plays tricks with the timing of events. He is not concerned with historical romance. If one concludes that his very full account cannot be accepted as entirely reliable—a conclusion one reaches reluctantly—this is doubtless due to his obvious weakness for the anecdotal, and to his regrettable tendency to present possibilities as actualities. He is certainly not rigorous enough to satisfy professional historians. He does not limit himself to facts and allow these to speak for themselves; instead, he often takes the liberty of attempting to interpret them, of composing them into an image, an idea. He does not accept Chance as the absolute principle in human destiny; he searches for meaning behind the absurd vicissitudes of life. One repeats that the chronicler is never untruthful; it is simply that *his* truth is of a kind one seeks in vain in the Zealand Directory and the Norwegian National Archives.

2

Three Cocks' Gules upon a Field Azure

I

Jens Munk was born on June 3, 1579. Shakespeare and Galileo were then fifteen years old. It was three years since Tycho Brahe had set foot on Hven and made his first observation there: a conjunction of the Moon and Mars. It was only two years since Queen Sophia had given birth to a boy who came into the world under the sign of Aquarius and was given the name Christian. And, finally, it was only one year since Mary Stuart's lover, the Earl of Bothwell, had died insane in the notorious royal Danish prison of Dragsholm.

Jens Munk was born in well-to-do circumstances on the Barbo estate at Arendal in southern Norway. Both his parents were Danish. His father was Erik Munk of Hiørne, a nobleman by birth.

His mother was Anna Bartholomaeidatter, a dark beauty, possibly with Jewish blood in her veins, and the daughter of a barber in Elsinore. Erik and Anna were not lawfully married. Nevertheless, they had two sons together, Jens and his older brother Niels—a serious matter in Reformation Denmark, where any breach of the laws of holy matrimony was regarded as the work of the devil. Even at the beginning of the century this sort of offense had been punished in accordance with the old city laws of Ribe: a woman who had lain with a strange man "must take her lover and lead him through the town, up one street and down the other, by that same member by means of which he had offended with her." With the coming of the

20

Reformation, the legislature lost its sense of humor and decreed the death penalty for adultery. In every market town, a number of trustworthy women were to make the rounds twice a year and milk the unmarried girls of the town to find out if any of them had secretly borne a child. A churl who had lain with a serving wench could expect to be hanged on the town gallows; the woman, publicly flogged. If the seducer was high-born, he lost two fingers, while the seduced lady was to be "immured for life." Consequently it was not to be taken lightly when, in a royal proclamation of 1580, the year after Jens Munk's birth, there appeared a warning to all "who lived an evil life with loose women, whom they maintained in their houses and kept as though they had been their wedded wives, to the not inconsiderable wrath of God, the profanation of holy matrimony, and the ill example of their fellow Christians."

This was precisely what Erik Munk was doing on his estate at Barbo. He was in no way ignorant of what he stood to lose. When he refrained from marrying dark Anna, weighty considerations were involved. From time immemorial it had been essential for a nobleman to make a noble match if he desired his title and property to pass to his descendants; otherwise the title could be abolished and the property confiscated upon his death. In this respect Erik Munk had painful experience to guide him; and it is here that his drama begins. His own father, Niels Munk, who owned the manor of Hiørne in Halland, had also lived with a bondwoman. But the old man had scorned convention and had led the girl to the altar. His fellow nobles, who still remembered that the Munk family had sided with the peasants and King Christian II during the civil war in 1525, were quick to seize on this pretext for revenge. The patent of nobility was withdrawn and the son Erik forced to start his career without title, a serious handicap for a man of ambition.

Erik Munk was a man of ambition. Above all things he wanted to get back the patent of nobility which had passed him by for such a ludicrous reason. The chronicler notes that he habitually wore wolverine fur, and recalls the words of the contemporary Archbishop Olaus Magnus, who said of the wolverine (or glutton): "Its flesh is without use, but the fur is magnificent and costly. Only princes and great men wear it. Yet I must not conceal that whosoever attireth himself in the fur of this creature can never desist from eating and drinking."

Erik Munk was such a glutton. His hunger, however, was the craving for land, and his thirst was for blood.

2

His history more than justifies these harsh words. As a young man he went to Burgundy and took part in the war between France and Philip II of Spain. In 1562 he was in Norway as the Governor of Vardøhus, the northernmost fortress in the realm. The following year saw the outbreak of the Scandinavian Seven Years' War. The Swedes advanced into Jämtland; on March 18, 1564, Trondheim fell, and fourteen days later the fortress of Stenvigsholm had to surrender as the result of defections and lack of gunpowder. But in Bergen Erik Munk had supervised the construction of a number of galleys; and on April 19th he boarded the *Dove* as the captain of a squadron of three ships. The canons of Bergen presented him with three casks of ale and wished him good fortune and victory.

And so it was to be. A week later the squadron made the most of a strong and favorable wind in the direction of Trondheim. En route they boarded three enemy sloops, putting the crews to death and taking but a few prisoners. On May 23rd they gave naval support to the attack on Stenvigsholm, which fell the same evening. The Danes were enabled to reconquer Trondheim . . . Romsdal . . . Norway.

It seems that Erik Munk took the news of victory in person to Copenhagen. At least, the annals bear witness to his presence there in this year, stating that "during a visit to Denmark an Erik Munk stabbed a man to death with his dagger in an inn." Shortly afterward Frederick II bestowed upon him the extensive Nonnesaeter convent lands near Oslo.

But the war continued. In 1567 Erik Munk was in command of an expedition of harquebusiers sent to relieve Akershus, which was besieged by the Swedes. When the men mutinied and refused to serve under him, he had five of the ringleaders arrested and executed. Then followed the assault on the Swedes. Absolon Pedersen relates how "with demiculverin he hunted the Swedes from their entrenchments like foxes from their holes"; while Edward Edwardsen describes how, at the head of his galleys, he "came up behind the Swedish camp, no farther than a bowshot from them at a spot where they were not entrenched, and so raked them that the blood flowed from the trenches down to the sea so that by this means alone two thousand men were slain." Once again Erik Munk sailed with the good news to Copenhagen; once again his presence is noted in the annals, where it is reported that in the year 1570 an Erik Munk killed a nobleman called Gregers Gram. That same year the King bestowed upon him the fief partly of Onsø Roads, near what is now Fredrikstad, partly of the lucrative Nedenaes estate near Arendal. Then Erik Munk journeyed back to Norway, taking a barber's daughter from Elsinore with him, and settled down at the manor of Barbo.

The war was over. Erik Munk had received estates and fiefs, but the glutton in him was not satisfied, for still no patent of nobility had reached him. He set to work to increase his revenues, built ironworks and sawmills, and sold timber to the Dutch ships which in ever increasing numbers tied up alongside his wharves. For his peasant farmers he was a harsh master. They complained that he overtaxed them, drove them off their farms when they could not pay, extended his lands by abolishing the old field boundaries, and forced his lawsuits through by bribing the judges. In the course of two years there was so much unrest that Frederick II had to send his prosecutor Mogens Svale to Norway, commissioning him to apprehend and arrest Erik Munk and convey him to Denmark.

Erik Munk received Mogens Svale on the Royal Farm at Nedenaes. There must be, he said, a mistake—surely the King did not intend to imprison him; the intention was surely to ennoble him. Mogens Svale returned to Copenhagen, his mission unaccomplished. That same year Erik Munk received the fief of Bratsberg. Four years later extensive additions to the Nedenaes crown fief were bestowed upon him.

But still no patent of nobility. There was no further point in fighting the peasants, and Erik Munk began to look around for another real war. By a stroke of good fortune, in 1577 King Stephen of Poland had offended Frederick II by seizing some Danish ships on their way to Danzig with salt herring. Stephen laid siege to the city because it would not swear allegiance to him. Erik Munk took charge of a squadron of ships, sailed southward, and drove Stephen off, using the old Akershus method of bombarding the enemy from the rear. Afterward he reimbursed himself for his trouble with a little plundering expedition to Polish Prussia.

Meantime, back in Norway, his bailiffs had continued the harsh treatment of the peasant farmers; and when he returned from his expedition the feeling against him was more hostile than ever. A John Mynster tried unsuccessfully to shoot him as he landed at Nedenaes quay, and the following year the farmers succeeded in getting their hated master summoned before the Council of Nobles. The charges involved violence, fraud, and the illicit extortion of taxes. Moreover, the worthy Jacob Lauritzen, a burgher of Skien, said that his wife Ingeborg Pedersdatter had been burned alive by Erik Munk, wrongfully convicted of witchcraft. Erik Munk moved quickly. The farmers had been foolish enough to have the indictment drafted by Kristen Jenssøn of Hiserø, who had formerly been Erik Munk's scribe at Bratsberg, where he had been dismissed because of discrepancies in the accounts. Erik construed his accusation as an act of personal revenge and had him condemned. The farmers had to withdraw the suit; in law, too, it is sometimes possible to fire on one's opponents from the rear.

Erik Munk exploited this victory to gain new wealth. Besides his extensive royal fiefs, he now owned the estates of Barbo at Arendal, Borregaard in Smaalenene, and Hiørne in Halland. But this was not enough. He was like those nobles of whom it is said that their hunger for land could not be assuaged until their mouths were filled with the clay of the grave. Constantly he acquired new domains: in 1580 alone he obtained the deeds of no less than twelve properties in Norway "for himself and his heirs in perpetuity." Then he came to grief. The following year the farmers again had him arraigned before the Council of Nobles. We possess their indictment, addressed to the Danish King and drafted on St. Olaf's Day, July 29, 1581.

The farmers' list of accusations was long and detailed: during the past winter Erik Munk had seized and imprisoned freeholders without trial. One poor farmer, Ulf of Hegland, he had put in hand-irons and had fastened him by a chain with his back to the wall so that he might neither sit not stand, but must hang by the hands, all on account of but one mark. The same he caused to be done to Biørn of Dalle. From Grym of Lysbal he had extorted two horses and three barrels of tar. He had ordered Biørn of Jordthvede to be flogged without cause. Gunlick of Lejland, who begged food for his children, he clapped in irons and struck with his sword, by reason that Gunlick would not pay him two calf skins in levies of war. He would not accept the farmers' butter tax in boxes, as was the usage, but forced them to fashion casks of beechwood or of oak, which trees are not readily come by, because they grow so high upon the fells. And then they must convey the butter down to Erik's farm Barbo in Nedenaes, and that for no reward whatsoever, a thing they would willingly perform were it not that they merely met with abuse, and it was sixty miles down to Nedenaes. Moreover he did abuse them with many ill words, calling them nothing but thieves and their womenfolk

25

whores. Therefore the commoners who live and labor in the parish of Raa, both old and young, women and children, do humbly and in the name of God entreat His Royal Majesty in His mercy to have regard unto their poverty and misery and part Erik Munk from them, for should he in this wise long rule over them, they would be forced, poor and unfortunate as they were, to give up house and home, women and children, and depart into another fief, or wherever else God might provide for them.

But the pleas of the thirty-one signatories were in vain. Nothing came of the matter. In 1581 Erik Munk was invulnerable. That little war in Danzig had borne fruit. Erik Munk set the peasants' indictment alongside another document he had received from the Danish King only a few months previously. It was the long-awaited patent of nobility:

> We Frederick II make it known, that whereas the well-beloved Erik Munk during the late lengthy conflict between Denmark and Sweden did serve Us faithfully and zealously, disposing himself to employment upon sea as upon land against the enemies of the realm and of Ourselves as was necessary, and as in a man of honor is needful, seemly and becoming,
>
> And to the end that his said service shall not remain without reward, but be to the honor, benefit, and well-being of his true and lawful issue,
>
> And whereas Our Royal Charter doth empower Us to give the unfree man noble liberty, as he may be deemed fit, We have of Our especial Grace and Favor, in this Our Letter Patent, given the aforementioned Erik Munk and his issue lawfully begotten, such noble liberty as is enjoyed by other knights and squires in this Our realm of Denmark, with escutcheon and helm, viz. three cocks' gules upon a field azure, such as standeth here in Our letters patent depicted.

With the King's letter in his document chest and three cocks

Erik Munk's coat of arms. (The Danish Peerage)

on his shield, the most sapient, most splendid, and most noble
Sir Erik now set out on the expedition which was to find its
true culmination many years after his death—one Whitsunday
in Hudson Bay.

3

Out toward the Barents Sea, east of the northernmost tip of
Norway and east of Vardøhus where Erik Munk began his
career as castle bailiff, lies the ancient Bjarmeland. Apart from
a few nomadic mountain Lapps, not a soul lives here; but on
the terraces of rock out toward the ocean, guillemots and little
auks breed by the millions. The short, rainy summer begins
when the rivers break up at the end of June and is already at

an end when they freeze over again at the beginning of September. Wherever the snow manages to melt away it reveals a marshy, half-thawed tundra or vast stretches of rocks interspersed with blue-green glacial streams. A reindeer may appear along the shore; the black and white snow bunting pipes in the stunted birch thicket; out over the ocean the sun burns behind the midnight fog. A ship might occasionally show itself out there, a pinnace or a solitary two-masted sloop followed by silent fulmars. This, however, was happening more and more often. For it was just about the time of the events recorded here that Bjarmeland came to the world's attention—and for a number of very strange reasons.

As early as 1555 English seafarers had found a way through to Archangel at the lower end of the White Sea; and soon the learned traveler Adam Olearius was to find English, Dutch, and Danish ships in the harbor there. They arrived with a miscellany of wares, which with the coming of winter were transported farther south by sledge, the ships then returning to Western Europe with dried cod, whale oil, and furs. Archangel was still a wretched trading post consisting of earthen huts and a few wooden cabins. But as trade increased, the town began to grow. A Russian boyar turned up as Governor; packing sheds shot up along the wet timber wharves; and in smoky alehouses mariners from Amsterdam sat playing backgammon with bear hunters from Novaya Zemlya.

The cause of this prosperity was to be sought many hundreds of miles to the south. After Sweden had captured the harbor town of Narva, the Gulf of Finland and thus the entire Baltic were closed to the Russians. The only place where the developing Muscovite state could then make contact with the Western world was at Archangel. The sea route along Bjarmeland's desolate coasts became the nearest way to civilization. But this route lay along the coast of Norway through Danish territorial waters, which led Denmark to exact toll of the ships using it. This, at least, was the Danish government's official explanation. The real reason was that Copenhagen observed with dismay how Russian trade was by-passing the Sound; and in one way or another it had to compensate for the consequent loss of revenue. The seriousness with which the Danes viewed the question can be gathered from the speed with which they acted. Narva fell in 1581. Only six months later instructions were issued for the seizure of foreign ships sailing to Archangel without the permission of the King of Denmark. The task was formidable, but one man was available who had previously mastered even worse assignments.

In the spring of 1582 the newly knighted Erik Munk sailed out of Oslo Fjord in command of a squadron. It was the fourth time he was to settle a matter of foreign policy from the deck of a ship. On this occasion too he acted with speed and resolution, and in the course of the early summer he had succeeded in tracking down and impounding three English merchantmen. But the bitterness of the Danish nobility on learning that the compromised Munk family had been reinvested with all its old dignity was great. Erik Munk appears to have fallen foul of some nobles who were taking part in the expedition, among them the powerful Christen Vind. On his return to Copenhagen the indignant lords sought to take their revenge. They told the King that Erik had sailed one of the prizes to his estate at Arendal in order to keep its treasures for himself. Erik Munk managed to get himself acquitted. Certainly he had sailed the foreign craft to Arendal, but naturally that was only a temporary expedient. There had been a gale; the weather was bad. The government in Copenhagen decided to trust him; and it also set about exploiting his action. On June 22, 1583, the suave diplomat Henrik Ramel got England to pay Denmark a hundred rose nobles annually for the right to sail to the White Sea. Shortly afterward France signed a similar agreement. These were not large sums; the significant thing was that Denmark had secured recognition of her territorial rights in the Norwegian Sea with all the consequences this was to have in the future.

Nevertheless, the noblemen did not forget the humiliation

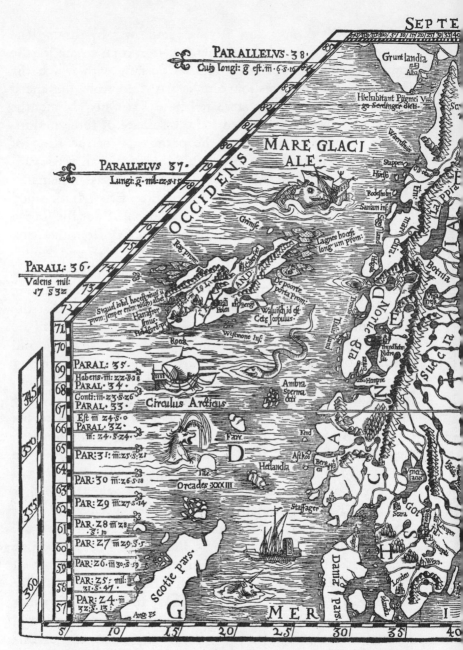

Knowledge of northern waters was still somewhat imperfect. Navigating by "charts" such as this, with sea horses, sea unicorns or narwhals, sea serpents and other monsters, and with Greenland driven into alarming

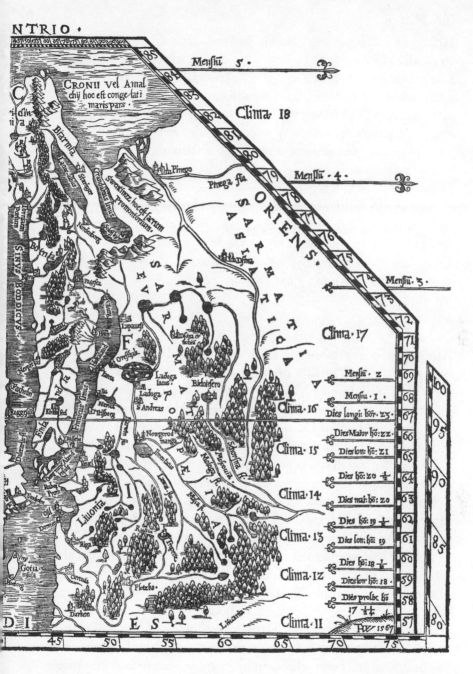

proximity to the Norwegian coast, Jens Munk rounded North Cape.
(Olaus Magnus)

Erik had inflicted upon them. Indeed, it is as though the die were already cast for the boy who at this time was taking his first steps on the home estate at Arendal. Erik Munk, however, sensed no threat. His position was stronger than ever. At the Council of Nobles in 1582, no one dared bring charges against him. Nor were any voices of dissent heard in 1583. In 1584, too, the silence remained unbroken.

But a new magistrate, Mogens Bardsøn, was silently at work, filing complaints, keeping lists of witnesses, establishing connections with influential aristocratic circles in Denmark, where there was no great love for Sir Erik. Not only the Norwegian peasants had it in for him: there was also a nobleman, Christen Vind. As time went by, one by one the heavy guns were brought into position. That was in 1585.

4

After four years of peace Erik Munk had once again been brought to law. On this occasion too we are in possession of the bill of indictment. Mogens Bardsøn had completed a solid piece of work; the wording is sharper and more concise than the previous one, but the main points are more or less the same. Erik Munk collects unlawful taxes and abuses his powers of war levy; he will not accept the old field boundaries established in earlier days by revered forefathers, but ranges over the fields with a compass in his hand making new boundaries regardless of witnesses or other evidence, and thereby increases his own lands in length and in breadth.

All this had been heard before. But Mogens Bardsøn had also established that Erik harbored on his farms and in other parts of the fief a great number of vagabonds, whores, and perjurers, who abused the poor peasants, whose only desire was to lead an upright and Christian life in accord with God's commandments and the custom of their forefathers. But if these loose harlots should bear children, they impudently and mendaciously imputed paternity to any peasant they chose. Thus

Erik Munk had charged Søren Hanneberg with having committed adultery with Anne Andersdatter. Søren denied this and was able to bring forward many witnesses in his support. But Anne testified to having lain with him; and as her testimony was supported by Erik Munk, the matter cost Søren his life.

According to the indictment, among the devices Erik used to rid himself of his enemies was that of alleging paternity, and then having sentence passed under the law concerning adultery. This accusation struck at Erik's weakest point. For who in the whole of Nonnesaeter and Nedenaes was unaware of the fact that the noble lord himself lived with a bondwoman, a barber's daughter who had borne him two sons out of wedlock? And now, by false testimony, he had caused an innocent person to be hanged for practically the same thing. The indictment closes, as the previous one did, with the peasants' threat to leave the fief if their pleas were not heard; but this time the threat need not be taken seriously. Mogens Bardsøn had calculated correctly. Erik Munk was finished.

We can follow his fall through court records preserved from the Council of Nobles in Oslo. The victor of Akershus was cornered, but he knew how to put up a defense. Throughout, Erik had a ready answer, silencing his accusers with ten facile arguments for every one they managed to stammer out, twice as quick, twice as telling. Had he caused a man to be hanged by the thumbs for one hour? That was possible. He had been carried away by his charitable heart. According to law the man had deserved the death sentence. Was Søren Hanneberg wrongfully put to death? That question should be put to the judges who sentenced him. Taxes? Field boundaries? Soldiers? What on earth would happen to the country's prosperity if the inhabitants themselves decided how much tax they would pay, or when they would furnish soldiers, and how much crown land they should secure for their own use?

Erik's eloquence only worsened his position. Eighteen judgments were pronounced at the Council in Oslo; all the judges were Danish noblemen; all the judgments went against him. Søren Hanneberg was to be exhumed and buried in consecrated ground. Halvor Kvammes was to get his land back. Herluf Sandø was to recover his forests. Jon Birketved was to get his meadow back. Jon Gunulfsen's claim for wages was upheld. Bergeraas Farm was returned to Oluf Engelbretsen. Knut Gregersen was absolved of the charge of having committed adultery with Dorthe Mortensdatter. Arne Ellufsen was to get back his salmon fishing. Twenty bucks were to be restituted to Sigvar Djønestad. It was agreed that Alf Thorgersen had been imprisoned without trial. Knut Hørve was to recover his wasteland.

And so on. Erik Munk's position as feudal vassal was already shaken when to the charges were added two terrible accusations from a higher power. Christen Vind had not worked in vain. The government in Copenhagen taxed Munk with having neglected the Royal Farm at Nedenaes and with having felled the crown forests for his own use. The noble judges upheld the government's case. Now they had caught their glutton.

On September 30, 1585, King Frederick stripped Erik Munk of all his fiefs and transferred them to Hans Pedersøn of Saem. A historian, J. Ber, left the record of the fallen lord's departure:

A royal man-of-war arrived off the coast and anchored at Sømskilen. The captain, with several officers, went and took the road across the plain to the Royal Farm. Erik Munk received them, invited them to dine with him, and treated them in splendid manner. In return the captain invited Erik Munk to eat on board his ship the next day. Unsuspectingly, he presented himself at the appointed time. While he was dining the ship weighed anchor, carried him off to Copenhagen, and delivered Nedenaes fief from a despotic and avaricious lord. Overjoyed at being rid of this tyrant, the commoners assembled on a little island near Sømskilen and passed the day there in merriment and carousing, as at a wedding, wherefore it is still known as Wedding Isle.

Erik Munk lost all his fiefs, but he still held his patent of nobility, and in 1585 there were strict limits to the liberties that could be permitted against a nobleman. He journeyed to Denmark confident that his title would protect him, firmly resolved upon vengeance, little suspecting what was in store for him. But before we follow him into the darkness, a backward glance should be given at the three people he had left to their fate at home.

Erik and Anna were never lawfully wed. In 1580 came the royal letter of proclamation against those who lived a wicked life with loose women, as though they were their wedded wives. This was the very year that Erik was ennobled; and as he knew from his own experience that a title could not be inherited by children begotten with a bondwoman, he felt no urge to marry Anna. Given the opportunity, he must find a noble partner. If he married the barber's daughter all his hard-earned privileges would be lost to his descendants.

In this respect Erik Munk showed considerable foresight. Only two years later, under pressure from the nobility, King Frederick set his name to a law which confirmed the old tradition and forbade noblemen to marry bondwomen, since this would be to the detriment and in contempt of the nobility of the realm. Should they nevertheless do this, then their children would be regarded as bond-folk, without the right to the family name or escutcheon, and without right of inheritance.

Accordingly, if Erik married Anna he lost his privileges. If he did not marry her he was guilty of adultery. He chose the latter course, and Anna had to give up all thought of marrying the man who had fathered her children. There was no place for them when Erik stood at the summit of his career. Still, all three had to share his defeat. After he had been taken to Copenhagen, they remained behind on the farm at Arendal.

35

Their life there could not have been pleasant, but at least they still had a home. A year passed, and they lost that too. On August 25, 1585, King Frederick sent strict instructions to Erik Munk's successor as vassal, Hans Pedersøn of Saem:

> Let it be known, that inasmuch as Erik Munk is found on several counts to have acted against Our subjects and thus also against Ourselves in unseemly manner, for which misdeeds We are minded in due course to bring him to justice, and leave to befall him whatsoever may by verdict and sentence be provided; and in order that We may obtain redress for that which he hath committed against Us and Our subjects: We pray thee, that thou in Our name take possession at once of all his properties, immovable as well as movable, and if he or the whore, with whom he has long passed his wicked, scandalous life, have carried away any property or goods personal, that then thou do with diligence investigate and search thereafter, wherever they may be found, upon his estate or with his whore, or wheresoever else he or she may have conveyed them, finding, inquiring, obtaining, and taking possession thereof, that We may thereby receive certain knowledge of them.

Hans Pedersøn of Saem set about the matter conscientiously, and in the autumn Anna had to move from Barbo. Of the rich furnishings of the farm, she was permitted to take only the bare necessities with her. She could find nobody to take pity on them and offer them shelter in Nedenaes. Together with her two boys, she sailed across Oslo Fjord to settle in Fredrikstad, the new town which the King had established to replace Sarpsborg, razed during the Swedish wars.

3

Dreams of the New World

When Anna Bartholomaeidatter settled down in Fredrikstad, Jens was seven years old. We do not know the age of his elder brother; we know what he was called and when he died, but beyond that very little is known. Niels Munk is a kind of figure frequently encountered in that hundred-year period running from the Reformation to the Thirty Years' War, a period ravaged by recurrent epidemics of typhoid, cholera, and smallpox. Of them there is just a glimpse of a name and a date on a grave.

Jens Munk's brother was one of these, as was also his mother. Of his father, even the date of his birth is unknown. The history of Jens's boyhood is full of the names of people remarkable only for the occasion of their death; so also in his later years they crowd about him, on the ice at Hudson Bay. Everything around him is obscure; only the man himself stands fully illuminated—the details of his boyhood are few and the chronicler must be content to reconstruct the more important features from such facts as are known.

What did the seven-year-old boy retain from those childhood years on his father's estate? Images of freedom and good living, horses and hunting, fine guests and discreet servants, a wineglass gleaming in the firelight, life *comme il faut*. All this he retained, and for him it coalesced into that vague notion of happiness by which every person lives his life in some form or other. In times of adversity his thoughts returned to his

37

early life; and when luck was with him this was the life he wanted to live anew. It is doubtful whether the seven-year-old child really felt the full impact of the misfortunes that struck the family. The Barbo estate lay near the sea where Oslo Fjord broadens out and becomes open water. Fredrikstad is similarly situated, though it is on the opposite coast. His father had had command of a squadron of ships and had sold timber to Dutch shippers. Moreover, in mountainous Norway, where there were scarcely roads at that time, let alone carriages, the least journey was made by boat along the coast. Quite early, the sea came to play a significant role in the boy's life. This was not greatly changed in Fredrikstad. There was a chance of hauling some sunken, waterlogged dinghy up from the harbor floor and calking the worst cracks with tarred rag; a couple of staves taken from the spruce forest and stripped of bark could serve as a mast and yard; and after wheedling a few worn-out shifts from the fisherwomen on the quay, doubtless to the accompaniment of a rain of jokes, the bastard child was able to tack together a passable lateen sail.

And there was a most desirable dinghy in which he could sail about in the approaches, riding on the gunwale and letting the sail fill, and steering out to sea. With the coming of spring it was easy enough to put out to the Whale Isles, to go ashore on the barren islands with their screeching oyster catchers, to pierce a gull's egg at both ends with a knife and voluptuously suck out the lukewarm, oily contents. Imperceptibly spring passed into the long, calm summer. All day long the boy would ride the glittering ocean, pulling aboard a struggling mackerel, leaning over the gunwale once more, following the hook with his eyes as it swirled toward the bottom, taking a glint of sunlight with it into the deep. A creak from the step of the mast, otherwise all was silent. Brown skin showed through the rents in his shirt; his neck burned from the sun. What can compare with the sea on a summer's day? On such days he might sink into a reverie: the boat would grow before his eyes, the poop rise up above its swaying stern, three masts shoot up from the floor with jib, foresail, and square sail; and he would take his stand on the bridge, feet apart. He was the admiral, and his craft not the rotten little tub dragged up from the harbor mud but the *Dove*, a sloop with eighteen cannon, or, better still, the caravel *Santa Maria*. The gleam he can just make out in the sun's rays to the west is not one of the Whale Isles, where he went collecting gulls' eggs in the spring. No, it is Stenvigsholm; it is the besieged Akershus; or, even better, it is the uttermost point of the unknown continent, it is San Salvador. Calmly he would stand with folded arms and observe how the New World slowly crept up out of the ocean as the caravel steered toward it in the breeze, and the crew sank weeping to their knees on the foredeck, whispering, *"Terra!"*

The New World! Scarcely a hundred years had passed since Columbus stepped ashore on San Salvador. Cargoes of slaves and silver had been ferried to Spain. Yet this very wealth was to mean the country's decline. The flow of silver made work superfluous; instead, the Spaniards bought their goods abroad. The silver stream did not end in Madrid, but in London and Amsterdam. For the first time since antiquity, the center of gravity of trade moved out of the Mediterranean. The Old World discovered the new one, but did not survive it. Italy was on the wane and Spain grinding toward a halt. Trade was being transferred to the Atlantic, where England and Holland were ready to take over the world market. In 1588, the same year in which Jens Munk played at being Columbus among the islands off Fredrikstad, a handful of English small boats and fishermen defeated the invincible Spanish Armada. By then Danish trade, too, had for some time been on the increase. One has only to consult the account books of the Sound Dues: in 1503 five Danish ships passed through the Sound; in 1588 the figure was 412. The diminishing importance of the Mediterranean weakened the position of the German cities as middlemen between north and south. By the middle of the century the power of the Hanse towns was broken, and the ubiquitous Lübeck cog was withdrawn from

39

Danish harbors. Frederick II regarded himself as "Ruler of the Sea"; and the remarkable thing was that here for once was a Danish king who could with justification regard himself as ruler of something. The realm had certainly been larger than it was in his reign, but never before had Denmark consisted of so much water. The Baltic, the Kattegat, the North Sea, and finally, after Erik Munk's swift action against the English merchantmen, the cold Norwegian Sea—all were recognized as Danish territorial waters. From Gotland to Iceland and from Rügen to Vardøhus Danish squadrons cruised incessantly; and foreign vessels meeting them respectfully dipped their topsail in honor of His Royal Danish Majesty. The first buoys were laid out in the Danish belts; the first beacons blazed at night on the Skaw, Anholt, and Kullen. The year 1561 saw the establishment of the first Danish maritime law, which the most High and Noble Prince, King Frederick II, caused to be published for the benefit of the common seafaring man. This was followed in 1568 by Laurens Benedict's sea charts and navigation manual, the first Danish nautical guide, wherein the best pilots recorded and described all the fair winds and characteristics of the sea, with groundings, depths, currents, channels, tides, and all else which it was needful for seafarers to know. In 1584 Kronborg stood ready in its light dress of sandstone, built for the Sound Dues, shipped thither from all the lands of Christendom. The new world which Christopher Columbus discovered was not simply America; it was the sea.

Rounding the point one day at Fuglevigen and seeing the houses come into view, the boy found the familiar scene completely changed. It was as though a cathedral with massive towers and spires had risen up in the center of the town during his absence. While he had been drifting about among the

Ships off Kronborg, when the castle was completed in 1584. In the background Helsingborg, Landskrona, and Hven. From a contemporary copperplate. (Braunius)

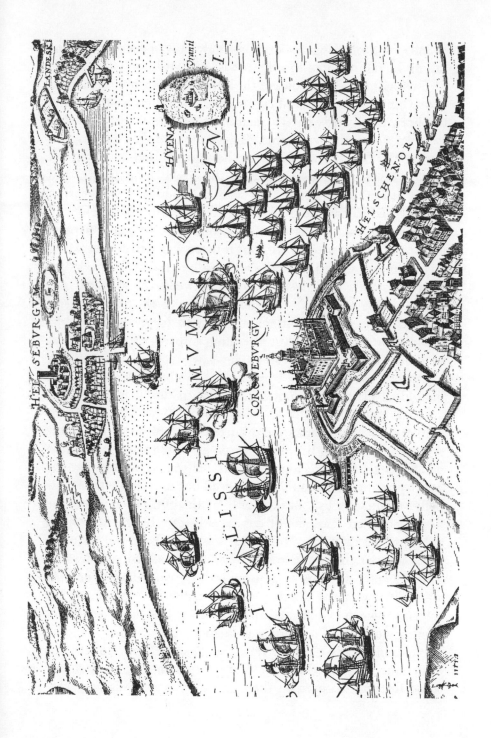

islands, one of King Frederick's new-built pinks had come sailing in and anchored in the roads.

Jens Munk steered toward the ship, noticing how it loomed above him, its shrouds and rigging silhouetted against the sky, the horizontal yards on the mainmast, the beautiful pennants hanging from the yardarms. The lateen sail's gaff reached toward the North Star, while the bowsprit jutted out from the prow, as sturdy in its timber as the great stout masts, and nearly as long. The beautifully painted figurehead of a roaring lion seemed to have to duck its head to find room. Along rail and tops the ship was dressed with bunting; pennants flapped under the gilded trucks. Although there was hardly any wind, a faint hum sounded from the rigging like the echo of a storm long subsided. Jens Munk stood between the thwarts and stared at this miracle. It was not the size of the ship that impressed him; he knew there were much larger ships in the world than these pinks; but one thing in particular caused him to gape, and made the ships he saw every day seem like wretched, old-fashioned barges. The hull was smooth. The individual planks were not corbeled with the quarter stepped outward and upward with each board. The pink was not clinker-built; the planks were butted edge to edge, the joints scarcely discernible beneath the pitch. The greater part of an oak forest must have gone into its construction, and yet the hull lay in the water as though carved out of a single trunk, its belly smooth as a fish, broken only by the gun ports, where the newly polished falconets of copper still caught the last of the twilight. Furthermore, the ship was not sharp-sterned; the stern was cut off some way in and replaced with a flat but magnificently appointed transom, which sloped up from the water line with the Danish coat of arms. The gleam of the gilded crown was reflected in the water, like some school of shining goldfish. The ship was fashioned in the latest mode: carvel-built. This must be how the *Santa Maria* looked: the same smooth hull, the same stern, the same high poop. He stood feasting his eyes on the sight; it was as if his very daydreams had been realized. He could sail right up to it, slap his hand against its tarred side. And yet at the same time it was now farther away than ever. His own visionary caravel had somehow now been destroyed, and with it all his visions of the New World. He was left with nothing but a rotten dinghy and never a hope of reaching San Salvador.

Up on the warship's quarter-deck, two officers were pacing to and fro, chatting in the mild evening. The sharp ring of their heels on the deck planks reminded him of his father, who not very long ago had walked to and fro on another deck. Where was he now? Why was he not the one to come sailing in? It was now three years since Erik Munk had left for Copenhagen, and still no word of him. What had they done to him?

A boatswain appeared and heaved a bucket of filthy water at the boy, as a sign to him to move on. He lowered his make-shift sail, took up a position in the stern with an oar, and began to scull in, just as he had seen the fishermen doing, with one hand on the oar and the other in his pocket. The dinghy left two gleaming lines behind it in the dark harbor. In the bilge water a couple of mackerel lay gasping for air. On the quay the fisherwomen stood gossiping. They already knew.

2

Jens Munk was born of defeat: shame was his father, and poverty his mother. After two years in Fredrikstad, Anna Bartholomaeidatter could no longer make ends meet. She found it impossible to afford an education for the two boys, who had long ago reached school age. A solution was found for Jens in Aalborg, where Sir Erik had a sister married to the city burgomaster, Frederik Christensen. He agreed to assist his distressed sister-in-law. This would put an end to sailing about the harbor. In the burgomaster's home Jens would be able to learn good manners; here he would get a sound up-bringing; here lay his only hope of becoming something great,

43

a clerk, perhaps, or even a priest. All other possibilities were excluded. For Anna, too, had heard the rumors which the fisherwomen had begun to whisper down on the quayside.

In 1588, Jens Munk sailed across the sea for the first time. It was not the New World that awaited him beyond the horizon, but Aalborg. To Jens, who had not even seen Bergen, which, with nearly fifteen thousand inhabitants, ranked as the largest city in the north, Aalborg with its close to seventy thousand people must have seemed like a witches' caldron. Here the sea had dwindled to a narrow streak of blue between green meadows. Farmers drove their cattle to market through groups of beggars and drunken mercenaries; stray dogs splashed through seas of stagnant sewage; roaming black hogs rooted among garbage and carrion; in short, a real city. Many of the houses showed the influence of the new type of architecture then gaining ground in the Danish market towns: long half-timbered houses with splendid windows, blue-painted frames and leaded panes, the whole broadside to the street; and in the middle of all a conspicuous gateway to the paved courtyard within, with its well and its willow tree. No idyl; but practical, modern, and expensive in appearance.

What sort of home awaited Jens Munk in these surroundings? As Anna Bartholomaeidatter had so rightly foreseen, life in Frederik Christensen's home was conducted with dignity and with due regard for the social proprieties. It was not one of the fashionable half-timbered houses; the third generation of city burgomasters looked on such follies with a skeptical eye. Frederik Christensen lived in one of the old-fashioned stone houses, which had gables turned toward the street. It was a house for people with traditions, reserved and formal, secure against life. The Middle Ages still permeated the deep, dim chambers: a handful of thyme thrust behind a shelf; women in velvet and white mantles; silence broken only by the brief quarter-strokes of the timepiece. The noise without did not reach within.

In this house Jens now had to find his place. In Fredrikstad he had roamed around more or less on his own; here he was introduced to an indoor existence hemmed in by prohibitions and obligations, by attention to lessons, by fixed mealtimes. The burgomaster was certainly not a man to tolerate backsliding. He shared the clear-cut views of his century regarding the problems of education: the important thing was to arouse in the young as early as possible a sense of gravity and piety, and transgressions had to be punished by beatings. If these were golden rules under normal circumstances, how much more suited were they not in this particular case. The correct and dutiful Frederik Christensen could hardly have felt sympathy for his brother-in-law's wild ambitions, which had ended in shame and misfortune; equally, he must have taken shocked exception to Sir Erik's domestic situation. His new foster child would have to understand that he was different from the other children in the household and offer thanks daily to Our Lord, who in His abundant grace and generosity had taken heed and led his erring feet to Frederik Christensen's stone house in Aalborg.

We must, then, visualize Jens Munk clad in black school gown, singing in church on Sundays along with the other pupils, or walking ahead of a funeral procession with a wax candle in his hands at the interment of a wealthy nobleman. Was this the price of ambition? For a nine-year-old the homesickness was inconsolable, the contrast too great. Aalborg made him long for the Norway he had lost; Frederik Christensen made him exalt his vanished father. It is extremely probable, as will become evident later, that Erik Munk had sometime told his sons the story of Christopher Columbus and his discoveries. In Aalborg the two men were so far removed from him that they gradually merged into one and the same figure; and this figure told him that it was impossible to achieve greatness in Aalborg. Nobody could live so far from the sea without losing his soul.

Three years passed, and he set off for home. In 1591 he turned up on the quayside once more; the bastard child had grown rather lanky, but was now decently dressed and strikingly quiet. He could read and write; but, alas, there was little to offer this courteous young man here. The situation in Fredrikstad had not changed in the intervening years; Anna Bartholomaeidatter still could not provide for her children. After a few weeks in the town Jens had to leave once more; but he did not return to Aalborg. One afternoon a strange ship lay in the harbor. For a warship of its time, it was not particularly impressive: a heavy, broad-bellied carrack, with a pair of cannon on the deck, but no pennants hanging from the yardarm. The master was Jacob Gerbrantzen; the boat was Frisian, had come from Portugal with salt and wine, and was now returning via England with grain, dried cod, and salt herring. Jens Munk knew that there the great convoys were prepared for America. That same evening he signed on with Jacob Gerbrantzen. The lord's son had become a ship's boy.

This time he probably learned the whole truth before he sailed away. Perhaps this partly explains his hurried agreement with Gerbrantzen. Anna could not conceal things any longer. For a long time it had been clear that the rumors which had reached the town three years earlier were true. The last hopes of seeing his father again had gone. The patent of nobility had not helped him in Copenhagen. For more than five years Erik Munk had been in chains in the dreaded State Prison of the Danish King on Dragsholm.

One summer morning in 1591 the carrack put out from Fredrikstad. On the quay the mother stood and waved good-bye. It was the last time these two were to see one another, for Jens Munk never returned to Fredrikstad, and Anna's role in his life was played out. She remained alone in the town for another thirty-two years, and still lived there as an old woman when Jens Munk lay trapped in the ice of Hudson Bay. Anna Bartholomaeidatter did not die until 1623, and was buried at the church out on the Whale Isles.

4

Can We See by Night?

From Oslo Fjord, Jacob Gerbrantzen put out into the Skager-rak, and the chronicler tells how they lay there for more than a week, with the sheets hauled in, riding out the bad weather from the southwest. Jens Munk fought against seasickness. He was sent down into the hold with a scraper to clean under the deck—Jacob Gerbrantzen held that no one knew a ship before he knew its bottom. When the wind at last shifted to the north, they sailed down through the Channel. The biography says that they put in to England, and the chronicler thinks that the port was Falmouth, which was then enjoying a boom consequent upon the West Indies trade. It was here that the skippers usually waited for good weather over Biscay. In Falmouth Jens Munk saw more ships than he had ever seen in his life. Three-masted frigates and caravels, galleys and ketches with forecastle and quarter-deck, low-lying, elegant galleons, small round-sterned Dutch boyers rigged with spritsail and forestaysail, slender fluyts with beautiful, rounded sterns, swift pinnaces with top-blinds and water-blinds—they all met here in Falmouth and lay a few weeks, rubbing planks with one another before sailing on west and south and east. Trans-atlantic sailors came in from the New World with salt in their beards and tobacco juice in the corner of their mouths and met silk traders from Amsterdam; the harbor was a jungle of masts and fluttering pennants; black, simian figures sat astride the yards, furling the bleached sails, and boys not much older than

Jens scaled the foremasts with rope ends between their teeth. These fellows won his admiration, for he had already attempted a turn up to the truck a couple of times in open sea.

One sunny day their course lay to the south again, and a couple of weeks later the carrack glided into Oporto. When the sacks of grain had been heaved ashore and the barrels of salt herring stacked up on the quay, Jens Munk signed off. In Oporto he had reached his goal for the time being, and with a letter from the master in his pocket he presented himself to one of the city's richest merchants, Duart Duez. The good manners he had learned in the burgomaster's stone house at Aalborg stood him in good stead now; Senhor Duez received him warmly and gave him a position in the warehouse. Six months later Jens had learned enough Portuguese to make himself useful in the office. Duart Duez noted his quick mind, took a fancy to him, and questioned him about his plans. Jens looked him straight in the eyes. He wanted to seek his fortune in the New World. Senhor Duez did not smile; he had a brother over there himself, who was also a merchant. His name was Miguel Duez and he lived in the town of Bahia, called by the Spaniards Baya de Todos los Santos.

A couple of months later a convoy was fitted out in Oporto, thirteen ships in all, nine Portuguese and four Dutch. They were bound for Brazil to fetch sugar for Duart Duez, and because of the danger of attack from pirates they were to sail in close convoy. For this reason three of the captains received military titles, even though they were all merchantmen. Jan van Bossen of Emden was made admiral, Roland of Flushing vice-admiral, and the level-headed Albert Jansen of Einkhusen rear admiral. Albert Jansen was captain on board the *Schoubynacht. Schoubynacht* was Dutch for "See by Night," a name particularly fitting for the ship whose task it was to ensure that the convoy kept to its course at night. Jens Munk was ship's boy on the *Schoubynacht*. In the biography he is called "cabin watch," which more or less means he was a servant in the officers' mess.

The thirteen ships left harbor with an easterly wind one autumn morning in 1592, the centenary of the discovery of America. That same year the French Count Ribolde equipped a heavily armed fleet of privateers in the harbor of La Rochelle.

2

Discovering America is a simple matter. Because of the sun's strength in the equatorial zones, the intense heat causes the air to rise; to compensate for the ensuing low pressure, a constant stream of cooler air moves in toward the equator from the tropics to the north and south. These regular air currents change direction on the way, however, owing to the rotation of the earth on its axis. Since the earth turns toward the east, the air currents in question are deflected in a westerly direction, with the result that all the year round north of the equator there is a steady northeast wind, known as the trade wind. Any ship from Spain would have a fair wind all the way to America. It was simply a question of slackening off the sheets and letting the wind have its way.

Standing on the fore-deck of the *Schoubynacht*, Jens Munk discovered that it was in fact easier to sail from Palos to San Salvador than from Fredrikstad to Aalborg. Instead of the wet, close-hauled passage of the cold northern waters, the eternal bracing of the sails, and the gale with rain in its wake, they now sailed on week after week with a calm, rolling, following sea. The sheets were lashed to the port side, and as there was nothing to do the crew passed the time on deck gambling and over mugs of ale. The unchanging tropical equinox reigned supreme; there were no clouds, no foaming billows. The only white against the blue sky were the ship's topsails, and the only white on the blue sea were the neat ruffs around their bows.

On board the *Schoubynacht* one week followed another without the sight of a foreign ship. The convoy's sole companion was the sun, which every morning rose vertically out of the sea far astern, and although the ships made rapid headway, and although the sun had to make the long detour up across the vault of the heavens, nevertheless it managed to overtake them every day at exactly twelve o'clock and eventually lay far ahead, hanging on the evening horizon like a red lantern before the ship's bowsprit, before diving down vertically into the water again. The earth was round; freely and weightlessly it was poised in space. But was that all? Did the sun revolve around the earth, or was it really the earth which circled the sun? In the city of Prague the young Johannes Kepler was making calculations based on the observations of Mars taken by Tycho Brahe from an island in the Sound: endless calculations based on twenty-one years of daily observations, until finally the great march of figures yielded its results at Easter, 1605. Every planet travels around the sun in an ellipse, the sun remaining stationary in one focus of the ellipse, and the areas swept out by the radius vector in equal times are equal. It was as simple as that.

So far everything had worked out in accordance with Jens Munk's wishes: he was on his way to the New World. In his ditty bag he had a letter from Duart Duez in Oporto, commending him to his brother, Miguel Duez, who was also a rich merchant.

Each day it got warmer, and as time went on it became impossible to find peace in the hot living quarters under the planks of the deck. The chronicler visualizes Jens Munk as he slipped up to the foredeck in the evening in search of a cool spot, and lay down in a coil of rope and peered up at the foremast. No longer did it inspire fear in him. For a long time now he had known every line and spar up there; he was the youngest person on board, and the tradition was that the lightest climbs highest. Up there one could see far and wide; it was from there that the enemy had to be spotted if Albert Jansen of Einkhusen was to get the cannon cleared for action in good time.

Then one morning the crew of the *Schoubynacht* noted a

50

strange movement of air over the ship; it struck them as mild and fresh and familiar; it made them think of grass and mud and the sweaty smell of stables. The old hands knew what it was. It was air from the land, drifting toward them. It was the New World, even though it smelled like the Old.

That same evening the convoy ran in to Baya de Todos los Santos. The bay opened out before the ships as though life itself were spreading its arms to receive them after the many weeks on the open sea. While the Governor exchanged words with Albert Jansen of Einkhusen, Jens Munk approached the Governor's black servant. It turned out that the Negro understood Portuguese. Jens Munk wanted to know where he could find Senhor Miguel Duez, brother of the well-known and prosperous Duart Duez in Oporto. The servant bowed; he was well acquainted with Senhor Miguel Duez, but as to his whereabouts, that was impossible to say. Miguel Duez had just left for Europe with one of his ships.

In these circumstances Jens Munk could not well remain in Bahia. A few weeks later he left the city once more on board the *Schoubynacht* and set out on the voyage which was to be the vessel's last.

3

The same sea, consisting like human tears of a neutral solution of sodium chloride, washes both the Danish and the Brazilian coast. The city was called Bahia, which in Portuguese as well as in Spanish means "bay." The full name of the city was Cidade de São Salvador de Bahia de Todos los Santos, Portuguese for "the City of the Holy Saviour on the Bay of All Saints." So many new discoveries had been made that it was becoming difficult to find names for them, and it became customary to name the new lands and places after the date on which they were found. Christovão Jacques discovered Bahia on November 1st, All Saints' Day. When, in the year 1532, Affonso de Souza entered another bay farther south and took it to be the mouth of a great river, it was January 1st, and he called it "January River," Rio de Janeiro.

But all that was during the Golden Age of Portugal. When Jens Munk arrived in the City of the Holy Saviour, sixty years later, Brazil was no longer Portuguese, and even Portugal was no longer Portuguese. In the course of a century the country had discovered and conquered one continent after another; in time it possessed practically the whole of India, Farther India, Africa, and South America. The caravels sailed out from Lisbon, and it seemed as if the small country around the mouth of the Tagus was intent upon spanning the entire globe. Then, in 1580, the fairy tale came to an abrupt end, not by wars of attrition but more simply: Portugal and all its possessions had been inherited by Philip II, King of Spain.

For a brief while Philip II ruled over an empire more than ten times as great as that of Alexander and Caesar. Apart from the Iberian Peninsula, he possessed Flanders, the new lands of America, three-quarters of Africa, and the Portuguese conquests in India, which extended as far as the Chinese border. Nevertheless, Philip felt himself hemmed in; whichever way he turned, his enemies threatened. Since Luther had unleashed the great religious conflict, almost half of Europe had fallen from the faith. Roman Catholicism, the holy *ecclesia universalis*, was forced onto the defensive. Philip, who owned nearly the whole world, saw the heretics advance and encircle him in the east and west, in the south and north. First he sent his magnificent Armada against the Turks, then against the English. In the name of the Holy Mother of God he burned Jews and Moors by the thousand on the squares of Spanish cities. But in the main, he turned north, against France, where a lengthy civil war persisted between the Holy Catholic League on the one side and Kings Henry III and Henry IV on the other. One of the Protestant strongholds in France was the port of La Rochelle on the Atlantic coast, where the Huguenots had formed a practically independent republic. The ruler was His Grace Ribolde, also called Ribolde de la Rochelle.

Map of the bay of Bahia. From a contemporary copperplate. (Barlaeus)

Ribolde de la Rochelle was greatly interested in sugar. In the year 1592 he equipped a number of fast pinks, appointed himself vice-admiral, and sailed out of La Rochelle harbor.

Barely one nautical mile from the Brazilian coast they sighted a convoy. The heavily laden ships lay low in the water; a few days earlier, they had left the City of the Holy Saviour on the Bay of All Saints. Afterward history recalled the name of only one ship in the convoy, and this was the *Schoubynacht*, and of all those who served on board the *Schoubynacht* it recalled only two men, the captain and his cabin-watch. The captain was Albert Jansen, of Einkhusen. He was that kind of person of whom history records only a name and a grave. The whole thing was settled before sunset. His cabin-watch had wanted to seek his fortune in the New World. This matter, too, was arranged by Fate in its own fashion before the sun went down.

At four o'clock in the afternoon Ribolde gave the order to open fire. The battle was brief, and a couple of hours later the true Gospel had triumphed once more. Albert Jansen's *Schoubynacht* had been set on fire, Jan van Bossen's ship sunk, and Roland of Flushing's vessel captured, disarmed, and occupied by a prize crew. During the execution of this task one of the French lieutenants caught sight of a hatch cover with seven survivors from the blazing *Schoubynacht*. He asked the vice-admiral if he should take them prisoner, but Ribolde replied that they had lost their ship and that he could not see any reason why others should share their misfortune with them. Dutifully the lieutenant asked if he should therefore have them executed. The vice-admiral answered tersely that they could be picked up by boat and set ashore on the coast.

Shortly afterward the two men on the French warship stood and watched the order being carried out.

The men began to row back. The black boat crept toward them like a large insect on the glittering surface, where the sunset blended blood with the glow from the burning *Schoubynacht*. The lieutenant looked toward the little group of captives left behind on the beach.

"Your Grace has a noble heart," he said. "The men have Your Grace to thank for the fact that they are still alive."

The vice-admiral made no reply, but stood looking into the

sun, which was sinking over the tropical forest. The Portuguese had never really succeeded in penetrating and colonizing these vast regions; their soldiers caught sleeping sickness and yellow fever and had to give up. The vice-admiral had heard that the forest still swarmed with hostile natives, who lay in wait in the trees with their blowpipes and poisoned darts. He took the view that you should not do today what you can get others to do for you tomorrow.

5

Larder and Cellar

When Ribolde de la Rochelle attacked the convoy the *Schouby-nacht* had been sailing northward for several days. The seven castaways whom the Frenchmen had set ashore in the jungle would therefore have to make their way to the south, if they were to attempt to return to Bahia. The distance could not have been very great, as the crow flies; nevertheless, progress was slow. They had to hide from the natives by day, and at night there were jaguars, crocodiles, and the large constrictor called anaconda by the Portuguese. Many days were wasted in attempts to find a way around swamps; heat and hunger exhausted them, for only occasionally were they fortunate enough to find bananas and bitter oranges; most of the time they had to be content with roots and stagnant swamp water. With their feet lacerated in the thorn thickets, bodies plagued by insects and leeches, and fever in their blood, they pushed on a little way south each day. We do not know how long it took them to reach their goal, nor how many of them perished on the way. We only know that the cabin-watch was among the survivors: "Meantime Jens Munk's plight was exceeding ill, and he suffered great tribulation, but did at last come in sorry condition to Baya de Todos los Santos," it says in the biography of 1723. One evening he covered the last stretch of the ridge, where Bahia lay facing the sea. When they had first come sailing to the city it had been as if the bay and life ashore had opened their arms to receive them; now he was coming from the north and sneaking into the city through a back door. Jens had told Duart Duez that he wanted to seek his fortune in the New World. Had he expected it to lead him to a palace? In the event, it was a cobbler's house, a painter's house, and a merchant's house. In the first he spent eleven months, in the second six months, and in the last he lived for four years.

In 1598 Jens Munk probably associated the idea of fatherland above all with his own father. During the seven years he had lived among strangers, no word of Erik's fate had reached him. Yet he could not believe that all hope had gone. Surely his father had long since got the better of his adversaries and broken out of prison, for no one could keep such a man penned in. Yet even if Erik had succumbed to the misery of his dungeon, there must at least be an inheritance waiting, which Jens Munk could claim and use in order to take revenge.

Now all the threads were drawn together. As Jens Munk returned home in the autumn of 1598 after his long adventure in the New World and, full of expectation, watched the coast of Zealand appear ahead, the drama inside Dragsholm had also reached its final scene.

2

Even in the darkest prison, says the chronicler, a back door stands half open to the light. In 1593 when the sick Erik Munk finally realized that the noblemen in the Council of the Realm had rejected his defense and turned down his plea to have his case brought to court, he had tried all possible ways of getting out of Dragsholm. He had engineered an attempt to escape which brought him nothing but more rigorous punishment. Year after year he sat in the dungeon, in the gloom, the stench, the chains, and suffering the insidious approach of madness. Broken and wretched, he wrote letter after letter in the hope of mollifying the mighty noblemen, the sole result of which was a curt statement to the effect that the matter had been dismissed.

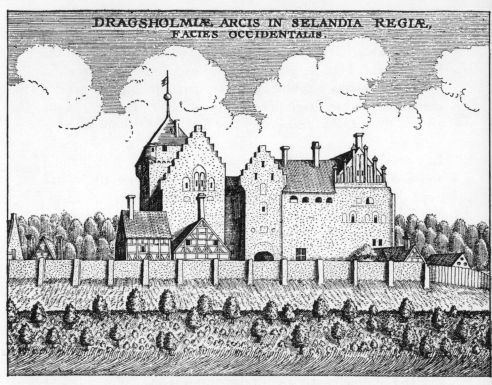

Dragsholm from the west. (Resen)

The end of Erik Munk's story is told by Eiler Brockenhaus, who compiled and printed an almanac with details of births, marriages, deaths, and other family occurrences among the aristocracy of the period. It is thanks to this almanac that we know the exact date of Erik Munk's arrival at Dragsholm, and it is here that we find the laconic announcement of his death: "Anno 1594 did Erik Munk hang himself at Dragsholm in the prison and was at that same place buried beneath the gallows."

Cut down by the executioner's assistant and flung into a hole in the ground under the gallows together with the remains of common thieves who had been hanged and murderers broken on the wheel—in this manner Erik Munk came to that

Dutch man-of-war. (Schoerner)

great, open country beyond the reach of his enemies. In those times it was usual for wolves which had been caught to be strung up on the gallows and afterward buried beneath them. In the eyes of his contemporaries it was hard to imagine a greater disgrace. Not only was Erik Munk an outcast of human society by virtue of his gallows grave: as a suicide he had also forfeited his hope of salvation; he was damned in eternity just as he had been in his life.

This was the news that awaited Jens Munk when the ship from Amsterdam moored alongside the quay at Gammel Strand in Copenhagen. He needed but to mention his father's name and every quayside loafer would hastily make the sign of the cross and begin to go into details with glowing eyes.

But Jens Munk does not seem to have been struck down by the cruel news awaiting him in Denmark. More likely it acted as a challenge, as a tremendous provocation. Now he was alone, and owned no more than the clothes he stood up in. This was his first time in Copenhagen. He did not know a soul, did not own a penny, but he was prepared to try anything to avenge his father and to secure his own advancement. No need for caution—he who is on the bottom cannot sink deeper.

His first action upon arrival in Copenhagen was to visit the Exchequer to claim his inheritance. At the Exchequer it was regretted that nothing was known about the matter. Not to be put off by this, Jens Munk wrote direct to His Royal Majesty. He was Erik Munk's son and he had come to Copenhagen to claim his inheritance. The King instructed his steward to refer the impetuous young man to Jørgen Bentsen, an elderly gentleman, who was alderman in Copenhagen from 1590 until 1605. Through him everything was finally revealed to Jens Munk. All Erik Munk's land and property had been confiscated by the State, which had also seized his remaining possessions and made them over to the Grammar School of Our Lady. However, in His gracious bounty, His Majesty had consented to a few small objects being set aside which the children might receive as mementos of their father. Alderman

Bentsen himself had charge of the bequest intended for Jens Munk, and a servant now entered with the objects in question: a silver tankard and some discarded clothing to the value of 80 rix-dollars. Alderman Bentsen kindly requested a receipt.

It was autumn, 1598. The King's instruction to the steward, preserved in the letter books of the Chancellery, was dated at Copenhagen on October 1st of that year. Jens Munk signed the receipt, stuffed the things into his ditty bag, and went out into the autumn sunshine. A silver tankard and some discarded clothes—that was what was left of the estates of Barbo, Borregaard, and Hiørne, of the extensive crown fiefs at Nedenaes, Bratsberg, and Nonnesaeter, of the scores of farms, which Our well-beloved Erik Munk had received for himself and his issue in perpetuity in token of his faithful service.

6

Hafnia Metropolis et Portus Celeberrimus Daniae

I

When Jens Munk saw Copenhagen for the first time, around 1600, the city which had been given the resplendent name "Hafnia Metropolis et Portus Celeberrimus Daniae" had only about twenty thousand inhabitants. It was bordered by water on all sides. At several points the water was quite shallow, and on warm summer days children could be seen paddling about among the carcasses of dead animals which the scavenger had not removed.

Framed in its glittering ring of moats and canals, the city itself was divided into seven divisions or quarters. In Jens Munk's days the quarters had other names, but by and large the streets were called the same as they are today.

Amagertorv and the surrounding streets were incomparably the most exclusive quarter in Copenhagen. People thronged here, both native Copenhageners and foreigners, and this gave impetus to the establishment of alehouses and inns. In the streets near the waterfront, drinking places abounded. To live is to quench one's thirst and to satisfy one's hunger. On the whole, rather more was drunk at these alehouses than was eaten. In the year 1600 coffee and tea had not yet reached Hafnia Metropolis Celeberrima; people managed on ale, wine, and brandy, especially the former. It was assumed that every adult required six quarts of ale a day, and an ordinary seaman in the navy had the right to five quarts daily.

Some of the alehouses gave rise to complaints. There one found "great moral laxity and disorderly behavior, with drinking at night, fornication, fighting, and other things inducive of God's wrath." But these everyday events were nothing compared with the excesses which occurred during the real gala days in Hafnia Metropolis Celeberrima. Besides providing the setting for the two weekly market days, Amagertorv was also the scene of the tourneys held by the Court and the nobility; and only three years before Jens Munk's arrival in the city there had been a spectacle, the like of which none of the inhabitants of the city had ever seen before.

On August 29th in the year of Our Lord 1596, a lanky hotspur of nineteen years, born under the sign of Aquarius, was to be crowned as King of Denmark and Norway. Everything was ready: to celebrate the coronation there were 1040 oxen, 3550 lambs, 3100 geese, 30,000 dried flatfish, 45,000 loaves of bread, 112,000 quarts of wine, and 35,000 drinking glasses. Foreign princes and ambassadors were invited to the city in such numbers that they alone had 2200 horses with them. In addition to this, the whole of the Danish and a great part of the Holstein nobility came with their wives, daughters, and servants. The streets were thronged with young warriors clad in velveteen kirtles with golden chains and silver-mounted daggers who came galloping along on the most beautiful silk-gray horses, decorated at head and rump with all kinds of plumes. And this was only the prelude. On August 29th, at nine o'clock in the morning, the coronation procession was to cross the tightly packed Amagertorv on its way from Højbro to the Church of Our Lady. The sun shone, and along the route stood the Civil Guard drawn up in full uniform; but all eyes were turned toward Højbrostraede. First to come into view was a drummer beating on two kettledrums of silver decorated with flags and the King's coat of arms. Then followed nine trumpeters with black cloaks hanging loosely over their coats of yellow satin and tight-fitting red velveteen hose. The sun glittered on the trumpets, which were of silver and decked with damask banners bearing the gold-embroidered arms of the King. After them came the Lord Chancellor with a nobleman on either side, and then, three by three, the whole of the realm's nobility with the Court younkers of the King and the Queen Mother, the ambassadors of the foreign rulers, representatives from Hamburg, Lübeck, and Danzig, the High Council from the duchies, and, riding at an ambling pace, the Council of the Realm of Denmark, the mighty men who had disposed of Erik Munk a few years previously.

The procession had long since stretched right across Amagertorv, and still none of the royalty had come into sight at the entrance to Højbrostraede. Behind the Council of the Realm came yet another kettledrummer with two silver drums, then fifteen trumpeters, then two heralds in expensively trimmed dress, then the four most senior of the Councillors of the Realm clad in long velvet cloaks and riding in single file with the regalia, the first with the orb, the second with the sword, the third with the scepter, and the last with the crown, which he held out in front of him so that the light could flash from its 970 inset diamonds and pearls. This was the signal: at once the great throng fell silent. Now everyone could see the nineteen-year-old youth who was the object of the celebration; he came riding in a chalk-white habit embroidered with gold and silver and silk and over that a black velvet cloak trimmed with wide bands of pearls. The intensity of youth marked his beardless, inexperienced face; in contrast to the white-haired Councillors of the Realm, he looked a mere student; yet he rode calm and self-possessed on his glossy gray horse.

Hafnia Metropolis Celeberrima. The inner harbor between Slotsholmen and the city, which were connected by Holmensbro and Højbro. Behind the gables down toward Gammel Strand stands the Church of the Holy Ghost, and out in the open country beyond Nørrevold one can see the outline of Rosenborg, although the construction of the castle had barely begun as the picture dates from about 1611. A section from Jan Dircksen's copperplate after the painting by Johan van Wick. (National Museum)

Three hours later, at exactly half past twelve, the procession returned in the same order as before. This time, however, the King was no longer clad in black and white, but in a kirtle of red brocade, and the 970 stones of the King's crown sparkled on his head as he sat his horse with the scepter in one hand and the reins in the other. Now he was no longer a nineteen-year-old student. He was Christian IV.

The fountain on Amagertorv began to flow with red and white wine; in the middle of the square a whole ox, stuffed with a variety of game and poultry, was roasted on a spit over an open fire. The celebrations were brought to their climax a few days later with two days' tilting at the ring, which likewise took place on Amagertorv. Within two days the King carried away the ring on his lance 206 times.

Because of these tournaments, which were repeated at intervals, the King was eager to acquire houses along Amagertorv. If, occasionally, he had to dispose of a property there, a clause in the title deed obliged the purchaser to maintain an armory providing jousting and single-combat weapons and a large room facing the square, where the King and his retinue could be accommodated at tournament time.

Such a property was the present No. 8 on Amagertorv. In 1594, two years before the coronation and five years before Jens Munk's arrival in Copenhagen, the then Crown Prince had commanded the Castellan to modify and improve this property, which the Crown Prince had given to a certain Henrik Ramel for his residence. The result was a magnificent palace, behind whose walls lived the enigmatic Henrik Ramel, of whom it was said that next to the King he was the most powerful man in the realm.

It was to this house that Jens Munk went after his encounter with Councillor Bentsen. He was a stranger in Copenhagen, he did not know to whom one doffed one's hat on Amagertorv; nor had he been present at the crowning of King Christian, who was almost the same age and would later come to play such a decisive role in his life. But he did know the puissant Henrik Ramel, for his name had come up in an earlier context. When Erik Munk had seized the English ships at the North Cape in 1582, the government had sent to London a diplomat who persuaded England the following year to acknowledge Danish suzerainty in the Norwegian Sea—the suave and dangerous feudal overlord and Councillor of the Realm, Henrik Ramel.

7

"What care I for the moon, while the sun is shining?"

I

Henrik Ramel was born the son of a rich nobleman in Farther Pomerania; he traveled widely in his youth, owned much and was to be given still more. He came to Copenhagen as a man of thirty-one, greatly impressed Queen Sophia, and became tutor to her eldest son, the five-year-old Prince Christian. Five years later, in London, he reaped the diplomatic rewards of Erik Munk's action in the Norwegian Sea.

Ramel was now the leading figure in Danish foreign policy. His wide experience and his eloquence in German and Latin impressed the foreign ambassadors; and when Queen Sophia came into conflict with the regency government after the death of the King, he succeeded, by a remarkable piece of tightrope walking, in maneuvering between the two parties. Upon the coronation of Christian IV he was given his seat in the Council of the Realm, and during the procession on Amagertorv he could be seen in his long velveteen cloak accompanying the Queen Mother's carriage on horseback. Henrik Ramel had mastered to perfection the art of being friends or enemies of the right people at the right time; and at the turn of the century he not only owned the stately house on Amagertorv, he also had a number of estates in Poland, along with Baekkeskov Abbey in Scania, the Deanery in Lund, Åhus fief unencumbered, the royal manor Fovslet in North Schleswig, the manor of Villand, and the Vallensgaard estate on Bornholm.

Face to face with this man there now stood a nineteen-year-old illegitimate son of a suicide father, whose entire fortune amounted to a silver tankard and eighty dollars' worth of old clothes. Jens Munk himself, however, did not see it this way; admittedly he was poor, but not like the hundreds of wretched creatures leading a beggar's life in the streets of the city. For him poverty was not a mark of fate but at most a temporary inconvenience; no mortal wound, but simply an insignificant scratch that would soon heal. He stood there as the son of Erik Munk: it went without saying that upon his arrival in Denmark he should seek out the most powerful man in the country, just as he had once approached the rich Duart Duez in Oporto. He belonged among these people who ruled over their fellow men and managed their affairs unimpeded by petty financial considerations. Full of the exuberance of youth, he explained his plans and outlined his qualifications. He had it in mind to offer his services on one of the ships with which the puissant Councillor of the Realm conducted his extensive foreign commerce. He felt it his vocation to command others, to control ships and destinies, to win riches and respect. He had, after all, noble blood in his veins, and sooner or later they would surely have to restore his old privileges to him. Naïvely and warmly, he told of his years abroad. Had he not already seen more of the world than any other citizen of Copenhagen, lived among the people of three continents, black and white, conquistadors and slaves? He spoke fluent Portuguese, had a knowledge of the chief commercial languages, Dutch and Spanish, knew what there was to know about shipping and chartering. What other people only knew from hearsay—of pirates and shipwreck, gales and waterspouts, the great-circle routes of the Atlantic Ocean—these were things of which he had personal experience. Now he was offering to place his experience at the disposal of Herr Ramel. He bowed submissively, secretly pleased with himself. The many years with Miguel Duez had taught him how to behave toward influential personages.

69

Henrik Ramel had listened to the young man's long report without attempting to conceal his boredom. Of course he remembered Erik Munk very well. Thanks to his intimate connections with the noblemen in the regency government, he even had a detailed knowledge of the intrigues which had occasioned that lord's downfall. But lost causes were not Henrik Ramel's affair; his diplomatic insight told him that Erik Munk's name was no gilt-edged security in contemporary Denmark; in short, he would have to disappoint this pleasant young man. There was no question of Jens Munk's obtaining an assignment of any consequence in his merchant fleet; but Henrik Ramel had no objection to signing him on as ship's writer if the young man would be content with that. That was practically the same as junior clerk, a menial occupation. Disappointed, Jens Munk was about to begin a new approach when he realized from the icy atmosphere in the room that the audience was over.

It is uncertain just when the two men met. The biography of 1723 mentions the year 1601, but everything seems to point to its having been immediately after his return home that Munk got in touch with Ramel. The biography mentions that in the course of the year 1600 and some part of the following year he made four voyages to Spain as ship's writer.

Commerce with Spain at that time constituted an important part of Denmark's foreign trade; it involved the so-called salt ships, often vessels of several hundred tons, which carried home the coarse bay salt used in great quantities for the pickling of meat in Copenhagen, where slaughtering was done only once a year. At about the turn of the century, however, this trade had declined considerably; there was trade with Iceland, Narva, and Newcastle, but only seldom did a ship come home from Spain. Wars and pirates had made navigation insecure, and few shipowners could afford to run the risk of losing ship, cargo, and crew. At the same time this situation had forced up freight rates, and there was good money to be made here. It is no surprise, therefore, that Henrik Ramel in particular should himself have taken a keen interest in the Spanish trade. He was practically without competitors, and it must surely have been on board one of his ships that Jens Munk made the four voyages in question. In spite of everything, the young man had been able to give a satisfactory account of his knowledge of things Spanish, and Henrik Ramel must have agreed on that basis.

The intention of becoming his own master with which Jens Munk had left Bahia had received a great setback. To raise the necessary capital, he would have to resign himself to working for others for a while. But things would have to move quickly; he was not prepared to waste time. He submitted to the bitter facts and agreed to become a ship's writer; but he chose the hazardous and well-paid Spanish trade, and he signed up for several voyages in succession. Four voyages in less than six months constitutes an absolute maximum for the sluggish merchantmen of the time, which often had to waste months slowly tacking their way forward. He was not content to sail in the summer only, but signed on for the hard winter voyages as well. That was something very different from the lazy life under Bahia's tropical sun; it meant frostbitten feet and skin flayed from the hands, but it also meant money. And as he had almost no expenses, every skilling could be laid aside.

During the following years he kept up the same savage speed. For the period 1601 to 1605 the biographer reels off no fewer than nine voyages to Narva, four to Danzig, one voyage to Amsterdam, and a further three voyages to Spain—the greatest possible number for this space of time.

These six years and the many thousands of miles sailed do not occupy much of the chronicler's narrative. But what, indeed, is there to tell? A seaman's life is humdrum, devoid of events. The ocean covers three quarters of the globe, but history prefers to keep to land. On February 17, 1600, Giordano Bruno was burned alive on the Campo dei Fiori in Rome; Jens Munk was at sea. On October 24, 1601, Tycho

Brahe died in Prague, exiled and bitter; Jens Munk was at sea. In France Henry IV was on the throne; in Spain a down-at-heel rag-and-bone man was released from the debtors' prison in Seville and made his way to Madrid to get his manuscript on the bold knight Don Quixote de la Mancha printed; in Frederik Christensen's stone house in Aalborg Anna Munksdatter died; Jens Munk was at sea. In 1603 Frederik Christensen entered into matrimony with the young Margrethe Jørgensdatter; Queen Elizabeth died; England and Scotland were united; William Shakespeare wrote *Hamlet*; Jens Munk was at sea. In 1604 Galileo turned against the teachings of Aristotle on the immutability of the universe, and the Inquisitors began to prepare the torture chamber. In 1605 the miller's wife in the town of Leiden, in Holland, was again expecting a child, which this time turned out to be a son, and was given the name of Rembrandt Harmensz van Rijn; Jens Munk was at sea.

Finally there was sufficient money saved. When he returned home from his last Spanish voyage, in 1605, he was finally in a position to take leave of Henrik Ramel. In Copenhagen he met his brother Niels, who the year before had joined the King's navy. As early as 1601 Niels was mentioned as the royal interpreter in Russian and was employed at the Chancellery. His knowledge of Russian can scarcely have any other explanation than that he sailed when young on the northern route to Archangel, which had once been opened by his father. He, too, was following in Erik Munk's footsteps. His presence in Copenhagen in 1601 made it possible for the two brothers to meet every time Jens returned from one of his voyages. This elder brother was Jens Munk's only contact in Copenhagen; the two young men found themselves in the same situation, felt the same humiliation and the same need for redress. Niels, in fact, proved to be his brother's only friend and ally for many years to come. In 1605 Jens Munk received a trade licence as an independent merchant in Copenhagen. Now there was money enough. Now he would have his own larder, his own cellar.

It was probably during this same year that he rented a house in Pilestraede. At that time the street still had a rural air; the west side was made up of the back gardens of the prosperous houses on Købmagergade; elder bushes and apple trees grew out over the hedge, and only the east side of the street had houses. Pilestraede had been paved for a considerable time, but it was regarded as part of the city's shabbier quarters, and was only in the fourth tax class. The young man obviously had to be modest in his choice of dwelling, but he preferred to be his own master in the fourth tax class than a lackey in the first.

This was in 1605. The very same year a thirty-foot narwhal was caught off Iceland, and its six-foot horn is said to have been sold for forty thousand rix-dollars, a couple of million Danish crowns in today's currency. Shortly afterward one of the King's new frigates was launched from Bremerholm, and quite naturally it was named the *Unicorn* for that lucky catch off Iceland.

2

The launching of the *Unicorn* was not the most important occurrence that year in Copenhagen. Greenland was redis-covered. In July, Godske Lindenow returned home from the west coast with a number of Eskimos, who were made to display their skill with kayaks in the canals. Lindenow had much to report about the Greenland silver mines, all of which gave Jens Munk much to think about. Hitherto his voyages had all been southward; but now the coasts of the Norwegian Sea began to tempt him with the promise of quite different rewards. His first move as an independent skipper was to approach a certain Børge Trolle. Børge Trolle had for long years sailed the Norwegian Sea and knew all the ports of call from Iceland to Vardø. He had the reputation of being a skilled captain, and he could hold his own both at tilting at the ring and at the drinking sessions afterward. "What care I for the moon,while the sun is shining?" was his motto. For some years he had been vassal in Erik Munk's old fief at Nedenaes, and so Jens Munk was able to begin his visit with a reference to his father.

Trolle had by now retired from his position on Bremerholm and seems to have made his living principally from his three ships: the *Black Dog*, the *Jack of Clubs*, and the *Jupiter*. Jens Munk purchased a share in one of these ships and began business on his own account. No information is available about his activities in the year 1606; at the outset he probably had to content himself with the home trade, which was less demanding in terms of capital. But the following year he sailed south to France and put in at the port of La Rochelle. Doubtless, as the chronicler suggests, there is an element of symbolism in the fact that on his first independent voyage Munk steered straight to that city in Charente Maritime controlled by the formidable Ribolde. Fifteen years previously Ribolde had set fire to the vessel he happened to be on and had left him to his fate among the natives in the Brazilian jungle. But the cabin boy had become captain; the condemned man was more alive than ever.

In La Rochelle he began to feel confidence in himself and in his destiny. The powerful Count Ribolde was a symbol of those smug noblemen at home in Copenhagen, who also imagined that he had been rendered harmless. There was something of his father's arrogance in the way he tempted Fate by making this voyage into the past; and when he returned home a few months later he behaved in much the same way. The trip to La Rochelle had also been a hazardous winter voyage, and it was not until December 15th that he rounded Kronborg on his homeward voyage. The following day he was unable to put in to Copenhagen because of ice. How was he to dispose of his cargo? For several hours he sailed to and fro in the approaches; then, disregarding all risks, he dropped anchor and discharged the whole of his precious cargo on the ice, from which he got carts and pole-bearers to transport it into the city. Luck was with him, and the event aroused such attention in Copenhagen that it was entered in the city annals.

Winter, which began early that year, proved to be severe and long. In January the King and Queen, Anne Catherine, had to cross the ice in order to get from Copenhagen to Malmö; and even by Easter the Sound was still frozen over. As soon as the ice broke up, however, Jens Munk set sail again; and this time the trip was not to the south, but northward to Husevig, in Iceland. Since the founding of the Icelandic Trading Company in 1602, commerce with that remote island had been flourishing. The Icelanders needed corn, cloth, iron, and timber and in exchange could supply dried fish, hides, eider-down, and large quantities of sulphur, essential for the production of gunpowder. In Husevig Jens Munk did indeed take on a cargo of unprocessed sulphur; but at the same time he probably attempted to gather general information about sailing conditions in the Norwegian Sea. Another journey to Greenland had revealed that Lindenow's silver mines contained nothing but rubble; the year before, however, a young English master mariner, Henry Hudson, had reached Spitsbergen in an attempt to find the Northeast Passage to China and had returned with sensational accounts of the enormous number of whales he had observed. Through centuries of intensive hunting the Basques had gradually driven the whales from the Atlantic Ocean; now, spurred on by Hudson's reports, English and Dutch ships moved north to where the new whaling grounds promised fabulous rewards.

When Jens Munk returned to Copenhagen after his summer in Iceland, in 1608, he had already made his decision. Now he had a little more money; he sold his share in Børge Trolle's ship and bought himself a vessel which cost him two thousand rix-dollars fully equipped. He had to be content with an old craft—it was impossible to get much of a ship for that sum of money, but it was better than nothing. At the same time he went into partnership with Jens Hvid, who likewise

75

was the owner of a merchantman. People shook their heads: this young skipper had big ideas.

Yet he was not the only one of his kind in 1608. The times were good. Jørgen Friborg had hardly finished two of the wings of Frederiksborg Castle when the King bought forty-one gardens outside Østervold as the site of the new Rosenborg; and his large brew-house on Slotsholmen was just being brought into commission. There was need for ale in Copenhagen, where people were preparing to pay homage to the prince. Ale and fireworks. The accounts of the Arsenal for this year reveal that seventy-six irreplaceable manuscripts from Søro Monastery had been found—unique records covering the whole of Danish religious, political, and economic medieval history. As a matter of form the King was consulted in regard to what should be done with the old manuscripts. His Majesty had not opened a book since he had been tutored, but he was categorically opposed to this valuable find being wasted. With his usual authority he replied that the seventy-six books should be delivered to the master of the royal fireworks, who was to use them in the manufacture of cartridge cases.

3

Initially everything went according to plan. When spring came Jens Munk and his partner had completed their preparations, and on May 21, 1609, the two ships left Copenhagen laden with small articles of trade. Their destination was Novaya Zemlya, in the Barents Sea, where they intended to buy the pelts of arctic foxes, polar bears, and ermine. This was the usual commercial objective of such journeys; but when one considers those voyages in the light of later events, there is no doubt that they also had other aims in view. Henry Hudson had found whales off Spitsbergen during an attempt to find a Northeast Passage. When Jens Munk conceived the ambitious plan of pursuing the same objective, what was more natural than to shape a course for the Barents Sea? He did not go to

Spitsbergen; he sailed to the north of Norway, to the waters he was acquainted with from the accounts of his father and brother. If there were whales off Spitsbergen, then they must also be found north of Norway; and as far as the Northeast Passage was concerned, he would be far nearer to a solution up there than Hudson was at Spitsbergen.

On his thirtieth birthday, June 3rd, the two ships sailed along the west coast of Norway. A few weeks later they rounded North Cape and sailed past Vardøhus, where Erik Munk had been castle bailiff in his young days. They saw no whales, but when they had passed Kildin it was evident that the arctic winter had been more severe than usual that year. The fairway, which by now should have been comparatively ice-free, lay before them filled with drift ice. They succeeded in forcing a way forward to the White Sea approaches, but then Jens Hvid would not go any farther. He suggested that because of the ice they should abandon their original plan of sailing to Novaya Zemlya and proceed south to Archangel instead. Jens Munk refused; for him a voyage to Novaya Zemlya was nothing very special. He had had experience of winter sailing before and had no intention of giving up his plans. This difference of opinion between them ended in compromise. Jens Munk could do what he wanted; meanwhile Jens Hvid would anchor in a natural harbor on the mainland and do a little bear hunting. In the biography, this natural harbor is said to be situated near to Kandmoss. This name does not appear on any map; presumably, it is a misspelling of Kanin Nos or Kaninnaesset, the long peninsula running northwest and sheltering the approaches to the White Sea.

It was a month since they had left Copenhagen. Jens Munk took leave of his partner, got under sail, and steered his old vessel into the bleak, ice-filled Barents Sea.

Ever since Jens Munk's father had captured the English merchantmen in approximately the same waters in 1582, this remote part of the world had been the scene of dramatic events. The Dutch would not give up their navigation in the arctic. In

77

1596 Willem Barents with a single ship succeeded in getting north of Novaya Zemlya, where he was forced to find a harbor for the winter; but as the ice remained the following spring, and provisions gave out, the ship had to be abandoned. With two open boats the wretched crew made their way southward; and a few days later it proved necessary to leave behind on an ice floe Willem Barents, the man who gave both his life and his name to the sea. Many weeks later, what was left of his men were taken on board a Dutch ship; by then most of them had perished from cold, hunger, and exhaustion.

The fate of the Barents expedition gives some idea of the difficulties encountered by shipping in these seas. Charts were non-existent; at the most Jens Munk may have had some Dutch aids with him, sketches by Gerhardus Mercator brought up to date by Jodocus Hondius and Abraham Ortelius; but they were full of errors. In addition to this, astronomical observations and the taking of bearings were made difficult partly by the clouds and fogs, partly by the strong refraction of light; and the practice of using a little quicksilver in a bowl as an artificial horizon had not yet been discovered. Nor could the compass be relied upon; because of the high magnetic latitude the needle's sensitivity was very poor; the iron nails of the ship caused a far greater instability than in other waters; and finally the many subterranean deposits of iron ore caused considerable distortion, which was intensified by the shallowness of the continental shelf. The Barents Sea lies five degrees of latitude north of the Polar Circle; spring is the best season, when there is little cloudiness, there is no wind, and the sun is already so strong that even at $-20°$ C. it is possible to work out in the open without head covering. But in May the cloud increases, the fog thickens, and the most unpleasant season—summer—begins. It is not particularly cold, but the air is heavy with water vapor; a constant drizzle saturates everything. Where navigation was earlier made impossible because of pack ice, ships now have to grope their way forward between shoals and reefs in visibility often less than the ship's own length. Ashore

The ships of Willem Barents in the Arctic Ocean. The image in the sky between them is a clumsy attempt to represent the well-known arctic mock-sun phenomenon, which is also referred to in Munk. (Gerrit de Veer)

on the low-lying land the tundra turns green beneath colossal swarms of midges; the blue forget-me-nots bloom between moss and lichen, and dwarf willows and junipers creep across the landscape in which countless pools gape leadenly at the gray sky. Only the upper layers of the soil are thawed out; a few feet below the surface the permafrost prevails, preventing drainage and forming endless impenetrable marshes. Many are the seamen who after months of struggling with the ice have reached the land here only to drown in the mud instead of the sea. The light is the same throughout the entire day, without shadow or contrast, and the hours are indicated only by the clock. Behind the gray, monotonous layer of cloud the disk of the sun is scarcely visible.

Jens Munk left Kanin Nos and stood out on the lonely voyage to Novaya Zemlya. During the whole passage he kept his logbook meticulously from hour to hour, and the biography of 1723 records the most important of its data. Thanks to this information, we can reconstruct the last days before the catastrophe with great accuracy.

In the early stages there was no drift ice of any consequence; and when Kanin Nos disappeared in the mist astern, they steered northeast by east before a light southerly wind. They still saw no whales, but on the morning of June 24th they sighted land. Jens Munk realized that this was not Novaya Zemlya but the island of Kolguev, which lies a few hundred nautical miles from the mainland. Taking frequent soundings, he steered in toward the coast and anchored in the mouth of a fjord, where at low tide he had seven feet of water. The island proved to be without vegetation of any sort, but on the west side of the fjord four wooden crosses had been erected and there was a similar one on the east side. Jens Munk concluded from this that there must be people on the island and that the Russians must trade with them. He dared not continue up the fjord in the ship's dinghy: the weather had thickened and the ship lay off an open foreshore. Instead, he sent some men ashore, but they met no human beings: "And they observed naught, except the spore of three or four bears and a fox, besides which lay the backbones of many Rosmer whales or walrus there."

When the wind freshened from the northwest that same evening their anchorage became too dangerous; in the event of a storm they would find themselves lying right in the middle of the breakers. Munk gave orders to set sail and put out to sea again. As he still wanted to head northward to Novaya Zemlya, he had initially to work his way to the west in order to get free of land. It is unlikely that the ship was very maneuverable; this was a difficult operation, and now it suddenly became mortally dangerous, for a few miles out they met drift ice.

It could not have taken Munk many moments to appreciate

the situation. There could be no question of pushing on against the movement of the ice; it was ten o'clock in the evening, and the wind was now blowing strongly from the west and pressing the ice masses of the Arctic Ocean in toward the land. As the minutes passed, the belt of open water between the edge of the ice and the coast was growing ever narrower; if they did not succeed in getting away quickly, the ship would be crushed like an egg in a vise. Munk had no alternative but to fall off on the starboard tack, his hope being that with the wind abeam and all sails out he might achieve sufficient way to round the north of the island and get into the lee of its opposite coast, where he would be protected from the drift of the ice for the time being.

The race against time lasted for the whole of that night. Jens Munk kept close in to the ice in order to avoid for as long as possible the dangerous reefs along the coast. The sails were as taut as sheet metal. To the windward the endless ice field disappeared into the fog, to the leeward the roar of the breakers got nearer and nearer. When they were forced close in to the land, the low coastline finally relented and on the morning of June 25th they succeeded in rounding the most northerly point of Kolguev and getting safely to leeward of the east coast of the island, where they dropped anchor in thirteen fathoms.

For the time being the ship was safe here. While the crew rested after their efforts, Jens Munk had time to consider the situation. The immediate danger had passed, but their position was still serious. If the wind changed they would be surrounded by ice in the matter of a few hours, with the result that the ship would either be smashed upon the coast or carried away by the drift into the unknown Arctic Ocean. In the latter case they would be lost. With a shipwreck they might perhaps be able to get ashore safely, but what then? Jens Munk was aware of Willem Barents's fate; as things stood there was no alternative but to give up Novaya Zemlya and start upon the return voyage as quickly as possible. From the biography it seems that Jens Munk weighed anchor that very evening and sailed southward along the east coast of the island, which according to his compass ran southeast by south, a misreading of several degrees. Fortunately, this coast was considerably less rugged than the west coast, and by diligent use of the lead they discovered that the bottom sloped steeply; only half a mile from land there was between 6 and 7 fathoms of water and a clean sandy bottom everywhere. On the morning of the 26th they again sighted ice and dropped anchor a mile from the shore in 8 fathoms in the hope that the ice would drift away. It must have been a cloudless day; by taking a reading on the sun at noon Jens Munk fixed their position at 69° north, while the compass variation was calculated at 2 points. This last entry is difficult to check, since of course the variation changes from year to year; but the fixing of the position is accurate; according to modern maps, Kolguev lies a little above the 69th parallel of latitude north.

From this anchorage, too, Jens Munk sent men ashore to investigate conditions, but again without finding any human beings. The only things they had with them when they returned to the ship in the evening were three cygnets, which were immediately eaten. They had then pressed on to the south coast of the island and found the narrow bay which cuts into the land, forming a natural harbor.

At this point the biography becomes rather vague, but it is most likely that the returning seamen described the good anchorage in the bay in question, and that Jens Munk then decided to make for it in the hope of finding better shelter from the ice than that offered by the bare, exposed east coast. At all events two things are clear: he weighed anchor on June 26th, and the course was southerly.

During the preceding days the action of wind and current had surrounded Kolguev with drift ice, and now Jens Munk was sailing his old ship south to save it from being trapped. The rigging was lit by an unreal gray light; behind the veil of stratus cloud the sun looked like the cold full moon; a fresh breeze was blowing in from the east. Because of the ice, the

Pink ice-bound
off Novaya
Zemlya. From
a contemporary
copperplate.
(Gerrit de Veer)

sea was completely without waves; on the other hand, one could scarcely make oneself heard up on deck because of the noise from the ice pack, which scraped along the ship's side with great crashing noises. Several hours passed, whereupon the noise began to subside; the wind blew as strongly as before, but they were making no headway at all. Jens Munk attempted to go about with the wind aft—but in vain. The four stout men who rushed to the tiller had to give up, for the ship would not answer the helm any more. The sails stood taut as drumheads; the howling of the wind in the rigging and stays seemed to have risen several notes, but the noise from the side of the ship had stopped. The ice still lay around them; the ship was motionless. All attempts to kedge it free were unavailing; the men put on more sail; they had reached the limit of what the masts and shrouds could stand, but it had no effect. On the contrary, the ship now began to turn beneath them independently of rudder and canvas. Jens Munk stood looking on helplessly, like a man relieved of his command. The ice had taken over; the ship was ice-bound. Then things began to move quickly. The old hull could not withstand the pressure of the masses of ice; it was a case of "rivet-sickness," a term used when the nails of a wooden ship, attacked by years of rust, gradually weaken until they reach the breaking point. What is serious about this type of corrosion is that inevitably all the nails below the water line reach this stage at the same time. This was no mere leak; the men could hear the water pouring into the hold where Jens Munk had his stores, his equipment, and his cargo. He himself rushed across and took over the pump, then realized that the work was pointless. He announced his decision. The dinghy was lowered on to the ice, and the crew and the skipper disembarked. All were silent; it was clear that nothing could be done. The ship was sinking.

8

A Certain Christian Frederiksen

In order to understand the background of the events which were now gathering momentum, it is necessary to speak of a man who had already sailed these waters ten years previously: a certain Christian Frederiksen of Copenhagen. On the evening of April 17, 1599, a frigate called the *Victor* had sailed up through the Sound. On board there were, among others, a nobleman by the name of Sivert Grubbe and a doctor of laws called Jonas Charisius, both of whom have given an account of the voyage. The commander of the vessel called himself Captain-General Christian Frederiksen. All on board knew that this was not the man's real name, but they kept their knowledge to themselves, since they had received instructions not to divulge his true identity under any circumstances on penalty of death.

Amid brisk salutes from Kronborg the man-of-war slipped into the Kattegat, and a few days later the weather was so clear and calm that Dr. Charisius could see both the coast of Norway and the church on the Skaw from the sterncastle of the ship. On April 20th they put in to Flekkerø, where the *Victor* was awaited by seven more ships, among them the *Roebuck* whose commander was that Børge Trolle who made over a share in one of his ships to Jens Munk a few years later. The entire squadron then proceeded north along the Norwegian coast; they ran into heavy rains with gales and cold, and it was difficult for the other ships to keep pace with the *Victor*, which

85

time and time again had to shorten sail so as not to leave the others behind. Nevertheless, during the voyage they succeeded in capturing two English vessels which were engaged in unlawful fishing, and at the beginning of May all the ships passed the snow-covered North Cape and assembled once more in the harbor of Vardø.

The rocky, barren island depressed the members of the expedition. A more wretched fortress, says Dr. Charisius referring to Vardøhus, was hardly imaginable. Erik Munk's old castle was only a square stone building, eighty feet each way, and surrounded by a tumble-down ring wall of slate, incapable of withstanding an armed attack. The population lived in miserable holes in the ground, together with their sheep and goats, and Sivert Grubbe recognized in the island's drunken priest a former student who had been expelled from the University of Copenhagen, an ignorant brute who passed the time away by brewing ale from the mash that he managed to beg from the castle. Worst of all was the overwhelming stench that hung over the island, and which came from the thousands of fish the inhabitants had hung up to dry outside their hovels. After a few days Captain Frederiksen had had enough, and on May 15th he gave orders to weigh anchor and proceed.

En route the squadron met a vessel from Copenhagen, the captain of which complained that he had suffered damage at the hands of some Englishmen in the neighborhood. One of the English ships was immediately traced and seized, and under thumbscrews the captain revealed that the others were to be found off the island of Kildin. But by the time the slow-moving squadron arrived here, the English ships had already retired to a bay farther east. Now Captain Frederiksen lost patience; he ordered all sail onto the *Victor* and left the rest of the convoy astern. Although in unfamiliar waters, he made straight toward the Englishmen, with the consequence that the *Victor* ran her keel on a submerged reef and was badly holed below the water line. The ship brought up with so sudden a jerk that every other man aboard went head over heels, writes the horrified Dr. Charisius. Meanwhile the Englishmen prepared to give the disabled vessel a broadside. This did not deter Christian Frederiksen. He refloated the *Victor*, stuffed oakum into the leak, and then, with badly damaged rudder and keel and with half the crew at the pumps, sailed straight ahead and boarded the English ships, the crews of which were overpowered, clapped in irons, and forced to see their ships taken prize together with all of the cargo.

By this time the *Victor* was half full of water, and the problem then was to get back to Kildin in the shortest possible time. When they finally got a favorable wind, however, a violent storm arose which made it impossible to put out to the open sea; the ships were driven in toward the rocks, and Dr. Charisius felt sure that his last moment had come. With an oath, Frederiksen was forced to release the two English captains, who knew the waters from earlier fishing expeditions and now piloted the ships free of the coast. On May 20th they put in to the harbor at Kildin, where the *Victor* had to be careened.

The repairs took a week, and Dr. Charisius found time for a description of the island with its Lapps, its reindeer, its blue foxes and stockfish. Thereafter they made their way back to Vardø. During the passage Captain Frederiksen captured yet another vessel, the Dutch master of which lost his life during a short exchange of fire. The burial took place on Vardø amidst great merriment. Everyone from the *Victor* got rolling drunk. The ship's chaplain, Herr Niels, could scarcely stand upright, and had to cut his funeral oration short. "Where he was born, I know not, just as little as I know who his parents might be; how he lived is likewise unknown to me, whereas on the other hand I know to the letter how he died; but as you others know as much on this point as I do, I have no need to expatiate upon it, and I therefore conclude my address herewith."

The following day the squadron started its homeward

voyage. Dr. Charisius observed a large number of whales drifting in the calm water as though they were dead. He pointed out his discovery to the captain, who stood for a long time looking thoughtfully at the whales. But then bad weather took over once more, fog alternating with gales, and at last Captain Frederiksen had to give orders for a black cat to be put into the sea in a tub with provisions of bread and fish for seven days. Naturally this appeased the gods, and on June 20th the ship finally put in to Bergen.

The festivities there lasted for eight days. On June 23rd, writes Sivert Grubbe, the captain invited all the noblemen who had accompanied him on the voyage to a party at the abode of the apothecary, Nicolaus de Freunt, "and there we were entertained right well. The comeliest wenches of Bergen were present, we danced roundly with them, and at last, when we had drunk our fill and danced sufficiently, we smashed all the apothecary's windows to pieces." On June 24th, writes Dr. Charisius, the burgomaster and Council were guests on board the *Victor*, where they received such a welcome that many of them were unable to walk home unaided. On the 25th, forty-four delinquents were flogged for the entertainment of Captain Frederiksen, while at the same time music was played, and Lutendrank, Hamburger ale, and all manner of confections and marzipan were served. The following night a display of fireworks was arranged at the ship, during which Henning Gøje was so severely burned that he lay blinded in his bed for three days. On the 26th Captain Frederiksen was guest at the burgomaster's; at every toast cannon-royal were fired in front of the city hall, and two of their musketeers were shot dead of a ramrod. On the 27th there were feasting and dancing on the quayside. On the 28th there were feasting and dancing at the abode of Lars Krusue, who had invited all the prettiest of the burgher-daughters. On June 30th, writes Sivert Grubbe, we did rest us after our drinking bout, for we had gone on in a

Captain-General Christian Frederiksen. (Frederiksborg)

continuous state of intoxication, so that our nature at last refused its service, and it was not possible for us to drink more.

By this time the whole of Bergen knew who the commander of the Danish squadron was. He called himself Christian Frederiksen, and in a sense he did not bear this name unjustly. His father had in fact been called Frederik, and he himself had undeniably been baptized Christian. His father was no ordinary Frederik, however; he was Frederik II. Equally, he was no ordinary Christian; he was Christian IV.

Fifty years later, on February 28, 1648, at five o'clock in the afternoon, this man died of cancer of the stomach in Rosenborg Castle in Copenhagen, lonely, bitter, and in debt. Defeat at Lutter am Barenberge, defeat at Rendsborg, Snoghøj, and Femern. Defeat at the hands of Tilly, Wallenstein, Torstensson, and Wrangel, Jutland twice invaded by the enemy and, even worse, by his own highly paid mercenaries, who plundered, raped, slaughtered, and burned wherever they appeared. The navy was lost; Halland was lost, Jemteland and Herjedalen were lost; Øsel and Gotland were lost. And anyone could see that their turn would soon come to Scania and Blekinge. Denmark was sinking, all the panes were smashed, and the coffers were empty. The institutions he established to provide the country with wealth—silk mills, sugar refineries, soaperies, tile-works, mills, and world-embracing trading companies—were all bankrupt. Even the crown itself, whose 970 diamonds glittered so magnificently in the sunshine that happy summer morning on Amagertorv, was in pawn with a Hamburg bill broker. Even within his own family he was alone. Kirsten Munk, his one-time mistress, had ended by making her old lover the greatest cuckold in the century; his favorite daughter, Leonora, had married the traitor Corfitz Ulfeldt; his eldest son and heir to the throne, Christian, had died of drink and dissipation the year before, and now cancer was consuming him as he lay there on his four-post bed at Rosenborg, evil-smelling, short of breath, stout, one-eyed in a literal sense as he had long been of soul, without appetite and bone-weary, tired of battlefields and cannon, tired of architects' plans and artisans' bills, of tarred ships and lily-white burgher-daughters, of ambassadors and councillors of the realm, of tilting at the ring and riding to hounds, of laughter and Lutendrank, of factories, prisons, shipyards, castles, and new-planned towns, of approximately twenty-three legitimate and illegitimate children. What had it all amounted to? The following day it transpired that there was not even enough money to pay for the funeral. There is a letter from a merchant complaining that he had never received payment for some cloth, part of which was used for His Majesty's own body, the lining of the coffin, and the draping of the corpse. Such was Christian Frederiksen's fate, not because he was a king but because he was a human being. His coronation tunic was red brocade embroidered with gold and silver and silk; his shroud they had to buy on credit.

But during those merry days in Bergen all these misfortunes still lay concealed beyond sight. The expedition around North Cape was the first great foreign venture of the twenty-two-year-old King. The pseudonym was chosen only as a pre-cautionary measure during the voyage itself; now that it was successfully accomplished, the news quickly leaked to foreign capitals. The expedition was a demonstration of power directed partly at Sweden and Russia, who had begun to levy taxes among the Lapps which were rightly due to the King of Denmark-Norway, partly at the Dutch and the English, whose merchant and fishing vessels had contravened Henrik Ramel's London agreement of 1582. Since Erik Munk's action in the Norwegian Sea, these waters had been patrolled almost annually by Danish men-of-war. But the voyage of the *Victor* was not simply a routine customs inspection. The young King had deeper intentions, higher aspirations. Under his father Denmark had ruled over more water than since the days of the Vikings. What, then, was more natural than that the son should outdo him and conquer still one more glorious sea?

At the time that he sailed to North Cape, it was still popularly believed that Greenland was connected to Spitsbergen, which in turn was thought to be part of a continuous continent extending toward Norway and Novaya Zemlya. The Norwegian Sea accordingly was seen as a great bay, bordered in the west, north, and east by coasts which had all been under the Dano-Norwegian crown from time immemorial. Toward the south, finally, lay those important outposts, the Faroe Islands and Iceland, which likewise were Dano-Norwegian. The moment seemed appropriate for bringing these waters under Danish suzerainty, together with all their resources of whaling and fisheries.

But not only that. With good luck Denmark-Norway might become the greatest power of the age, and Christian IV its mightiest monarch. At this time, trade with the Orient in pepper and pearls had long enjoyed a boom. But the Spaniards and Portuguese jealously watched over the seaway to India around the south of Africa and imposed on all foreign ships tariffs which reduced profits to nothing. For this reason the English and the Dutch began to seek a seaway to the east which lay beyond the reach of the Spaniards and Portuguese. Such an alternative route had necessarily to be sought to the north either of America or of Asia. This was what sent the ships of John Davis nosing their way about the ice-filled strait between Greenland and Labrador. This sent Willem Barents groping his way through the unknown waters between Kildin and Novaya Zemlya. Both attempts were known to King Christian. He realized that if he succeeded in transforming the Norwegian Sea into a "Mare Nostrum," Denmark would control both these gateways to the paradise of the Orient, and could levy dues in comparison with which the otherwise quite lucrative Sound Dues would be a mere nothing. This Northwest or Northeast Passage should preferably be discovered by Danish ships.

These were the perspectives behind the King's expedition of 1599, which he would undoubtedly have continued still farther east had he not had the misfortune to damage the keel

92

of the *Victor*. He did not forget his black cat. As he sailed south from Bergen, however, and the sea air gradually began to sober him, he returned to his aspirations. First, the Norwegian Sea must be cleared of all foreign vessels on unlawful errands; then lines of communication must be established as soon as possible along all the coasts; and, finally, expeditions must be dispatched with the objective of finding the passages in the northwest and the northeast.

During the years that followed, these plans were put into effect in the sequence indicated above. Patrolling of the Norwegian Sea was extended and intensified; in 1602 the Icelandic Trading Company was founded; and in 1605 Lindenow was sent to Greenland. Now there remained only the last and most important item: the voyages of discovery themselves.

Such was the situation in 1609 when the King heard of a young master mariner from Pilestraede who had ventured up into the dangerous waters off Novaya Zemlya on his own initiative. Why? Christian Frederiksen recalled his own hardships up there scarcely ten years previously, and he listened thoughtfully as the dramatic reports came in.

2

Jens Munk's first task after the shipwreck was to bring the crew and the lifeboats, along with their provisions, safely ashore. This accomplished, he tried to judge their position. Here the biography is uncertain in its figures. It reports that Jens Munk calculated the distance to Archangel as 124 Danish miles, corresponding to 580 miles. This is indeed the approximate distance between Kolguev and Archangel, but Jens Munk was hardly in a position to calculate this distance. Moreover, it is unlikely that he worked in Danish miles. This follows from some figures a few lines farther on in the biography, where a day's march is put at 14 Danish miles, or 65 miles—an unusually long stage. The figure is correct if one uses the unit which for Jens Munk would have been natural:

93

the nautical mile. That gives a day's march of approximately 15 miles, and the 124 Danish miles mentioned above then is seen to be not the distance to Archangel, but the distance from the southernmost point of Kolguev to Kanin Nos, where Jens Hvid awaited them. This was the distance Jens Munk needed to know; this was the one his logbook could give him; and it is in fact approximately 124 nautical miles.

This corresponds to a little over 223 km. This was the distance between the shipwrecked crew and their salvation— a distance to be covered in a rowboat across open sea with fog and drift ice, and with all the men crammed together on the thwarts around an unreliable compass. All must have been aware that the chances of survival in these conditions were extremely slight. The greater was their relief, therefore, when some days after the wreck two of the crew returned with astounding news: there were people on Kolguev.

The strangers turned out to be fifteen Russians who had come to hunt wild geese on the island. Their vessel was a so-called "lodie," a single-masted boat, open, but high-built, with the individual planks held together with reindeer sinews and manned by fourteen oarsmen and one steersman. Jens Munk approached them, but was told that nothing could be done to help, which must have been clear even at first sight: the lodie was far too small to take on the Danish seamen. They were back where they started; there was no alternative but to attempt to reach Kanin Nos with their own boat. While the Russians worked away plucking geese and salting them down in great wooden casks, later to be sold in Kolmodgraa, Jens Munk's men began to rebuild the ship's boat with fragments from the wreck. A mast was rigged up with a scrap of sail; most importantly, the boat's gunwales were raised all the way around so that it could take all the shipwrecked men aboard and still have some sort of freeboard. Almost two weeks went

Russian lodie in the Barents Sea. From a contemporary copperplate. (Gerrit de Veer)

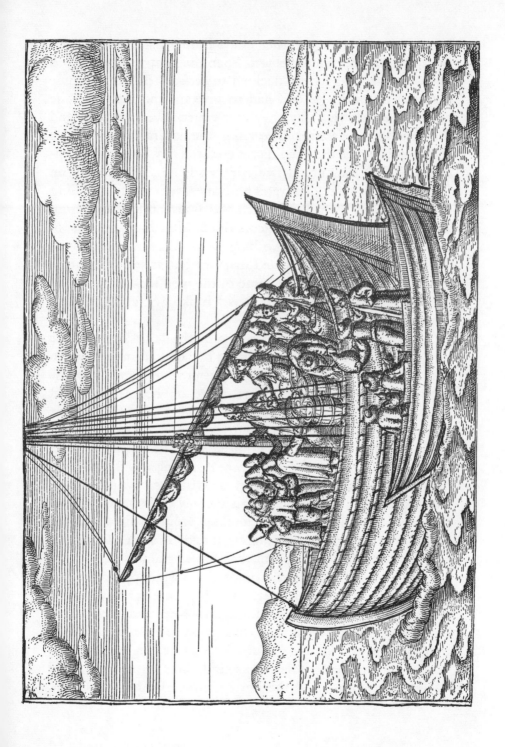

by on this work; the weather got a little warmer and the ice began to retreat from the coast. Then the boat was ready, and on July 17th Jens Munk decided to set sail. But after a time they ran into drift ice and had to give up and return to the coast. The following day they made a renewed attempt, and this time they succeeded in reaching the natural harbor on the south coast which they had discovered the day before the shipwreck. There they found five Russian lodies, which were on their way to Novaya Zemlya. The Danes went hunting, killing one polar bear, the pelt of which was fourteen feet long from head to rump, and which contained fifty-three pounds of melted fat, according to the biography. On the morning of July 19th they again observed drift ice out at sea, but within the bay it was so warm that some of the men took to the water to bathe. The following night Jens Munk gave orders to leave Kolguev.

The chronicler gives an account of the long journey: the jury-sail puffed by the wind and lit by the low sun; the men taking hourly turns at the oars and moving about with the utmost caution. How many are there on board? Surely at least ten or so—even now they were too many, but they had no choice. The overloaded boat lay deep in the water, with only an inch or two to spare at the raised gunwales. A rash movement, a gust of wind, and they were lost. Kolguev disappeared below the horizon. At the tiller Jens Munk sat with his compass. After a time everyone fell silent; only the rhythmic stroke of the oars could be heard; and all around, almost up to shoulder height, the ice-cold water glinted in the sun. Occasionally, as they passed through banks of mist, the world suddenly shrank; enormous ice floes loomed up and disappeared again in the fog; the tholepins creaked. Then the fog disappeared as quickly as it had come, and they met clear weather again, a pale-blue world of sea and sky. It seemed to the men as if each stroke of the oars took them into the very heavens themselves, while the sun went endlessly around them in a great tilted circle. As it approached the northern horizon for the second

Polar-bear hunt on the Barents Sea. Winter. (Gerrit de Veer)

time, showing that they had rowed without pause for forty hours, a blue-gray streak appeared ahead. Skilfully allowing for currents and for compass variations, Jens Munk had succeeded in calculating their exact course. He had stayed at the helm for the entire journey. When one of the men asked him if the gray-blue streak on the horizon was another bank of fog, he did no more than shake his head. The men turned around uncertainly; some murmured a prayer. It was not fog; it was Kanin Nos.

On the evening of July 21st the two captains met again

97

after exactly a month. A few days later those of Jens Hvid's crew who had gone hunting polar bears returned to the ship, and the voyage to Archangel was resumed. Jens Munk occupied himself with drawing up a navigational report on the approaches. His notes are the earliest we have from his own hand:

He who would run to Podienske or the roadstead of Archangel, he must keep the white sand dune approximately 2 feet west of the church tower of St. Nicholas, and continue thus until 7 fathoms are reached. After which, when he runs in through shallows he shall use the tower of St. Nicholas due south above the forest. Afterward there stands a large eminence hard by the strand, this shall he keep in line with the tip of the tower of St. Nicholas, and then run south by west until he comes to a white sand dune where the soldiers hold watch. Then he must go southeast by east across to the eastern rampart, dead ahead toward the forest, and then follow this, for the most part where the land is steepest.

Jens Hvid remained at Archangel for nearly three weeks, trading; not until August 18th did he get under sail again. The homeward voyage passed without incident. On September 26th they reached Copenhagen, where Jens Munk took leave of his partner and his crew and went ashore at Gammel Strand, as poor as when he had first arrived in the city ten years before. During his absence Copenhagen had acquired an adornment which could be seen for many miles around: a new spire had been erected on the Church of Our Lady, completely clad in copper and two hundred feet high with a glorious gilded crown at the top. The times were still good, yet here and there there were signs of unrest. Prices were rising; money no longer had the same purchasing power; the King had devalued some of the currency. From time immemorial a silver dollar had stood at 66 skillings; suddenly it rose to 68. And on the evening before Christmas Eve, the tide flooded many cellars, streets were under water, and goods in the Weighhouse were inundated.

Polar-bear hunt on the Barents Sea. Summer. (Gerrit de Veer)

Four days later a gale blew up; His Majesty's fleet came un-
moored, and many merchant ships were severely damaged.
Wise people in the city took this as an omen of impending
disasters. It was Christmas, 1609.

3

Jens Munk was again at the bottom of the ladder. The efforts
of ten years had been in vain; he had lost everything he owned,
and nothing had come of his great ambitions. Yet now less
than ever could he abandon his old dream. It is not adversity
but success that makes us modest creatures, says the chronicler.
The poorer Jens Munk was, the greater his desire for wealth,

99

power, and glory. He threw himself anew into the struggle to win recognition. But this time he did not go to see Henrik Ramel, or Børge Trolle, or indeed any of the others who had known his father in the days of prosperity. He had finished with these cold, suave noblemen; he knew their game. They had no intention of helping the son of the man whose downfall they had engineered. But was there not another powerful man, of whom it was said that he looked sympathetically upon ambitious young people, even if they were only commoners? It was worth a try. That same winter Jens Munk walked over Højbro, passed by the baying wolf at the gate of the palace, and obtained an audience with His Royal Majesty King Christian IV.

By this time the King already knew of Jens Munk from hearsay. There had been talk of him in the city. People thought that the young man had been soundly punished for his overweening pride; he had defied Providence more than was proper in a simple commoner, and he had only himself to blame for his misfortune. At the same time the miraculous operation by which the thirty-year-old skipper had rescued his crew in those bleak polar seas had reached the King's ears— no mean sailor, apparently, to be capable of such an exploit. Conversation at the palace naturally turned to the Barents Sea, whose many dangers His Majesty knew from his own experience. Which of the two men initiated the plan for a new expedition into those ill-starred waters will probably never be known; but what can be said with certainty is that the declared purpose of the voyage this time was the discovery of the Northeast Passage. Both men took an interest in this. For the King such an expedition constituted the last and most important part of his long-term Norwegian Sea project; he only needed a capable and experienced man. For Jens Munk, support from the King was the last chance he had of realizing his plans.

In the early spring of 1610, the instructions of Christian IV for the voyage came to hand. This lengthy document, preserved in the Norwegian National Archives, reflects the fact that His Majesty was personally familiar with these waters. With the two ships *Angelibrand* and *Rider*, Jens Munk was to proceed to a harbor in the north of Norway, and on approximately June 10th or 12th sail east and seek Novaya Zemlya on the 69th or 70th parallel, and then follow the land up to the 76th parallel, or as far north as the ice permitted, and there seek for train oil or whatsoever else there might fall out, until September, unless he had earlier taken on full cargo. Furthermore, on that same voyage (insofar as opportunity might present itself, and they could make progress in the ice) he was to run in to Vaygach one or two days' sailing and gather information as to the opportunities of this said land, so that he might on his return humbly and respectfully render a true and detailed relation on all these things. And when it was time to make for home from Novaya Zemlya, the two ships which were to be sent on the said journey, should they have become separated because of storm or bad weather, were to meet at Kostin Saurk and accompany one another thence to the royal castle Vardøhus.

The King might equally well have said that Jens Munk should find the Northeast Passage. The island of Vaygach, with Yugor Strait at one end and Kara Strait at the other, lies between the mainland and the group of islands called Novaya Zemlya. This was approximately the most easterly point Willem Barents had reached sixteen years previously, and it was supposed that beyond this was a sea route that led direct to China —which in a sense it did. Only Vitus Bering's Siberian expeditions more than a hundred years later were to show that it was considerably longer and more difficult than had been conjectured in the time of Christian IV.

However, the King also had other wishes. With his customary attention to financial considerations, he had taken care to stress in his instructions that the expedition should cover its own costs by seeking "train oil or whatsoever else there might fall out." The King's intention here was that Jens Munk should do some sealing and walrus hunting and render down the blubber; but the words probably also covered a desire for information about the incidence of whales in these waters. The King had not forgotten the sight of the gigantic school which Jonas Charisius had pointed out to him on the return voyage from North Cape, nor was he unaware of the growing efforts abroad to organize whaling on a large scale in the north. Opportunities for enormous profits existed here, and he was therefore anxious to obtain early and expert information about these waters which lay under his suzerainty.

Jens Munk's new expedition was to be a voyage embracing trade, hunting, and exploration, like the one he had undertaken the year before at his own expense, and like those which the English and the Dutch also sent to the north at this time. The two ships assigned to him were both well suited to this. The *Angelibrand* had already proved itself in arctic waters, having accompanied Lindenow's Greenland expeditions in 1606 and 1607. The King had bought it in England in 1605; it carried a crew of sixteen and had a capacity of forty tons. The *Rider* was a pinnace and consequently somewhat smaller. On the other hand, it seems to have been quite a new ship, since it is not mentioned in the Bremerholm records for this year. Even in this first arctic expedition it can thus be seen that Jens Munk uses a large "mother ship" and a smaller, fast "scout" vessel, exactly the same simple but appropriate combination he was later to adopt for the expedition to Hudson Bay.

Special attention was given to the manning of the ships. Jens Munk himself was to be captain of the *Angelibrand*, and for his first mate he was assigned Anders Nolk, who had had command of the smallest of the ships on the Greenland expedition of 1606. His second mate and interpreter was named Hans Brok, who must similarly have been an experienced mariner; we shall hear more of him later. Hans Brok was to be one of Jens Munk's most trusted men on the expedition to Hudson Bay. The captain of the *Rider* was one Knud Madsen, who had Anders Oluffsen and Johan Stenger as mates; in the

Bremerholm records, the latter is reported as having been shipwrecked in 1604 in an escort vessel off the west coast of Norway, so that he also probably brought with him experience from the Norwegian Sea.

Most noteworthy, however, is another name on the crew list of the *Rider*: once more we find Jens Munk's elder brother Niels, who is specially designated in the King's instructions as "Our Russian interpreter." His appointment may seem modest, and yet he probably played a substantial role in the planning of the whole expedition. In all probability it was Niels who brought the King and Jens Munk together after the events at Kolguev. The fact that both brothers are given command of a ship on this important expedition leads one to suppose that the plan for this expedition was their joint work, the result of years of careful preparation in secret. Theirs was a kind of partnership, in which each exerted persuasion upon the King to mount the expedition. Jens Munk had acquired experience and qualifications in practical seamanship; Niels first as a royal interpreter in the Chancellery, then as an official on Bremerholm, for his part acquired insight and influence in administrative circles. But they both had precisely the same objective: some outstanding achievement with which they could win back the lost glory of the family. The facts clearly reveal their intentions. It is no mere coincidence that Sir Erik's two bastard sons now return together to the Norwegian Sea and follow anew in his forgotten wake. But the future presages itself in a remarkable way on the spring day when they embark. It appears, from the Bremerholm files, that alongside the *Angelibrand* and the *Rider* on that selfsame day there lies a third ship which is to sail southward under Captain Bruun to take part in Grand Admiral Ulfeldt's tour of the Baltic. It was the *Unicorn*.

So one forenoon in June, Jens Munk rounded North Cape for the second year in succession. The sea lay calm and clear, reflecting rocks and clouds. A year ago he had loaned it two thousand rix-dollars, and now he had come to claim the debt.

This time the attempt must succeed. He was far better equipped: from the mainmast of the *Angelibrand* flew the royal naval colors; a short distance away the newly tarred hull of the *Rider* gleamed in the sunlight; and instead of the timorous Jens Hvid he was accompanied by proved arctic voyagers. Had he not cause for confidence? Despite misfortune and adversity, he had in a mere five years succeeded in working his way up from ship's clerk to commander in chief of a unit of the royal fleet; and if he continued at the same pace, his final objective could not be long delayed. The course was east by north; ahead lay the island of Vaygach, pointing the way to China and India, a whaler's wealth, the acclaim of the people of Copenhagen, the King's recognition, and sweet revenge over his father's enemies. Crowd on more sail! Things are moving at last.

A few days later, when they had passed Vardøhus, it became apparent that the arctic winter this year had again been severe. The facts had to be faced: they saw no whales, and the Barents Sea was full of drift ice. Munk sought a passage in the shallow channel between ice and land, and groped his way back and forth in the fog along the coast. The sailor who took the soundings in the bows of the *Angelibrand* grumbled that the lead would melt if he went on heaving it up and down as fast as this! Finally Jens Munk hove to because of the imminent danger of running onto one of the submerged reefs which had once torn open the bottom of the royal ship *Victor* in these same waters. He anchored the *Angelibrand* and sent the *Rider* north on a reconnaissance. Two days later Niels returned with the depressing tidings that the way to the east was blocked everywhere by ice. Jens Munk made a new attempt off the shore. He made the men work without changing watch; he himself clambered aloft into the crow's-nest to look for openings in the ice. They hacked a way through with axes and boathooks, but gained little more than a cable's length or two in twenty-four hours. The men began to complain; they had taken too little clothing with them to resist the biting cold.

From up in the crow's-nest there was now almost as much ice to be seen to the west as to the east, and behind the misty veil of stratus the sun looked like the full moon. Munk remembered only too well Kolguev the year before; he had nothing against risking his own ship, but he could not gamble with the King's men-of-war. So he listened to the complaints of the crew, and one evening, when neither the *Angelibrand* nor the *Rider* had advanced a yard in the course of the day, the order was passed from man to man and from ship to ship: the captain had given up—they were going back to Kildin.

When they arrived there, the island was overflowing with stockfish. One could scarcely breathe for the stench; they were the big cod which, unlike the "bergfish" or "klipfish," were dried unsalted and therefore much sought after in Copenhagen, where people were only rarely able to serve fresh food. Jens Munk decided to take two shiploads back with him. It should have been whales, the sea passage to China, three red cocks on a field of azure. Instead—stockfish!

The biography of 1723 makes it quite clear that Jens Munk had been turned back once more on the threshold of his great destiny. "Nor could he undertake anything on account of the much ice, which came drifting, and because the men had not provided themselves with clothes against the cold. Therefore must he run into Kildin with the ship and load it with fish." But the story did not end here. On the contrary, there now occurred an event which was to have the most far-reaching consequences. The King would not rest content with the unsatisfactory outcome of the expedition to Kildin. Some time after their return to Copenhagen Jens Munk was unexpectedly given a mission, the prospects of which were infinitely greater than those of any of his previous ventures. Just when he thought he had suffered a decisive defeat, he got the greatest chance of his life.

It was 1610. In Rue de la Ferronerie in Paris Henry IV was stabbed by a schoolteacher; the execution of François Ravaillac lasted for more than an hour and ended with his being torn apart by four horses. In Copenhagen the construction of Rosenborg was now under way; all through the summer a great host of craftsmen and laborers could be seen in the park, where peach vied with quince, mulberry, and fig, and bricks were stacked among Anne Catheriñe's Provence roses, and the King himself could not resist going over to lend a hand and getting a little plaster on his clothes. The fourth Christian sat more soundly in the saddle than the fourth Henry. Denmark's nobility, the clergy, and the Council of the Realm with the worthy fifty-four-year-old Chancellor at its head had humbly knelt down before Christian's son and sworn eternal fealty, and the prince had sat there stiffly watching the show. A seven-year-old boy. In the evening it turned out that the King had done right in handing over the old manuscripts to the fireworks makers. Not an ounce of the priceless parchment was wasted: "There was let off a great display of fireworks made in the likeness of diverse creatures and many hundreds of rockets and squibs, which ascended into the air, and charges of gunpowder, which were laid down in the earth and thundered, so that the whole city shook thereat, all of which passed off without scathe."

But Rosenborg and the festivities cost money, and when Jens Munk came home from the Norwegian Sea with his stockfish, the King had further devalued the currency, making it easier for him to pay his bills. Inflation set in quickly, however, prices rose, and the skilling fell. From 68 to a silver dollar, instead of the previous 66, the value of the dollar now shot up to 74 skillings. The effects were widely felt; an uneasy atmosphere reigned, and wise women put their heads together and talked of imminent misfortune.

Then there came unexpectedly a portent, which even His Majesty could not ignore. On December 20th there occurred

The harbor of Kildin with ships in the roads, dog sleighs, reindeer, stockfish hanging out to dry, and three well-developed inhabitants. From a contemporary copperplate. (Van Linschoten)

an eclipse of the moon. This time it was not only the wise women but also the learned astronomers of the realm who could see that something was portended. Anxiously they noted in the almanac that the effects of this phenomenon would certainly extend until the year 1611, "for after such an eclipse there usually follows a great war and terrible bloodletting with murder and fire."

Amidst these warnings the new year began. On February 3rd the child Christian Ulrik Gyldenløve was born, in all probability the King's first illegitimate son; and on March 1st he appointed another bastard, the thirty-one-year old Jens Munk, as royal naval captain in his fleet with an annual salary of two hundred dollars, to be reckoned from the coming Easter Day. It appears from the archives that more people were enlisted into the navy at this time than ever before. Throughout the whole of March a feverish activity reigned on Bremerholm. In the rest of the city tension mounted. Prices rose, and rumors abounded. Then it turned out that the sages had again been right. On April 4, 1611, the clear portents of two years were fulfilled.

The news spread like wildfire through the light spring evening. It was Jens Munk's big chance. Christian Frederiksen had declared war on Sweden.

9

The Ships in Krabbeløkke Bay

When Jens Munk left the house in Pilestraede on March 1, 1611, and made his way down behind the anchor forge, across the city moat, and in through the Bremerholm Gate to take his oath of allegiance, he stepped into a separate world. Bremerholm was a city within a city, a state within a state, with its own congregation and its own priest, its own laws, its own judges, and its own hospital "where so many faithful servants of the sea rested their enslaved limbs with sighs and with longing made over to God their repentant souls."

The name derived from the sixteenth century, when the government brought in a team of shipwrights from Bremen and "ordained for them a place on the Holm east of the palace." This holm, which today comprises the quarter between Nyhavn and Havnegade, was in ancient times an independent island in the channel between Amager and Copenhagen; in the time of Christian IV it was separated from the city by a moat—a waterway that has since been filled in and made into a street, which still bears the name of Holmens Kanal.

Access to Bremerholm was by means of a drawbridge immediately east of the anchor forge, later Holmens Kirke. Here there was a lively traffic of carriages and pedestrians throughout the day. Under Christian IV the population of Bremerholm reached a figure of 3000 seamen and 800 craftsmen, who consumed annually 480 barrels of salted herring, 1000 cart-loads of dried fish, 3000 barrels of bread and 7200 barrels of ale, all of which had to pass through the Bremerholm Gate. The nobility were to be freely admitted, but the gate had to be locked each evening at seven o'clock; and the master of the watch had instructions to examine the night watchman, before he was posted, to see if he were red in the face, which was regarded as a sign of intoxication and resulted in the unfortunate man's being mercilessly placed upon the wooden horse with a pair of iron weights attached to his legs.

This wooden horse stood outside the guardroom to the left of the gate. On the opposite side, behind a high board fence facing the water, was the timberyard, where the masts and planks for shipbuilding were stored. Most of the timber came from Danish and Norwegian forests, where the buyers from Bremerholm had first choice, but the choicest timber for deck planking and floor timbers had to be brought from Pomerania.

Some way farther out on the open, wind-swept stretch lay the shipyard itself. The men worked in a smell of tar and fresh oak shavings, the air echoed with the ring of broadaxes and rivet hammers. The yard consisted of several scattered work-places for the blockmakers, the gun-carriage builders, and the wood carvers, and a couple of sheds in which tar, pitch, and blacking were melted. The ships were constructed on the bare foreshore, where for a long time they lay looking like stranded whales with the herring gulls wheeling over their projecting ribs. At this time two men-of-war were built annually. The King attended every time the keel to a new one was laid in the name of the Lord, just as he always came to watch its launch-ing from the slipway to the accompaniment of kettledrums and bass drums.

For the most part the shipwrights were foreigners, like the famous Scots, David Balfour and Daniel Sinclair, who lent their names to the navy's finest ships. Their annual pay far exceeded that of a naval captain, and in practice they had greater

A new ship being launched from the stocks. Launching took place as soon as the ship was planked up to the sheer strake and could float. The remainder of the work with the sterncastle, the fitting out, the deck, and the rigging took place on the water. From a contemporary copperplate. (Witsen)

authority than anyone else on Bremerholm; even the victualing master and the admiral of the holm had always to bear in mind that in the event of disagreement the King would side with the shipwrights. Christian Frederiksen had observed that there is always a dearth of skilled craftsmen, while the world is always full of bureaucrats.

The chronicler describes the approach of evening on Bremer-holm. The last journeyman had left the half-completed new construction on the stocks; the place that had been filled with busy craftsmen lay deserted, and the silence was broken only now and then when a convict clattered down toward the beach with his rubbish. From the ramparts the red western sky could be seen behind Copenhagen, where the spire of the Church of Our Lady rose, serene, above the low houses huddled together at its feet. It was impossible to count the roofs; seen from out here, the city looked large and extensive. Yet one only needed to turn one's gaze northward across the gleaming water to see an even larger city with still more, still higher spires.

Out here in Krabbeløkke Bay the fleet of King Christian IV lay at anchor. The dark, smooth surface of the water accentuated the curved lines of the ships' hulks; together, they constituted the capital city of that overwhelmingly greater part of Denmark, which consisted of nothing but water. Masts and rigging formed an impenetrable network against the sky; bronze cannon and brass mountings flashed like distant windowpanes in the sunset, until the moment came when darkness fell, and the watchman hauled down the flag, lit an anchor lantern, and began his melancholy pacing back and forth, audible far away on land.

The tall ships in Krabbeløkke Bay were famous far and wide. Some of them had just reached home from Greenland, Gotland,

Bremerholm, about 1611. After Johan van Wick. On the left the gate in the ramparts and the bridge over Holmens Kanal. Just within the entrance to the right lies the timberyard with planks for shipbuilding; two ships are under construction on the beach and not yet planked, a three-master is being careened, farthest away lies the long rope walk with sail loft and office, and beyond this can be seen the ships in Krabbeløkke Bay.

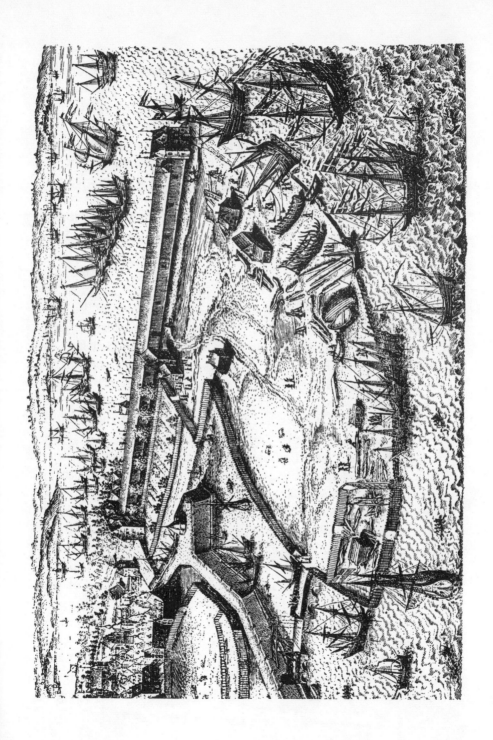

England. Others were soon to make their long way south along the African Coast to Ceylon and Farther India. No two of them were identical. They were often given pet names, sometimes poetic like *Blue Dove* and *Little Angel*, sometimes humorous like the *Crab Louse*, the *Come Along*, the *Cow*, the *Milkmaid*, the *Little Lucky Pot*. The King, too, had flights of fancy when a new ship was to be named. When Daniel Sinclair completed the navy's hitherto largest man-of-war, one of the few in Denmark built with a double gun deck, it was called after the King's mother, Frederick II's formidable widow, who silenced the nobility and the Council of the Realm throughout half a century; thus the fleet's most fearsome dispenser of thunder and destruction sailed the seas under the name *Big Sophia*.

In other places, however, the ships from Krabbeløkke Bay inspired more respect than humor. Duke Henry of Brunswick believed that there was not to be found another such fleet *in tota Europa*; the Frenchman Peleu spoke with respect of *ces merveilles de l'océan, ces puissantes forteresses flottantes*; a Venetian, the Cardinal Bentivoglio, reported in his *Relationi* in 1636 that the Danish navy had at its disposal some of the world's best ships and seamen; and a contemporary Dane, Tyge Kristensen, said that His Majesty had diverse fine men-of-war built comparable with the best that ever sailed the sea. Figures from the Bremerholm accounts support these words. At the time of the coronation in 1596, the Danish fleet consisted of 22 types of vessel; by 1611, when Jens Munk was commissioned as a naval captain, this figure had trebled. Altogether, the names of 276 ships of various types are known from the navy of Christian IV. In his time it was one of the world's largest; today only its memory remains. Faded copperplates give some idea of the appearance of the ships; dusty logbooks give us a glimpse of the life aboard them.

Not all the King's ships were equally impressive. The navy included many single-masted sloops with only a few cannon, while the main force consisted of large frigates which might have over fifty cannon, and which were usually rigged with foremast, mainmast, and the little mizzenmast with the lateen sail. Among the largest were the *Three Crowns*, the *Oldenburg*, the *Norwegian Lion*, the *Dragon*, the *Spes*, and the royal ship *Patientia*. These were about 190 feet long and 23 feet wide and had a displacement of approximately 1300 tons. It was no less than 165 feet from their keelson to the flag truck on the mainmast. Their crews consisted of 150 seamen and a corresponding number of soldiers; the total sail area amounted to 6000 sq. ft., and it must have been just as laborious to raise the main yard as to haul the heavy forged-iron anchor inboard. Jon Olafsson describes the *Patientia* with its mainmast constructed from 9 tree trunks, its 72 copper cannon, its multitude of flags and pennants waving from masts and yards, and costly coverings draped over the rails. Astern, the ship was fitted with a double galley with small gilt pillars on the outboard walk, where the officers enjoyed standing and toasting one another as the ships sailed abreast.

Nine tree trunks to the mainmast is perhaps exaggerated, though timber was not spared when David Balfour and Daniel Sinclair went to work. The curved oaken ribs in a frigate were 21 inches thick on average, and so close that one could not drive a coin between them. On both the outer and inner side they were covered with $4\frac{1}{2}$-inch planks of oak, forming altogether a massive ship's side two and a half feet thick. Jon Olafsson says that it needed 60 men to carry the rudder of the

One of Christian IV's largest men-of-war in a fresh breeze. The ship, which unfortunately is not named, has a double gun deck, and even the two tops are armed with small cannon, which peep out from among the King's monograms. The two spritsails on the bowsprit are taken in, because the ship has the wind abaft the beam. The same applies to the topgallants. The upper deck is packed tight with soldiers, drummers, and trumpeters, on the upper gun deck gunners are seen conversing in pairs; pennons and flags fly from all the masts and yardarms, and the high sterncastle is lavishly ornamented with turrets, coats of arms, and carvings. (The Print Collection)

Pearl. For a long time this figure was thought to be an exaggeration, but when Swedish archaeologists raised the rudder of the contemporary *Wasa* from the bottom of Lake Mälaren it was found to weigh 4000 kg.

A frigate of medium size could be provisioned for three months at sea; there were three meals daily on board, and every meal had to start with a prayer and end with a hymn. The men ate at their places in the mess; each had his own earthenware bowl, wooden spoon, and wooden plate, while the more expensive pewterware was reserved for the officers. To offend the cook brought the death penalty, so the food could not have been very exciting. A normal ration, the so-called Bremerholm rate, consisted of two herrings for three men per meal. On the meat days, Sunday, Tuesday, and Thursday, a pound of salt meat was supplied to each man, and in addition to this a loaf of bread, a pound of butter, and a cup of peas every Saturday. At least that is what was stated in the regulations; but on long voyages, when the ship had lain hove-to for weeks on end in bad weather, the crew had to dig their teeth into other delicacies: a roast rat caught down in the storeroom, or old ship's biscuits, crawling with white maggots; all good filling stuff.

The consumption of ale was large, often 14-16 pints daily per man. It has been supposed from this that the sailors of Christian IV were in a constant state of intoxication; this is an exaggeration, for the ale was Danish-brewed and not especially strong. This consumption was due to the everlasting salt food which was served, and the serious shortage of fresh water, rather than any chronic drunkenness. There were rarely fresh-water tanks on board. Each man had his own supply in a canvas container which served him as a pillow at night, partly to provide him with a little comfort, partly because he feared that his neighbor might take a drop of the precious contents— even though the punishment for this meant swinging from the bowsprit with a rope around one's neck. To replenish his supply, each man slung out a sheet in the rigging on rainy days, laid a lead ball in the middle, and placed an earthenware jug underneath. Each drop was precious out here, though there was water, water everywhere.

In these circumstances it was difficult to maintain proper hygienic conditions on board. Fleas and lice had to be borne with. Mice and rats were equally difficult to get rid of; but from time to time cockroach hunts were organized, the prize for 1000 being a bottle of brandy from the cook's locked pantry. This must have given the crew a gay evening now and again; the annals of the navy record instances of a single "catch" of this sort bringing in 32,500 cockroaches. Efforts were made in other ways to maintain cleanliness on board. If it was discovered that a hard-pressed seaman resorted to the popular night-time expedient of relieving himself in one of the cannons, the delinquent was mercilessly keel-hauled. No one with sores or serious boils was allowed to use the "privy." Yet, a seat there might also expose one to a certain amount of danger, as on the occasion when a certain Peter Alkmaar on the *Pearl* complained that he had been badly burned in his rear parts by a cannon-shot fired from the ship's bows. This was the kind of risk one ran in the navy of King Christian IV. The men attended to the call of nature beneath the ship's figurehead, often represented by a white-painted angel of deliverance.

10

Captain in the Royal Navy

When Jens Munk made his way across the city moat and in through the Bremerholm Gate on March 1, 1611, it was to take his oath of allegiance as a newly commissioned captain in the royal navy. This new life, with its new responsibilities and new authority, would set him quite apart from life as lived on the gun deck. Jens Munk had served his apprenticeship on Jacob Gerbrantzen's crayer, he well knew how a simple sailor lived at sea; but these were not matters which a captain of the royal navy normally needed to concern himself with, let alone have knowledge of.

His world was situated behind the mainmast, in the dignified sterncastle, where the ship's officers had their cabins, suitably elevated above the turmoil of the sail deck and the stench of the gun deck. The captain and his lieutenant had supreme command over the seamen and the soldiers respectively, they received special fare, and only in emergencies did they show themselves in parts of the ship other than the pillared gallery-way. For the rest, their luxury was limited to a bunk, a carved wooden chair, a brazier of bronze, and an unpainted oak table, where copperplate charts and parchment-bound logbooks lay spread out between one or two lusterless pewter tankards and perhaps a single, faintly gleaming, brass sextant. Their pay varied between 150 and 400 rix-dollars annually, depending upon their origins. Captains who were commoners did not enjoy nearly so many privileges as nobles and, irrespective of their qualifications, had to see themselves bypassed time after time where promotion was concerned. The officers were responsible for carrying out the mission set out in the King's orders, but they had not necessarily received any training in nautical matters, nor did they always have knowledge even of such subtleties as reading and writing. The well-testified reticence of certain individual ships, when it came to battle, indicates that the navy's weak point was in its corps of officers. It was true of the King's fleet, as it was in some measure of his own person: a feeble head was set on a powerful frame.

The link between the sterncastle and the decks was the boatswain who, although he seldom received more than fifty rix-dollars a year, was the most important man on board so far as the daily routine was concerned. In contrast to the officers, he had to be a man of wide experience; he was in charge of the practical navigation, directed the setting of the sails, and was responsible for the maintenance, graving, planking, and winter warping of the ship. His badge of rank was the little silver whistle he received upon his engagement, which he wore constantly around his neck until he passed it on to his successor on the day of his retirement. It was upon the piercing signal from this silver whistle that the yards were braced, the anchor weighed, and the helm put hard over; otherwise it was strictly forbidden to whistle on board, since this would inevitably provoke the storm with its terrible whistling in the masts and rigging. The only exception to this rule was the boatswain, who after several days of absolute calm might permit himself, in strict privacy, tentatively and quite softly, to whistle a little tune.

The boatswain belonged to a special group, halfway between the officers and the crew, who ate by themselves, even though the fare was the same as for the rank and file. This group additionally included the ship's chaplain, the surgeon, the writer, and the musicians. On the royal ship there were twelve musicians, on an ordinary frigate not less than three. Their instruments were trumpet, cornet, shawm, lute, and drum.

Seaman draws water in a bucket outboard. The cannon ports are open, on the upper deck soldiers and musicians are visible, the heavy cable hanging down across the picture is the sheet for bracing the mainyard, and the four shrouds can be seen firmly secured to the deadeyes on the ship's side. Detail of the picture on pages 116-117. (The Print Collection)

Their most important duty consisted in sounding the trumpets in periods of bad visibility, so that the melancholy strains of their hymns revealed their presence to the other ships of a convoy in fog. When the time came to leave a harbor, it was the trumpeters who alerted the men in the town and summoned them on board; in addition, the musicians did service at devotions; and when the voyage was over and the tall ships slowly glided into Copenhagen's harbor, the city people could stand on the ramparts ashore and listen to the harmonious, brassy thanksgiving.

While the musical King Christian demanded much from his players, it was different with the ship's chaplain and surgeon. The latter was rarely very competent, and his tools were limited to a few knives, tongs, and a chest with various herbal preparations. A surgical operation on the open sea was a matter which required both strong nerves and a strong arm, particularly on the part of those assisting. When Jon Olafsson had his hand crushed one day during firing, he watched aghast as his superiors placed themselves around him with tears in their eyes, while the ship's surgeon prepared his instruments:

My captain ordered six men to lay themselves upon me and hold me down, while Surgeon William treated me in the customary fashion. But I begged him, that none should lay hands on me excepting in the utmost need, for it was for me sufficient that the chaplain and the others were in attendance. The ship's surgeon said that he had never met a more long-suffering being, but that was due alone to the Grace of Our Lord. The surgeon had to use his tongs to break the fingers at certain points and with his blunt instruments pick out the splinters of bone, clip away the singed flesh, saw off the crushed fingers, and pry into the hand itself between each finger and each joint with diverse instruments for wood splinters and pluck them out. He said that there were more than 300. The captain bade him not to torture me so before his eyes, but he answered that it was necessary.

Where the ship's surgeon proved deficient, the ship's chaplain had to step in—often a somewhat thirsty person who had deserted theology prematurely. He drew his pay from the collection box nailed up on the sterncastle, through which the crew sought to appease the Almighty's wrath with an occasional small offering. A week of wind-force 10 might well provide this humble servant of the Lord with quite a nice little salary. But he had a full schedule: every Sunday and Wednesday there was divine service with a sermon, and devotions twice a day with communal morning and evensong and prayers for the salvation of the King and the ship. While the vessel was under sail it was a capital offense to mention the devil's name on board.

This was the world within a world, the state within a state into which Jens Munk stepped on March 1, 1611, as he strode across the drawbridge and passed the sentry on Bremerholm. From the gate he continued alongside the timberyard, through the shipyard and past the great slipway, where the convicts crawled around in their chains. Finally he reached the high building at the end of the ropewalk and went into an office where a number of newly appointed captains and boatswains were already waiting. Through the north windows of the hall one could look out across Krabbeløkke Bay; the water shone peacefully in the spring sun, the tall ships rocked to and fro at their moorings. After a time Grand Admiral Mogens Ulfeldt read out the form of the oath itself, while the large assembly repeated the words, sentence by sentence, in an irregular, droning rhythm:

> We hereby promise and swear, every one, that we will be true and faithful to our most gracious Lord and Monarch, King Christian the Fourth, King of Denmark and Norway, His Royal Majesty, likewise His Majesty's realms and lands, in all manner of means, and assist in succoring and defending the same to the utmost of our abilities and with life and blood, and against all harm and adversity shield and guide, and entirely to abide by these duly read articles, and in all manner of means to conduct ourselves as good, loyal servants, and as befits honorable gentlemen of war and seamanship, so help us God and His Holy Word.

These solemn words became a bloody reality. A month later the Kalmar War broke out.

Once more it was a question of the Norwegian Sea. Sweden had exacted taxes in the foggy Bjarmeland of the midnight sun; in 1607 Karl IX had called himself King of the Lapps, and the following year he granted the burghers of Gothenburg charters to sail to the Northlands.

This was too much for Christian IV. Admittedly, these considerations are generally thought to be an excuse only for his declaration of war in 1611. He wanted to conquer Sweden, and one pretext was as good as another. Yet the King did mean what he said: these coasts belonged to Denmark and Norway; he had been there himself. The previous year he had sent an expedition up there to seek a seaway to China. But if the Swedes established themselves at the approaches to any such passage, his plans would be upset. It was thus no mere pretext; it was deadly serious. When Christian IV lost his head, it generally was.

Besides stockfish, Jens Munk may also have brought back secret reports on his return from the luckless voyage to Kildin; his brother had of course acted as Russian interpreter on the expedition. It is enough that six months later the King went to war to get rid of the Swedish taxgatherers and traders. He would attack Sweden's eastern bastion, Kalmar, and at the same time another section of his army would move up from Halland and take Elfsborg, at the mouth of the Göta River. Once these border obstacles had been removed, the two armies were to advance in a pincer movement and converge on Sweden's heart at Jönköping.

A necessary preliminary to all this was that Sweden should be cut off from the rest of the world. To this end, a unit of the navy was to blockade the narrow coastal stretch between Halland and Bohus Len, where the land jutted out into the Kattegat. Here lay the fortress of Elfsborg, so that the blockading ships could support the army's land attack at the same time.

All this was meticulously prepared, long before the King put his signature to the declaration of war. On March 1st, the very day Jens Munk reported to Bremerholm, a letter was dispatched to the young nobleman Jørgen Daa, requiring him to report to Copenhagen without delay. Six days later he was appointed admiral of a squadron with Jens Munk as his lieutenant. He had nothing like the breadth of experience of the sea which his subordinate had, but he was a nobleman. The two men were given the frigate *Herring Ness* at the head of seven other ships. Peiter Holst became captain of the *Black Dog*, Steffen Sørensen of the *Mackerel*, Anders Nolk of the *Red Lion*, Peder Jacobsen of the *Turtledove*, Johan Petersen of the *Prodigal Son*, Mads Brage of the *Cat*, and Frans Brockenhuus of the *Star*.

On March 26th prayers were held for the departing fleet, and before the end of the month the ships were dipping their bows in the Kattegat (or the West Sea, as it was then called). The larger part of the navy had accompanied the King to support the attack on Kalmar, and it was not a particularly powerful unit that remained for Jørgen Daa. Two of the ships, the *Herring Ness* and the *Prodigal Son*, are first named in the Bremerholm accounts for the previous year, so they may have been brand new; and the *Mackerel* was built by David Balfour in 1607. But the *Black Dog* was an old ship which the King had bought from Børge Trolle; and the *Red Lion* and the *Cat* had already been with Lindenow to Greenland, the former appearing as early as 1596. Its complement was forty-eight men, so that in spite of its name it did not belong among the navy's large ships; the *Cat* was even smaller, with a crew of only twelve men.

There was some sense in sending the small men-of-war to the western point of attack. The many rocky reefs and islets in the waters off Elfsborg prevented the use of larger frigates, but under certain conditions the small ships could penetrate right into the Göta River. Their fire-power was also small: the *Red Lion* roared with a mere six cannon-royal; there were twenty-two cannon on the *Star*, though the ship itself was "not much worth," as was stated in the report from the Swede who captured it a year later.

As the ships were small, so were their captains young and untried. Apart from Peiter Holst, not one of them was older than the thirty-four-year-old King, who had over-all command. The Kalmar War was a young man's war—a bloody story, in brief. Sweden, it is true, was led by the sixty-one-year-old Karl IX, but a few months later he died and the war was carried on to the end by his renowned son, Gustavus Adolphus. It went splendidly; Gustavus Adolphus was sixteen years old at that time.

Ideally, Jørgen Daa, the commander of the squadron, would arrive off Elfsborg before the Swedish men-of-war based there would become suspicious and put out to sea. The plan was successful; even at the beginning of May the blockade was effective and the Swedish West Sea fleet was locked in. The Danish ships lay rocking on the waves in a circle between the islands; the squadron had been further reinforced by the *Crocodile*, which saw to the provisioning. Ashore, the army had likewise begun its siege. No wagons and no ships slipped through with supplies for Elfsborg. Thus it went on day after day, week after week, until on the night of May 23rd-24th a shout suddenly sounded from the lookout up in the crow's-nest of the *Herring Ness*. Shortly after, a crowd of white sails appeared in the gray summer night. The Swedish ships were attempting a sortie.

The naval unit which the Swedes had lying at Elfsborg was largely equal, if not superior, to Jørgen Daa's little squadron. As well as a number of fireships and gunboats, it consisted of six men-of-war, the largest being the *Hector* and the *Blue Serpent*, each with twenty-eight cannon; also the frigates *Crab*, *Jonas*, and *Fransiska*. The vessel that would prove most interesting, however, was not one of these.

Among the ships that bore down on the Danes that night, and which Jens Munk set eyes on for the first time, was a small, fast, single-masted sloop, whose destiny from now on is linked in remarkable manner with his own. This Swedish ship took its strange name from a predatory fish, common enough even today in the North Sea. It is slimy and eel-like and up to three feet long; its mouth is surrounded by a round suction disk, and it lives by attaching itself to cod, mackerel, and salmon, which it then literally sucks in, until only the skin and bones remain. It is the lamprey. The second of the two silent principals in the drama in Hudson Bay now suddenly appears over the horizon, flanking the Swedish attack on Jørgen Daa's squadron, and bearing the name *Lamprey* in large golden letters across the stern.

With the other Swedish ships, the *Lamprey* took the Danes by surprise. Naval strategy at that time was based on two fundamental principles: get into a position where the deadly effect of a broadside could be fully exploited, and at all costs to keep to windward of the enemy, since whoever drifted down to leeward was clearly and hopelessly lost. Because the prevailing wind over Denmark is west, particularly in the summer, Jørgen Daa normally had no difficulty in observing these basic principles during his blockade of Elfsborg. But circumstance and the skill of the Swedish admiral intended him to offend against both of them that night.

It was still a summer night. What little wind there was came from the east. The enemy was also able to exploit a powerful current. The Danes thus came into the lee, and since they lay at anchor, the current also ensured that their bows were turned toward the attackers. While the enemy had sufficient momentum to maneuver across the current and deliver a broadside, the Danes lay parallel to the current and, initially, could only use their forward cannon. As the Swedes came into sight, Jørgen Daa noticed one after another of his ships cutting their cables. Whether this was an act of cowardice or done in the vain hope of achieving greater maneuverability, it is not easy to say; the result was that the current rapidly carried those ships out of range. Only one ship besides the *Herring Ness* maintained position with its anchor holding fast.

Jørgen Daa thought that if he could hold out until daybreak the wind would probably freshen in their favor; but many hours still remained. With two ships against six and unable to maneuver, the Danes had to suffer a murderous bombardment before they succeeded in warping the ships across the current and replying. Every single cannon was brought into use, and the men on the gun deck worked for their very lives. Shortly before sunrise a light wind arose from the west, as anticipated. Immediately the position was reversed, and the Danes lay to the windward. The ships which had drifted away now bore down upon the scene of battle with sails spread, and the Swedes quickly sought cover under the cannon of Elfsborg. The blockade had held.

No details are available of Jens Munk's role during this hazardous encounter, but as Jørgen Daa's second-in-command he was among those under fire from the Swedish cannon. There was no reason to hold back; Jens Munk had been aware from the very first day of what was at stake. For him the battle for Elfsborg was a true replica, an almost literal repeat, of the accounts his father had given him as a boy at home on Barbo: the story of Stenvigsholm; the story of Akershus. In both cases there had been a strong shore-based fortress occupied by the Swedes; in both cases Erik had laid siege to the fortress from the sea with a naval unit, and in both cases the enemy had been forced to submit. The reward for victory had been the patent of nobility. At Elfsborg Jens Munk was faced with the same mission, the same enemy, the same struggle, and if like his father he conquered, it would be the same victory followed by the same reward.

No, there was no reason to hold back. All extant sources agree that Munk was conspicuously active from the very beginning. On May 28th he seized a Dutch merchant ship with supplies for Elfsborg; on July 21st he led a landing party which razed Gothenburg to the ground; and shortly afterward

Jørgen Daa made him captain of the *Black Dog* in place of Peiter Holst. Since Peiter Holst, as already indicated, was the eldest and most experienced captain in the squadron, the post could not have been insignificant. Furthermore, there was another reason for giving Munk this particular ship: he was familiar with it. In all probability the *Black Dog* was the same vessel that Jens Munk had had a share in five years before and which he had sailed to the port of La Rochelle. Since then there had been years of adversity and loss; but now, at the decisive moment, fortune had sent him the same ship with which he had, as a young master, avenged himself on an old and mortal enemy. The superstitious captain knew an omen when he saw one.

Nevertheless, Munk's achievements in the course of the summer could in no way disguise the weaknesses of the Danish position, which had been revealed during the battle. They had too few ships; they were too weak to mount an attack; and they were barely strong enough to maintain their blockade. This position deteriorated further when the army gave up the siege of Elfsborg at the beginning of June. Jørgen Daa immediately requested reinforcements from the King, since "he feared that the fleet off Elfsborg otherwise would stand in a very dangerous position." The King's answer was negative. "You must needs assist yourself with the ships you have. Pray God for favor, and stand against your enemies as best you may."

A few weeks later Jørgen Daa even received orders to transfer two ships to the King; and on July 2nd Frans Brockenhuus sailed away with the *Cat* and the *Crocodile* to Kalmarsund. Apart from God's favor, Jørgen Daa now had only seven small ships to rely upon, and once more he begged the King for reinforcements. Christian promised that Lindenow would reinforce the West Sea with the *Victor*, the *St. Michael*, and the *Crocodile*, but for weeks the lookout on the *Herring Ness* sat watching in vain. The three ships had received counter-orders en route, and Lindenow never appeared off Elfsborg.

Such was the situation as the summer drew to a close. For the fourth month the small ships lay rocking on the waves between the islands; Jens Munk's great destiny was still undecided. On the gun deck the men were becoming restive, growling darkly about the dry ship's biscuits. And now autumn was imminent, with cold, gales, darkness. Then one day a land patrol returned with ominous news. The Swedes were preparing a devastating attack upon the weakened Danish squadron. When Jørgen Daa in the greatest haste sent a new appeal to the King for reinforcements, the answer for the third time was "no."

11

The Storming of Elfsborg

I

While Jørgen Daa and Jens Munk held the Swedes at Elfsborg with an inferior force, Christian IV had not been idle. Three weeks after the outbreak of war he arrived at Kristianopel and assumed command of the attack planned on Kalmar. On May 3rd he began the siege; on May 26th he opened up a breach in the wall; the assault began, and at five o'clock the following morning his personal standard floated above the ramparts. With the exception of the fortress itself, Kalmar had fallen. The King was unable to prevent his mercenaries from sacking the town.

Scarcely a month later, however, Karl IX appeared before the ramparts, and on June 17th attacked. Simultaneously the Swedes attempted a sortie from the city fortress. But the enemy were forced back, and three days later Mogens Ulfeldt crowned the Danish victory by forcing his way around the north of Øland with the main fleet and entering Kalmar with troops and provisions. The King probably thought that he could now do without a number of ships; and the following day he gave Lindenow orders to sail to the assistance of Jørgen Daa—orders which were later withdrawn for unknown reasons.

With the arrival of the fleet, the position of the Swedes became hopeless; Karl withdrew his siege troops to Ryssby, and on August 2nd Krister Some surrendered Kalmar Castle. The enemy's eastern wing had collapsed; Christian IV was able to return to Copenhagen and grapple with the problem of Elfsborg.

Here the position was more serious than ever. The Danes still had the fortress under blockade, it was true, but Jørgen Daa saw clearly that his squadron could no longer prevent the Swedes from breaking through if they attacked. In the middle of October he tried a fourth appeal to the King, "for the Swedish fleet which is lying before Elfsborg is being reinforced with all dispatch," and on this occasion Christian IV understood the menacing nature of the situation. On November 5th he sent off his own ship *Victor* with instructions that Jørgen Daa must overcome the Swedish fleet or set it on fire.

The *Victor* gave Jørgen Daa the reinforcement he needed. The King's old ship, which had borne him around North Cape in its time, was still one of the best craft in the fleet. The crew consisted of seventy able-bodied men, and the forty-four cannon gave the vessel a respectable fire-power without reducing its seaworthiness. The *Victor* arrived off Elfsborg in the middle of November, and on the evening of the 27th Jørgen Daa gave the order to attack. Taken partly from the ships and partly from the Bohus fief, a landing fleet of sixteen boats had been assembled, which were to be sailed into the harbor of Elfsborg covered by the cannon of the *Herring Ness* and the *Victor*. The first of the boats was commanded by Jens Munk, the next by Johan Petersen, and immediately in their wake came Anders Nolk with the fireship, an old barge crammed to the gunwales with highly inflammable wood chips and tarred rags. Munk had orders to destroy the enemy flagship, the twenty-eight-cannon frigate *Hector*. The Swedish seamen poured burning tar over their attackers, but the Danes succeeded in boarding the frigate, and after a short hand-to-hand struggle the Swedish crew had to leap ashore and take refuge in the fortress. Munk gained possession of the ship's colors, and the *Hector* was taken. But the enemy had blocked the harbor entrance, so that only the smaller boats could slip in and out;

and as the wind was in the west, they stood no real chance of taking their large prize with them. Anders Nolk made fast the fireship alongside the *Hector* and set fire to the old rags; in the space of a few minutes the flames boarded the flagship and shot up the rigging. The burning ship shone like a torch in the night; showers of sparks flew out over the black waters of the harbor, thronged with Danish landing boats, and ashore the glare lit up the massive walls of the fortress.

The Danes were compelled to delay their withdrawal from the burning ship in order to prevent the Swedes from returning and putting out the fire. "The Danes remained on the ship, until such time as the blaze was so clear, that the Swedes on the fortress could distinguish them," it says in the biography of 1723. They probably held out for some time longer, for when Jens Munk gave the order to retreat, eighteen of his men had fallen to the Swedish bullets. At this stage the whole of the Elfsborg River was lit up, and Jørgen Daa no longer needed to fear a sortie.

At the beginning of December the King had the squadron recalled, and on the 12th Jørgen Daa weighed anchor. On the voyage home, snow and frost set in; a severe southeast gale blocked the waters between Kullen and Elsinore, and the largest of the ships, the *Victor*, the *Herring Ness*, the *Turtle-dove*, and the *Black Dog*, had to give way before the storm and put in to Kalundborg, where Jens Munk supervised the stripping of the ship's rigging.

The winter of 1611-12 was harsh and long. The annals report that even at Christmas the Sound was ice-bound, and the ice remained right up until well into March; but the war continued with undiminished severity. The day after Christmas, Christian IV had rejected the peace offer of Gustavus Adolphus; and at the end of January he turned upon Nya-Lödöse, where he was unable to prevent the male population from being put to the sword. Thereafter, he continued up into Väster-Götland, where he was unable to prevent every farm in an area as large as Zealand from going up in flames.

134

Finally he reached the town of Skara, where once again he was unable to control his men.

It seemed as if both kings had discovered that it was more rewarding for them to do battle apart. Gustavus Adolphus meanwhile wreaked havoc on an alarming scale in Scania; but with the arrival of spring the campaign had to be brought within firm bounds once more. The Danish plans were the same as in the previous year: a dual attack was to be carried out from Kalmar and Elfsborg respectively, both aimed at Jönköping, but this year Christian IV would lead the western wing.

Once again a detachment of the fleet was needed off Elfsborg; as early as February 2nd Jens Munk was sent to Kalundborg to supervise the preparation of the ships left there the year before. A month later, when they had been careened, graved, and rigged, he was appointed commander of the squadron. He had to send the *Victor* to Elsinore for further orders, while he himself returned to Gothenburg with the remainder of the ships and placed himself under the command of Jørgen Daa. The latter had already had assigned to him two vessels which had not seen action at Elfsborg before, the frigate *Leopard* of 1604 and Frederick II's old twenty-two-cannon *Raphael*, which had also taken part in the King's North Cape voyage.

On the very day the Sound was clear of ice, Jørgen Daa steered north; and on March 12th the two men met once more off Elfsborg. This time their task was appreciably simpler. Within the harbor of the fortress lay the charred ships which the Swedes had been unable to reclaim; the Danish squadron was substantially stronger, and the land forces were also much larger than in the previous year. It was clear from the smallest details in the provisioning on the gun deck that the King's attention had been transferred from Kalmar to Elfsborg. He sailed with the *Victor* from Elsinore on the morning of May 4th and without a moment's delay began the siege of the Swedish fortress.

135

The odds were weighted. Against the Danish mercenaries, nearly twenty thousand men altogether, the commandant of the fortress, Oluf Stråle, could not muster more than four hundred, of whom many were wounded or in poor health after the extended siege. But Christian had a chivalrous nature, if it suited his plans; he offered Oluf Stråle a safe-conduct for himself and his men if he would surrender the fortress. Oluf Stråle answered dryly that this was no Kalmar, and that in future he would answer only with powder and shot. The same night Christian Frederiksen gave the signal for the assault.

2

Christian IV reached Jørgen Daa's squadron on the morning of May 4th. His plans were simple: Elfsborg was to be attacked before Gustavus Adolphus received news of his arrival and came up with reinforcements. This was the way the King had surprised and conquered Kalmar the previous year, before Karl IX had appeared on the scene. They had to establish a bridgehead immediately on the Swedish coast, and the operation was to be led by the man who had earlier shown himself capable of pressing an attack right under the walls of the fortress. Jens Munk received orders the same night "to put in as near to Elfsborg as possible."

From a year's experience of siege he knew every detail of the lie of the land. Old Elfsborg stood on a high rock on the southern bank of the Gotha River, approximately on the western outskirts of present-day Gothenburg. Westward along the river out toward the sea the landscape was dominated by two heights, Käringberget and Billingen. The former, which Jens Munk calls Kjerlingbjerget in his logbook, is at an elevation of 150 feet and lies about two nautical miles west of the fortress. The latter is slightly lower and lies less than one nautical mile from the ditches within range of the enemy cannon.

Munk realized that the attackers from the sea had to take possession of these heights which commanded the approaches;

only then could they proceed with the encirclement of the fortress itself in conjunction with the forces of Jørgen Daa. During the night of May 4th-5th he went in under Kjerling-bjerget with the *Black Dog*, turned broadside on, and started a bombardment of the Swedish positions, maneuvering exactly as his father had once done at Akershus. The enemy soon had to evacuate the important height, and the following day Munk landed at the head of two hundred men, whom he set to work constructing fieldworks and trenches. The work was carried on under heavy fire, and Munk lost fourteen men; but during the night of May 7th-8th the trenches were complete and the remainder of the Danish forces could be set ashore.

In less than three days a bridgehead had been established and the King's order executed. On the following night Jens Munk and Jørgen Daa together sailed into the Gotha River itself, passed the fortress, and forced their way up the river for some distance, where they succeeded in sinking some barges that were endeavoring to bring supplies and men to the besieged garrison.

Elfsborg was now cut off completely. When Jens Munk returned at daybreak, the King had consolidated the position at Kjerlingbjerget, and Munk received orders to go ashore with a hundred sailors and take the batteries on to the next height, Billingen. "During this labor he lost a part of his company," states the biography of 1723, "but His Royal Majesty was standing by, from which they derived no small comfort, and most of all when His Majesty had caused one measure of Rhenish wine to be served to them, and thereto one whole cask of Rostock ale, in which His Majesty did himself bore the hole with his poniard."

The episode is clear evidence that Christian IV was in close contact with Jens Munk at this important stage in the attack and had a personal knowledge of his part in the operation. On the same occasion the King made him responsible for landing the ship's cannon which were to take part in the bombardment of Elfsborg. On May 10th Munk again put in to the river

137

with the *Black Dog* and anchored in a shallow cove at the foot of Billingen, scarcely one nautical mile from the fortress. On the following day he managed to get four cannon-royal brought up to the battery, the next day two more bronze cannon were dragged ashore, and the same night, at the head of his sailors, he forced his way to within a mere three ells of the rampart, where he laid mines, with the loss of four men.

It was May 13th. The preliminary attack was over; the Danes stood in a tight ring around the fortress; the breaching could now start. Jens Munk took a few days off as captain of the *Herring Ness* to escort some ships transporting supplies from Marstrand down to the camp. The expedition passed off without mishap. On his return he embarked on the *Black Dog* again, sailed into the Gotha River, and took part in the bombardment of Elfsborg. Here the situation was desperate. Upon hearing reports of Christian's arrival, Oluf Stråle had given orders to sink the Swedish men-of-war, so that they should not fall into Danish hands. His only hope now lay in holding the fortress until Gustavus Adolphus arrived with reinforcements. But the Swedish King was far away in Scania. Day by day the toll of fallen and wounded in the fortress increased; there was practically no food left, and all day long the cannon balls battered against the walls. After a week's bombardment the Danes succeeded in opening a breach. It was May 22nd; a large part of the eastern tower had collapsed into the moat. Oluf Stråle had scarcely four hundred men left. At sunset the artillery fire from the ships and the surrounding heights ceased; the light summer night shrouded the land; a heifer bellowed in the distance. Suddenly the silence was shattered by a fanfare of trumpets, and over from Jørgen Lunge's camp the air resounded with wild cries. The assault on Elfsborg had begun.

No evidence is available to show whether Jens Munk himself took part in the attack; most probably he covered the land forces from the *Black Dog* out on the river. The first wave consisted of English mercenaries who charged forward from

The siege of Elfsborg. Immediately in front of the fortress can be seen the cannon which Jens Munk has brought ashore; the ships lying at anchor in the river must be Jørgen Daa's squadron. From a contemporary copperplate. (The Royal Library, Stockholm)

three sides toward the open breach in the wall, where they were met with cascades of boiling water and blazing pitch. With their jackets in flames the Englishmen fell among their dead. Jørgen Lunge ordered the German regiments into action, but they suffered the same fate. The battleground was littered with dead; powder smoke billowed in the glare of the burning pitch. The King decided to throw in his regiment of life guards; a fierce hand-to-hand struggle followed under the partly shattered eastern tower, but Oluf Stråle set fire to the ruin, which crashed down, burying the regiment under a welter of blazing timbers and molten lead. The attack was again thrown back, but the cost was high; the fortress stood in flames. When Christian IV threatened to cut down the whole garrison if he was forced to make a fresh assault, Oluf Stråle capitulated and at daybreak was accorded safe withdrawal, accompanied by the few soldiers still alive, "with flags flying and drums beating." The only prisoner held back was a Danish deserter from Kalmar. The King felt that the soldiers ought to have some fun after their hardships, and handed the fellow over to them. The drunken mercenaries passed the following day breaking him on the wheel.

The next forenoon Jens Munk walked at the King's side, as Christian IV with his senior officers marched into the fortress. After many years of poverty, toil, and humiliation, Munk's great destiny was at last within reach. The fanfare sounded from the silver trumpets of the King; the procession moved off. In the evening the thirty-two-year-old sea captain entered the great event in his logbook. It was May 24, 1612, forty-eight years to the day since Erik Munk's conquest of Stenvigsholm. History had repeated itself.

3

With the fall of Elfsborg, Denmark had conquered the two frontier fortresses that barred the way to any further advance. From Kalmar, Gert Rantzau had already begun to press northward into eastern Småland, and Christian IV now made hasty preparations for moving into Väster-Götland in order to join up with him near Jönköping. First of all, however, the great booty at Elfsborg had to be secured against any attack from Gustavus Adolphus. Besides forty cannon, it consisted of the six men-of-war that lay sunk in the harbor by the fortress. The day after the victory Jens Munk set to work to organize the salvage operation. At the same time he took leave of Jørgen Daa, who was to go hunting pirates in the North Sea with three of the Danish ships. Munk himself was appointed commander of the remainder of the squadron, which was to assist the King during his further offensive. Jens Munk was clearly assigned

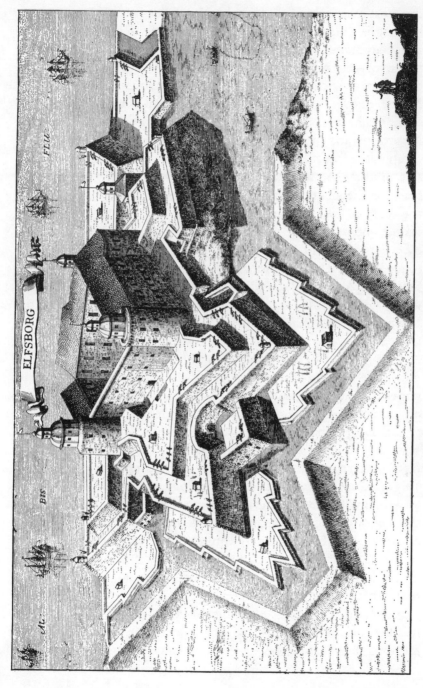

Elfsborg after its reconstruction. (Dahlberg)

the most martial task. He was leading a fleet of galleys manned by English mercenaries up along the Gotha River past Bohus and Gammelmose and on to the Berre Rapids. The decisive phase of the campaign had come. The Swedes offered no resistance; victory was waiting at Jönköping. But when Jens Munk reached Vänern an epidemic broke out among the soldiers; he did not have enough boats to carry the sick to Marstrand and instead had to go ashore and set up a temporary camp in the forest close to the shore. Within the space of a week this idyllic spot was transformed into a place of horror and fear, for the sickness spread rapidly. Jens Munk went around the tents noting how one soldier after another fell to the invisible enemy. In the middle of June he was himself attacked by the plague and "could no longer be a witness to the fortunate and victorious actions of his worthy King," as the biography states. When Christian IV appeared, shortly afterward, he gave Munk sick leave and had him taken back to Elfsborg, from whence he was to be conveyed home to Copenhagen.

Jens Munk reached Elfsborg in the last week of June. In the meantime the salvage work here had been concluded. The largest of the ships, the *Hector*, was clear as early as June 4th; on June 26th the last of the enemy ships was refloated, ready to sail for Bremerholm. A sloop lay ready and seaworthy off Elfsborg during the very days when Jens Munk returned from Vänern, and as the Danish warships not taking part in Jørgen Daa's North Sea sweep had long since been sent down to Mogens Ulfeldt in the Baltic, everything seems to suggest that this was the vessel that carried the fever-stricken captain back to Copenhagen. Jens Munk was on board the *Lamprey*.

At the beginning of July he went back to Pilestraede, where he lay sick until far into the autumn. The biography reports that "that renowned King bore such great favor for this His true servant, that He did Himself have prepared for him all manner of medicaments to which attention the good man ascribed his restitution"—new evidence that Christian IV knew of and appreciated his service at Elfsborg, and that Jens Munk might with good reason expect a just reward after the conclusion of peace.

This was now imminent. While Jens Munk lay ill in Copenhagen, the war with Sweden gradually petered out, brought to a halt by a power that had at its disposal far more dangerous weapons than Gustavus Adolphus and Christian IV. It was not only Jens Munk's soldiers who had to contend with boils instead of bullet wounds at Vänern; invisibly and impartially the plague moved through both armies. On July 30th Mogens Ulfeldt arrived from the Baltic with twenty-one men-of-war, in which for the most part "the crews were simply dead, so that there were scarce so many living and sound as might work the ships." About the same time Christian IV stood finally outside Jönköping; the great victory was within reach, yet the King had to withdraw, because there were not sufficient healthy soldiers to move up the siege pieces. The autumn brought only scattered engagements. In November the Danes accepted Gustavus Adolphus' offer of talks, and two months later peace was signed at Knaerød. Sweden gave up all its demands on the northern territories and Finmark, relinquished all claim to taxes from Lapland, and undertook to pay the Danish King one million rix-dollars in ransom for Elfsborg.

The King had achieved what he had desired, and even secured liberal payment for his war. Jubilation knew no bounds; the whole country was in a state of exultation. It was Christian's first victorious war. And yet there was no cause for fanfares: it was also Denmark's last.

But no one suspected that in 1613. The conclusion of peace at Knaerød was celebrated with great festivities in Copenhagen. It culminated in a service of thanksgiving in the Church of Our Lady, during which the captured Swedish colors, including the three flags which Munk had taken on board the burning *Hector*, were hung beneath the vaulting of the church. Jens Munk himself was present at the ceremony and heard the names of those men who were to be knighted or otherwise rewarded. Letters patent and distinctions rained down, and with good reason the King was particularly openhanded toward his officers from Elfsborg. A million rix-dollars in ransom was an enormous sum of money, and what was more logical than to reward those who had risked their lives to secure it? Now came the prize of honor for all those captured vessels, for toil and sickness, for sieges, fieldworks, and flags from burning ships. Jørgen Daa received Holbaek Manor in fief; Jørgen Lunge was knighted, appointed Constable of the Realm, and given Bohus fief; and so on. Many other names could be added to this list of favors, but they are of no importance here. For the list did not include the name of Jens Munk.

So one searches for his name in other archives. There was at the same time a whole series of promotions on Bremerholm: masters became captains, and captains became admirals with appropriate salary increases. But neither did this list include the name of Jens Munk.

About Candlemas, 1613, shortly after the thanksgiving service in the Church of Our Lady, Jens Munk again made his way across Bremerholm. He still bore the marks of his long sickness. However, spring was coming. He was on his way to the scrivener's office to collect his usual half-yearly pay. The clerk handed him the pouch with the one hundred rix-dollars. Embarrassed, Jens Munk turned away and counted the money over with his big hands. The clerk banged impatiently with his knuckles on a note. Munk turned; it was the receipt. It required a signature. The clerk looked on outraged, while the other man laboriously wrote his name under the amount. A clumsy lot, these seamen.

12

The Neighbor's Daughter

The Peace of Knaerød was a turning point both in the history of the country and in the life of Jens Munk. Just as the Danish victory simply served to herald that uninterrupted series of defeats which have characterized Danish history ever since, so it meant for Jens Munk the end of those great ambitions of his youth. At Elfsborg he still had a chance of advancement; after Elfsborg the dream was over. The King did not knight him as he did the commander of the land forces, Jørgen Lunge. There was no patent of nobility.

Why not? Christian IV was not unaware of the part played by Captain Munk. In the decisive phases of the battle the two men were in personal contact, and His Majesty missed no opportunity of expressing his appreciation. A cask of ale for his sailors when they were tired; a box of medicaments for him when he lay sick. Christian IV was well aware of the importance of a royal gesture. But a patent of nobility . . . Munk was an excellent man, efficient, reliable, and energetic; but there was that unfortunate story of the father and his "loose" woman. Jens Munk was and remained a bastard. Could one raise him to noble rank without arousing a storm of indignation? The fact that the King himself in his long and active life had fathered a number of illegitimate children, all of whom were ennobled, must not confuse the picture. Not only in his own eyes, but also in the eyes of his contemporaries, Christian IV was a custodian of virtue and morality. He was committed to the puritanical view of marriage that was preached in his churches.

Even if the King—with the sense of justice which despite his excesses was part of his character—did perceive the limitations of this view, and even if, in his sincere appreciation of his naval captains, he was often moved to great generosity, any attempt to ennoble Jens Munk would certainly have met serious opposition. In the Danish Council of the Realm there still sat people who had contributed to the downfall of Erik Munk; and it was clear that they could count on widespread support from their kind if they opposed such an appointment —an appointment which would undo what had once been decided, and which might provoke awkward claims for rehabilitation and compensation. In 1613 Christian IV could not afford to cross the powerful nobility of the realm more than was absolutely necessary. There could be no knighthood for Jens Munk—no manors, no fief. Ale and medicaments, yes, but any further reward would have been both a moral and a political impossibility. The King might as well ennoble his dog.

How did Jens Munk take this setback? He had spent fifteen years of his life seeking to win back the lost glory of the family, and the disappointment was bitter. In his youth he had been headstrong and ambitious like his father; but he did not possess that single-minded ruthlessness which his father injected into his plans. His many years of conflict with the nobles were not attended by acts of violence as his father's were; he did not seek to elevate himself by destroying others. Erik Munk had had to execute his own men to get them to obey commands; in the history of Jens Munk's many voyages there occurs not one instance of mutiny. At Kolguev he sacrificed his ship, but he saved his crew. The following year he harkened to his men's complaints about the inhuman struggle with the ice, and returned to Kildin. When it came to the point he had no influential friends; apparently he had no flair for flattery. Naïvely, he believed that in the end everything was a matter of courage. He was not afraid of cannon-fire, but could be

146

wounded by a remark. To think of Jens Munk as a noble is therefore like imagining a left-handed person trying to write his name with his right hand. One thinks of him, instead, aboard one of his ships. He is no baron—he is a captain. Not particularly articulate, yet friendly and sincere, he is in his manner in tune with the type of life he has chosen for himself, secretly admired by the crew as he slops across the deck in his sea boots, throwing an anxious glance up at the mainyard, muttering an order to the steersman and passing on with head bowed, as though apologizing for the superior experience and expertise which are nevertheless obvious to everyone. A simple man, and like most heroes strikingly unheroic. Composed and genial, marked by that good humor that is fostered at sea, where evil has ample play in the fury of the elements and does not need the assistance of men.

Precisely these qualities, which he may have inherited from the quiet Anna Bartholomaeidatter, just as he had inherited his hatred of humiliation from his father, made it possible for him to come to terms with the disappointment that followed Elfsborg. When he got on his feet again after months of sickness, the ambitious fever of youth had also subsided. The biography bears no traces of rancor. Not a word of that stinging affront; not a word of the King's infamous betrayal; only humble thanks for medicines received—something which stands in marked contrast to the expansive claims and expectations of the past. Jens Munk felt that the King had saved his life. This he could not have done with any number of manors. What were they worth when all was said and done? To own is to lose, the war had shown him this. And had he not been sufficiently near to triumph to be sensible of that burned-out feeling which also hangs over the battleground? Now he felt the feebleness vanish and his strength return. A new spring was on the way. And when he went down to Bremerholm to fetch his pay, it was with something of the same feelings with which he had once collected his father's silver tankard from Councillor Bentsen. His name was not among the illustrious in the Church of Our Lady, but what was the loss of a patent of nobility for one who had been on the point of losing life itself?

One event from these years seems to lend weight to the chronicler's assumption that Jens Munk had completely given up hope of regaining his father's title. He got married—the girl is a commoner, Kathrine Adriansdatter, and they are lawfully wedded. We do not know the exact date of the wedding, though it is unlikely that it took place in summer. It was a little winter's tale; and if we are to judge by the ages of his children, which are approximately known, it must have taken place immediately after the Kalmar War, or at a point in time when the King's negative decision was a *fait accompli*. He had once been in a position to choose one of the rich daughters of Miguel Duez; and if he had become a nobleman, he would have had to find himself a girl of noble birth. Now he took a simple mariner's daughter. He had known girls on both sides of the Atlantic; now he was marrying the daughter of one of his neighbors. There is only one explanation: he succumbed to the old family failing and took the girl he loved; but in contrast to his father and grandfather, it cost him neither title nor blood.

In 1614 Jens Munk was to be found at the Yuletide party of the Danish Company, together with his friend Jørgen Daa; apparently he still had hopes of becoming a merchant, and exchanging a man-of-war for a merchant vessel. But in 1614 this goal was further away than ever, and he had to be content with serving on Bremerholm. There are also grounds for believing that the King, far from any desire to ennoble him, rather wished to stress his inferior status. It is clear that the role assigned to him in the years after Kalmar betokened a retrograde step in every way. Much more than ever before he had to subordinate himself to the nobility. Those posts that did come his way were in every case minor ones.

It began only a few weeks after the conclusion of peace, when Munk received orders to sail to Øland with five ships and bring back Christian Friis, a nobleman and future Chancellor, who had become governor at Borgholm Castle when the island was conquered by the Danes. At Knaerød it was decided to return Øland to Sweden, and for this reason Christian Friis together with his distinguished retinue was to return to Copenhagen. The captain had to vacate his stern cabin and let the fine passengers move in; and little was seen of him during the voyage. Indeed, hardly anyone knew who he was. Munk had to swallow this indignity, on which occasion there was less distinction between him and his lowliest boatswain than between him and the governor's children.

Nevertheless, the voyage passed off without incident; Munk sailed from Krabbeløkke Creek on March 2nd, and only a few weeks later he was back again with the party from Øland. Nor were there many free days in Copenhagen on this occasion; Christian IV did not spare his men, and he had decided that Jens Munk should serve another group of nobility, this time certain diplomats who were off on a mission to Spain. Again this was quite a modest assignment—it was stated in the royal instructions that apart from his usual work as captain he was to act as "interpreter and quartermaster." He was qualified to be the former by his knowledge of the languages he had acquired in his youth; the latter implied something in the way of a functionary, whose duty was to be at the disposal of high-ranking personages and take care of their accommodation and conveyance. Once more it was a very distinguished company that installed itself in the captain's sterncastle. The chief object of the mission was to protest at the increase in privateering by Spaniards in the Norwegian Sea, where the terrible Mendoza, whom Jørgen Daa had sought in vain to neutralize during the Kalmar War, wrought greater destruction every year. Two ships were placed at Jens Munk's disposal for the voyage: one, the King's familiar old *Victor*, the other the Swedish man-of-war *Hector*, which Munk had himself helped to capture in Elfsborg harbor. On April 16th he sailed up through the Sound on his way to Spain.

The intention was to complete the journey in one stage, and

149

the ships must have had favorable wind on the passage, for scarcely two weeks after their departure the northern coast of Spain appeared above the horizon. They now sailed straight down into the great Mediterranean summer. Flashes of lightning blazed at night in the heavy darkness; Jens Munk stood on deck and observed how the *Hector* momentarily came to sight with every detail of the rigging silhouetted against the black sky. After ten years' absence he had again returned to the waters he had sailed with Ramel's salt ships, and before that with Albert Jansen of Einkhusen.

A wind sprang up; and late in the evening of May 6th the Danish men-of-war reached the approaches to La Coruña. The biography makes much of the fitting reception:

Upon their arrival the Governor sent his boat to meet them without delay, in order to learn who they might be; and as soon as he had informed himself thereof, he caused a salvo of welcome to be given with the cannons. His son with a company of nobles at once came on board in order to bid the emissaries welcome, and to conduct them ashore. The Governor met the emissaries on the beach, and as soon as they had set foot on the land he caused six pieces to be fired. Thereafter they were conducted into the city and quartered and entertained right well in his own palace. The courtiers were quartered out in the city among the most distinguished inhabitants, and treated right nobly for nineteen days, until a bidding came from the Court.

Jens Munk had taken his logbook with him and continued to make his entries ashore. On May 24th the company set out on the journey to Madrid. The Governor made arrangements for them to pass through his province without customs restrictions, but in Villafranca the noble lords were required to pay 1100 pieces-of-eight in duty on their clothes, so they cannot have been in rags. On June 14th they arrived at the capital and were accommodated at the Court's expense. The remainder of the month passed in negotiations. It is improbable that Jens

Munk took part in these; in all likelihood that experienced man of the world Jacob Ulfeldt could cope with the Spanish, and Munk's work during these weeks was limited essentially to the supervision of supplies and lodgings. On the other hand, he did participate in the magnificent farewell audience which took place on July 3rd at the palace of El Escorial.

Many things suggest that relations between these eloquent noblemen and their reticent quartermaster were not particularly cordial. It is remarkable that the whole of this high-born company chose to make their way home overland; even at that time a sea voyage was usually preferable to the month-long ride from Madrid to Copenhagen. Nor would it come as any surprise if Munk had difficulty in falling into his role. He had had to resign himself to remaining a commoner, but this in no way placated his feeling toward the class in which he saw the main cause of his own and his family's misfortunes.

It was probably with a sigh of relief that he took leave of Jacob Ulfeldt and his retinue. Two weeks later he arrived back at his ships in La Coruña. Now he was in his proper element once more; and, like the outward passage, the home voyage proceeded in record time. One evening in mid-August the *Victor* and the *Hector* glided once more into Krabbeløkke. The news quickly spread that it was Captain Munk, returned home from Spain.

2

If Jens Munk was weary of sailing with noblemen, the King on the other hand was in no mind to replace his efficient quartermaster. Christian IV was no great judge of men; he did not notice that in the relationship between Munk and the nobles the scene was set for a conflict which would be certain to take an explosive turn sooner or later. Were there rumors that the diplomats had not found their quartermaster particularly companionable? We do not know, but even if this were the case, it would not have mattered in the eyes of the King.

Munk had always taken good care that they arrived at the right place and time; he was a splendid captain, not rude and uncultured like so many others, but well fitted to the task—a man of whom one need not be ashamed. That was the important thing. Any personal disagreements the gentlemen must please compose among themselves, that was not the responsibility of His Majesty. In brief, it was the King's will that Jens Munk should again the following summer place himself at the disposal of the nobility of the realm.

On this occasion the journey was northward to Archangel. Jens Munk had been entrusted with the frigate *Herring Ness* on board which there was a large company consisting of the Russian ambassador, Ivan Mikhailovich, and his suite of thirty-five persons, together with a number of Danish nobles proceeding to Russia to convey the felicitations of the Danish King upon the accession of the new Czar Michael. But this time Jens Munk seemed to have taken good care that at least he was not alone with the puissant lords. With him on board the *Herring Ness* he also had his brother Niels. The biography mentions that he "had commissions of His Royal Majesty to execute." As a pretext for taking Niels with him Jens Munk simply needed to point out that they required a man who could act as interpreter between the Russians and the Danes.

For this position Niels Munk was admirably qualified. It was not the first time he had been on the route to Archangel. He had long since been an expert, like his father, in the affairs of the northern territories, and the two brothers could not have rounded Vardøhus and Kildin without recalling their fruitless efforts in the pack ice four years earlier, when they were investigating the possibilities of whaling, while incidentally seeking a sea route to China. The sources are silent about Niels Munk's activities in the intervening years, and his role in the Kalmar War is unknown; but it is clear that his brother's setback had also affected him. Revisiting the Norwegian Sea put new life into the two men's long-cherished plans to try whaling up there. Both the Dutch and the English were already earning fortunes in whale oil. More than ever before, Jens Munk was interested in finding an independent livelihood and being rid of the everlasting noblemen. The fact that he now had his brother at his side, who must have shared his feelings, did not soften his attitude. It was no wonder therefore that the tension, which may have been present the year before, led to an open clash on this occasion.

Among the Danish noblemen who were to convey the King's congratulations to the new Czar was a certain courtier named Knud Gyldenstjerne. Not very much is known about him; he was four years older than Jens Munk, owned several estates in Denmark, and as a reward for his participation in the Kalmar War had been given Vestervig Abbey in fief, which he exchanged for Bergenhus Castle in 1619. This last circumstance was fateful. Nowhere is there evidence that Jens Munk met this man more than twice in his life. The first time was on the way to Archangel in 1614; the second took place six years later at Bergenhus Castle, at a low point in his turbulent life. On this latter occasion the highborn Knud Gyldenstjerne received him with a studied malice that as a rule one reserves for one's worst enemy. His conduct cannot be interpreted as an expression of haughty indifference. It was an act of revenge.

What incident inspired such feelings of hatred in Knud Gyldenstjerne that they remained alive for six years? Why was it that from this moment on complete silence surrounds Niels Munk's name in Danish politics and in the archives of the Danish Chancellery? Why did he die in the prime of life three years later? Why is there no information about his place of burial, no funeral sermon? What was the reason for Jens Munk's ceasing to act as quartermaster immediately after the voyage to Archangel?

The enigmatic episode on board the *Herring Ness* is difficult to isolate, but everything suggests a violent clash. We have mentioned Munk's feelings toward the high lords, who on their side had scarcely forgiven Erik Munk's son his triumphs at Elfsborg. A token of his triumph, irritatingly, followed him both on the journey to Spain and on the passage to Archangel: firstly, in the shape of the prize ship, the Swedish *Hector*, and secondly in the shape of his own and Jørgen Daa's famous flagship the *Herring Ness*. Then there was the actual situation on board ship: the confrontation of the captain, the man in control, and a group of men who by virtue of their high social position were accustomed to command. This was a situation fraught with danger. Both parties ventured to express their minds. Whether it was a case of Munk in the end resigning as quartermaster, or of the King finally realizing the untenability of the situation, the consequence of the voyage was the same. Between Jens Munk and a number of leading figures within the nobility there reigned from this time on a cold hatred.

On August 23rd he returned to Bremerholm. The King had now cast off Kirsten Madsdatter, who had comforted him during the difficult period of the Queen's death; now he was known to have taken a fancy to Karen Andersdatter, said to be with child by Gyldenstjerne at the time. She was well known; her father was a clerk on Bremerholm. Then there were the usual everyday events: on October 23rd a fire in one of the merchantmen; on November 5th, the launching of the good ship *Unicorn*, which had been rebuilt and lengthened. But all this was overshadowed by the tales of sailors who had been to Iceland or to the Faroe Islands during the summer. The terrible Mendoza was on the rampage again, taking hostages, burning down settlements, and making off with loot. Reliable eyewitnesses declared that he had talons instead of nails, that he breathed fire and brimstone, and that sharp knives and iron spikes grew from his elbows and knees.

The wild rumors contained a grain of truth. During the Kalmar War the King had sent Jørgen Daa in vain to hunt Mendoza, and since then piracy in the Norwegian Sea had rapidly increased. Merchant ships were seized or sunk; the pirates came ashore where opportunity offered, tortured defenseless prisoners to get them to tell where they had hidden their silver, and carried them off to Algiers, where families were broken up and sold separately as slaves. Negotiations with Spain had proved fruitless; other means had to be resorted to. But Christian IV had difficulty in finding men for this unpleasant task; his noblemen found it altogether more comfortable to take part in visits to foreign courts than to hunt pirates on the open sea. Only Jørgen Daa was willing, and in the spring of 1615 the King decided to send him out for a second time. It was natural that Jørgen Daa should offer the post of second-in-command to the man who had held the same position during the blockade of Elfsborg. He knew of the critical state Jens Munk was in after the voyage to Archangel and perhaps wished to proffer his friend a helping hand. Munk agreed; for him, restoration to his old post was a welcome opportunity of asserting himself in the face of his powerful enemies. Unfortunately, Jørgen Daa's squadron was not as large as during the glorious time at the Gotha River; sufficient officers for only two ships could be obtained. On the other hand, the two men were given a free hand to use any means for the accomplishment of their objectives. Jan Mendoza was to be brought to Copenhagen dead or alive.

3

At the end of April Jens Munk again joined his old comrade in arms on Bremerholm. The King had lent them his famous *Victor* and a fast pink, the *Jupiter*, built by David Balfour. Jørgen Daa and Jens Munk themselves went aboard the former, while the latter was placed under the command of Klavs Povlsen and Johan Sem, both of whom were well qualified for their task. The first had participated in Jørgen Daa's first attempt to catch Mendoza; the other had commanded the *Jupiter* the previous year on an expedition. Within a week the two vessels were supplied with provisions and ammunition, and on May 5th Jørgen Daa gave orders in the name of the Lord for the anchors to be weighed.

The ensuing events are reported in no fewer than three

sources. As usual, the biography of 1723 gives a copious extract from Jens Munk's logbooks; and in the National Archives Jørgen Daa's personal and hitherto unpublished report to the King is preserved. Furthermore, the Icelander Jon Olafsson noted in his memoirs the rumors he heard on his arrival in Copenhagen in the spring of 1615. Thanks to these three accounts, we can form a fairly accurate picture of the dramatic expedition.

Shortly after their departure a violent northerly gale arose, so that it took Jørgen Daa five days to round Kullen. It then came to his notice that a number of pirates were assembled in the Faroes who did great harm and injury to His Majesty's subjects by murder and plunder. After he had passed the Skaw, therefore, he laid course for the northwest. In the waters between the Shetland Islands and the Faroes they sighted a fishing boat, went alongside, and brought the two members of the crew aboard the man-of-war by force, in order that they might pilot them in to Suderø. On May 20th they reached Kvalbø, where Munk went ashore to gather information. It seemed that they had been more fortunate than they could have dared hope. Only fourteen days previously two pirates had set out from Kvalbø. The inhabitants knew the names of both of them from bitter experience; one was an Englishman called Thomas Tucker, and the other was Mendoza himself.

It was now necessary to act with dispatch. The people of Kvalbø were rather vague about the pirates' further moves. Mendoza was said to have sailed to the northern territories; Tucker, after seizing three fishing boats, had similarly "put to sea" with them. The very next morning, when the wind "had turned to his favor," Jørgen Daa set sail, and in the waters near Store Dimon they met some fishermen who told them that two pirates were reported lying in a haven at Strømø. In his account Jørgen Daa calls this harbor Wessbindhaffn, while in the biography it is called Vesper-Havn. Undoubtedly, Vestmanhavn on the southwest of Strømø was the place in question.

156

Jørgen Daa hurried on, "and thus had God and the wind ordained, that when I came thereto the 22nd of May the freebooters had unfurled their flags, the admiral on the main top and the vice-admiral on the foretop, and when the 'Jupiter' first came into harbor, they thought to have a free ship at hand, but when I followed with the 'Victor' and unfurled the flag, then did their courage wane."

It was Tucker's men who had taken shelter in Vestmanhavn; in all, five ships lay there, two of them the pirates' own, the three others their prizes from Kvalbø. They had no chance against the Danish men-of-war in the closed fjord. When the *Victor* suddenly appeared, ten Irishmen fled ashore with a ship's dinghy and drew in close to the cliff. Jørgen Daa sent fifteen musketeers after them, but the Irishmen succeeded in getting away to Thorshavn, where subsequently they stole a fishing boat and put to sea. Meantime the remainder of the pirates had put themselves on the defensive. Jørgen Daa sailed the *Victor* quite close in to them. A single broadside was sufficient; the cannon killed three of their men and wounded four. Tucker was not among them. The day after, all were led with their hands tied behind their backs onto the upper deck of the *Victor*, where Jørgen Daa and Jens Munk conducted the court. Eighteen persons (according to the biography there were only nine) won acquittal by agreeing to sign on with the *Victor*; they were able to show that they had served with the pirates under duress. The rest were sentenced to death by hanging. Jørgen Daa and Jens Munk had a busy time; the execution took place that same evening within the harbor, where a gallows was hurriedly erected. According to the biography, thirteen men were condemned; Jørgen Daa mentions eight. A Moor among them saved his life by acting as executioner.

Barely fourteen days after their departure from the Sound, Jørgen Daa and Jens Munk had captured their first prize. The three fishing vessels were released, while one of the pirate ships with its stolen treasure was sent down to Copenhagen.

The other was to accompany the *Victor* and the *Jupiter* on their expedition. Reinforcement might come in handy, now that it was Mendoza's turn.

On May 27th Jørgen Daa stood out from Vestmanhavn. The people of Kvalbø had told them that Mendoza had set sail for the northern territories, and it is not unlikely that by using appropriate means the Danes were able to get their prisoners in Vestmanhavn to supplement this information. In any event they steered a northeasterly course, passed North Cape, and reached Vardøhus on June 12th. Here there was no intelligence of Mendoza, and Jørgen Daa continued the voyage eastward. The lanes were ice-free; and two days later, when he was approximately at the same latitude as the island of Kildin, he met a merchantman from Flensborg, who lowered a boat at the sight of the friendly man-of-war and rowed over to them. Jørgen Daa and Jens Munk received the master in the *Victor*'s poop and listened in silence to his brief tidings: Jan Mendoza lay inshore at Kildin.

It was the forenoon of June 15th. Jørgen Daa gave orders to crowd on more sail and headed quickly toward the island. No pirate ships. The people ashore explained the situation. The Flensborg master had told the truth: Mendoza had lain in the roads for two days, but he had sailed away six hours previously—according to the biography, indeed, it was only three hours before. He had two ships at his disposal; he himself was on board a pink, which he had equipped with six cannon, and he was furthermore accompanied by a sloop, which was likewise well armed.

Now Jørgen Daa had smelled blood. Once more he set sail immediately, and during the following five days he systematically searched the waters east of the island. All search proved fruitless, and on June 20th a severe gale sprang up from the northwest. Little by little the two ships had come right over to Kanin Nos at the approaches to the White Sea, where Jens Hvid had once awaited Jens Munk's home-coming from the voyage to Kolguev. Then late in the afternoon the lookout in the swaying crow's-nest on the *Victor* sighted two ships, to windward, running before the wind and scudding south into the White Sea. Jørgen Daa was certain that these were the pirates and took up the chase. The crews of the *Victor* and the *Jupiter* were ordered to splash water on the sails, regardless of the wind force; bonnets were drawn under the mainsails and stunsails set at the sides, and on the *Victor* they hoisted the red provost-sail on the foremast, which signified that the ship was on a royal punitive expedition. So began the wild pursuit. The sea heaved around the two ships like green mountains with snow on their peaks; their upper deck tilted like the roof of a house, so that down on the lee side the bulwarks and cordage tore through a belt of seething spume.

Jørgen Daa was right: it was Mendoza who lay ahead. Already it was clear that the foreign ships had also begun to increase sail on sighting the Danish men-of-war in an effort to get away. Later it was learned that Mendoza had been on his way to Kanin Nos, where he intended to lie in wait for a Dutch merchantman homeward bound from Vaygach. But the Danish pursuit did not last for long; Klavs Povlsen had set more sail than his vessel could bear, the wet canvas stood taut as flexed metal plates in the gale, and shortly afterward both of the *Jupiter*'s masts were carried away. With the rollers sweeping in over a chaos of ropes and torn Lübeck canvas, the ship lay heaving, a defenseless prey to the waves. Jørgen Daa reported: "Meanwhile the 'Jupiter' lost both its topmasts and the one top overboard, so that it lay past all hope, and in the meantime there was come upon us a fog and dark weather, so that I took myself back to the 'Jupiter' again, since I dare not sail from His Majesty's ship, for I feared that other harm might come to it."

To give the order to turn about was difficult for Jørgen Daa, but there was nothing else to be done. Out in the drizzle the foreign ships disappeared; Mendoza had escaped. But that same night, in spite of rain, storm, and the rough sea, the *Jupiter*'s crew succeeded in repairing the worst of the damage and set up a jury-rig. "On the morrow," says Jørgen Daa "when the sun stood in the northeast, there came a Dutchman and informed me that the freebooter together with his pink was somewhere near Crytz Island." When the *Jupiter* was more or less maneuverable again, Jørgen Daa took leave of Captain Povlsen and set course for the position indicated. A few hours later his lookout again observed two topsails on the horizon.

This time Mendoza did not attempt flight. He saw that his pursuers had only one ship left, and he prepared for battle under what for him were the most favorable conditions. "Yet by this time I had reached him in the 'Victor' and was come so near as to have him under my cannon," says Jørgen Daa. However, it was Mendoza who fired the first cannon-shots, and at the same time he brought his sloop to windward of the *Victor*, so that he was in a position to fire on the Danes from two sides. The impact of the cannon balls on the water caused spray to rise to the height of the crow's-nests on the ships; if any cannon balls struck it was the sheerest fluke, for the motion of the ships in the heavy sea made it impossible to take proper aim. The musketeers had better opportunity: "Mendoza had good musketry and knew full well how to twist and turn his ship," it states in the biography, and Olafsson has an anecdote telling how the pirate had the Danish cannon balls, which struck his ship, carried down to his cabin so that he could judge their size: "It happened that the pirates had a Danish cabin boy, and Mendoza asked him if he believed that his countrymen, the Danes, had still larger cannon on board. The boy answered that he believed this was so; he knew well their practice of first firing the smaller cannon and thereupon the larger ones. This boy was desirous, indeed, of sending them all to the devil," comments Olafsson.

The battle ended in Mendoza's favor, for in the end the *Victor*'s main topsail was damaged to such an extent that Jørgen Daa had to withdraw the vessel in order to carry out repairs. However, Mendoza's ship must also have been badly knocked about at this stage, for the pirate did not press home his advantage, but remained hove-to at the place of battle. It took the crew of the *Victor* seven hours to repair the torn rigging, but just as this work was nearing completion, a joyous announcement rang from the crow's-nest. Limping across the waves, with its three-quarter jury-rig flying in the wind, the *Jupiter* now came heading straight for Mendoza.

Immediately Jørgen Daa got the *Victor* under sail again, and the Danes closed in on the enemy from two sides. "And therewith had I become too strong for him in navigation and all things," he says in his report. The *Victor* fired two broadsides, and this time finally succeeded in striking Mendoza's pink below the water line. The pirates on board his sloop discovered that he was in difficulties and saw their chance to slip away. Mendoza himself had no alternative but to make for land and run the ship aground before it sank. He began to heave valuable clothes and chests overboard, and Jon Olafsson with his taste for dramatics believes that this was a stratagem: the pirate threw his treasures overboard so that the pursuing ships would be delayed in an effort to save them. Both Jørgen Daa and the biographer are more objective: Mendoza jettisoned the precious pieces of clothing because of a leak in the ship's side; the heavy chests were offered not as bait but as an attempt to make the ship lighter and bring the hole above the water line.

Even now, however, the battle was undecided. A well-aimed cannon-shot from the fleeing Mendoza struck the *Victor*'s bowline and the main topsail again came down with yard and all. The Danes managed to retaliate by holing Mendoza, but then the pirate got away from them in toward Kanin Nos, keeping the wind right aft. His ship was so waterlogged that the *Jupiter*, in spite of its jury-rig, had no difficulty in following him. Meanwhile the crew of the *Victor* replaced the ropework and hauled the yard aloft for the second time. Mendoza succeeded in running his pink aground in a calm cove below Kanin Nos; but as the cove was too shallow, the

Danes had to give up their attempts to come within shooting range of him and dropped anchor in four fathoms. In the evening a new northwesterly storm with hail and snow broke upon them, which lasted the whole of the following day and forced Jørgen Daa to a cease-fire. The men had enough to do with laying extra anchor chains to prevent the ship from running aground in the roaring breakers.

When the storm subsided the red flag still flew from the main top of the grounded pirate ship. Mendoza had not given up the struggle; he lay outside the range of the Danish cannon and had utilized the pause to go ashore and build a redoubt on the hilltop from which his men could rake the beach with fire and cover the disabled ship. The day before Midsummer, Jørgen Daa sent two men ashore in a dinghy to exhort him to give himself up. Olafsson says that Jørgen Daa's servant Morten and a musketeer called Gotschalk were those concerned.

Mendoza received Morten and Gotschalk with food and ale; that is probably why they lingered for a long time with him, continues Olafsson, at which the admiral became so annoyed that they came near to being punished when they finally returned. The two self-indulgent parleyers reported that Mendoza was minded to fight to the last man, though he was willing to go on board the *Victor* and negotiate with Jørgen Daa, if the Dane first sent along his lieutenant as a hostage, unarmed and without companions. Jørgen Daa agreed to Mendoza's offer, and Jens Munk had no objection to going.

It was Midsummer Eve, one of the few nights of the year when the red midnight sun does not even brush the northern horizon but turns off its course as if suddenly thinking better of the direction it has chosen. On the Danish warships the men stood watching as Jens Munk was rowed ashore. It was so quiet that the noise of the steady oar strokes could be heard all the way in. At last they reached the beach; the dinghy was made fast, while Jens Munk clambered ashore. Soon after, with a feeling of uneasiness, the men on board saw their little lieutenant disappear up among the stony hillocks, alone and un-armed.

This was a dangerous move which Jørgen Daa had taken in the hope of avoiding the final battle. The risk was obvious, the prize doubtful; and, indeed, the result turned out to be what one might have foreseen: Mendoza did not come on board. Ashore on the beach lay the ship's dinghy; the men waited in vain; hour after hour passed, and the tide went out. The men on the *Victor* and the *Jupiter* stood gazing anxiously across the barren landscape. Mendoza had failed to appear; but that was not the worst, for neither did their lieutenant. They had fallen into a trap: Jens Munk was a prisoner of Mendoza.

13

The First Retort

Jan Mendoza had lived for many years on plundering and slaving; a wealth of experience had taught him that one can wage war with other means than cannon-royal. His favorite technique was to take hostages and threaten to subject them to torture; then, as a rule, the rest was easy.

Mendoza had not intended for one moment to go out to the *Victor*. He informed Jens Munk that if Jørgen Daa wanted his lieutenant back with nails and limbs intact, he would have to let him get away with his ship, his booty, and all his men.

Jens Munk shrugged, unperturbed. He had complied with Jørgen Daa's request and rowed ashore, well aware of the likely consequences to himself. It had been agreed between him and Jørgen Daa that, should he not return, his friend would announce by a cannon-shot from the *Victor* that he was going ashore with his musketeers. But while Jens Munk spent the night in the pirates' camp, with no break in the silence outside other than the cries of the guillemots down on the beach, he had ample opportunity to go over the many weak points in this agreement.

Jørgen Daa had all too many reasons for delaying his attack. It was by no means sure that a landing party would be able to rescue his lieutenant, and anyway the pirates would have plenty of time to put their hostage to death. Secondly, even from a purely numerical point of view the situation was by no means favorable to the Danes. If one collates the figures from the biography and from Jørgen Daa's report, it is evident that even after the loss of his sloop Mendoza had an appreciable force. During his sojourn behind the enemy defenses Jens Munk was able to satisfy himself that the pirates numbered at least eighty men; and it is unlikely that the total complement on the *Victor* and the *Jupiter* substantially exceeded this figure. During the Kalmar War the *Victor* was manned by seventy men; but then the King himself was on board. The crew of the *Jupiter* was no more than about a score. In Vestmanhavn, Jørgen Daa had signed on some of Tucker's people, but it may be assumed that about the same number had been left in Kildin as crew for the captured pirate vessel. Finally Jørgen Daa realized, says Jon Olafsson, "that his men were all too little skilled in war, and this apart, there were many on board who were not good shots." The most likely implication here is that the two ships were manned largely with seamen from Bremerholm, while the number of soldiers was small. The Danish force was not sufficiently strong, and this probably was the real reason why Jørgen Daa and Jens Munk had risked so much in order to achieve a surrender through negotiation.

Such was the situation on Midsummer morning at sunrise. Everything was quiet; behind the earthworks Mendoza's men lay with their muskets; midway down on the beach the oarsman sat waiting near the overturned dinghy; a little farther out the pirates' pink was firmly aground, and out where the gleaming water became dappled and dark blue the Danish warships swung at anchor.

Then the hills echoed with a cannon-shot. The guillemots rose screeching from the shore. There was only one shot, but that was sufficient; Jens Munk recognized the largest of the cannon-royal on the *Victor*. Jørgen Daa had overcome his misgivings, and now it was neck or nothing.

In the handwritten report preserved in the National Archives, the Danish admiral describes the effect which the cannon-shot had in Mendoza's camp; the extract is important, because we encounter here the first authentic statement handed down from the taciturn Jens Munk. Jørgen Daa writes:

"Meanwhile my lieutenant remained somewhat long therein, and so I fired off a piece. Then said my lieutenant to them: If you do not let me pass on the instant, then will there be made a feast of it, and that not of the best."

The free and easy spirit of this remark is characteristic of Munk. He must have been able to give these simple words an unmistakable ring of authority, for he succeeded in turning the tables and frightening Mendoza. The pirate agreed to release him if he would inform Jørgen Daa of the conditions for a truce. This promise Munk was able to give without difficulty. The dinghy was refloated, Munk slopped after it in his sea boots, climbed aboard, and was rowed back to the *Victor*. As to the pirates' conditions, Mendoza required that they should leave his ship where it was until he could refloat it when the spring tide came. Then he would sail to Kildin with the Danes, from where he and his men were to have a free conduct. If Jørgen Daa refused to agree to this, he would fight to the last man.

Even if Mendoza's new conditions assured the Danes of his ship and his remaining booty, they were unacceptable to Jørgen Daa. It was Mendoza himself, not just his spoils, which they were to secure according to the King's instructions. There was no alternative but to try to attack.

As mentioned, Jørgen Daa had none too many soldiers; and, furthermore, the *Victor*'s cannon could not be brought into play. Mendoza had taken care to place his redoubt out of their range, and because of the heavy draught of the ship and the gently shelving sea bed it was impossible to bring it nearer to land. Jørgen Daa therefore went aboard the smaller *Jupiter*, which they succeeded in taking to three fathoms so that its cannon could provide sufficient cover for the landing party.

The troops were to be led by Jens Munk. The mission was the same as it had been once before, at Kjerlingbjerget and

Billingen. The enemy was to be stormed and driven from the redoubt on the hilltop, which would then be used as the base for the final assault. During his somewhat involuntary stay ashore Munk had been able to investigate the position: his plans were ready, and late in the morning he assembled his forces on the beach to the sound of trumpets and the roll of drums.

It is Jon Olafsson who mentions the drummers, but in all probability there was no time for any show of music. The beach was under heavy fire from Mendoza's musketeers, and the moment the Danes leaped ashore they had to run and take cover at the foot of the hill. It was from here that Munk gave instructions for the assault. But before they reached Mendoza's redoubt, yet another obstacle had to be overcome—a snow-drift halfway up the hill which had survived the winter. Stuck in the snow up to their waists, several of the Danish musketeers were easy prey for Mendoza's men. Still, Jens Munk succeeded in getting most of his men across this hurdle and up to the top of the hill, where they leaped down into Mendoza's trenches. A fierce hand-to-hand struggle began, but the Danes were in the majority. At the sight of the onrushing sailors, many of whom had now thrown down their muskets and substituted long ship's knives, Mendoza and the greater part of his following took to flight, and in a short time Jens Munk was master of the redoubt. While the pirates withdrew to their grounded ship, he distributed the shovels and mattocks they had left behind among his sailors, and they began in great haste to extend the redoubt to provide cover in the direction of the pirate vessel, which for obvious reasons had not been done before.

In the meantime Mendoza had assembled his scattered forces, and he now aimed the ship's cannon at the redoubt ashore. But Mikkel Vibe's pink was no man-of-war; the six cannon were all mounted on the upper deck, and when the Danes had completed their digging, it was an easy matter for them to keep the pirates off the cannon with their muskets. At the same time Jørgen Daa, who had followed the progress of the battle from the *Jupiter*, succeeded in getting two of the ship's cannon onto the beach, from which they started a systematic bombardment of Mendoza's ship.

The pirate had now come under double fire; he was unable to offer further resistance, and as his vessel was grounded in very low water, there was imminent danger of the Danes setting it ablaze. He had to bring himself to send his master, Walther Brahe, with an offer of negotiation. According to the biography, Jens Munk received Brahe on the newly taken hilltop. Their conversation did not last long; Jens Munk recalled Mr. Brahe's mirth when he had found himself in the hands of the pirates a few hours earlier. Now he curtly declined the proposal; neither he nor Brahe had authority to negotiate. Mendoza must personally approach His Royal Majesty's admiral, Jørgen Daa. When Walther Brahe returned to the ship with this message, the Danes resumed their fire; but this time the firing was brief. A few minutes after Brahe's return, the red flag was lowered from the main top. The men on the redoubt ashore and out on the *Jupiter* and *Victor* saw the pirates lower a boat and row over to Jørgen Daa. The battle was over. The tall man who now climbed up onto the deck of the *Jupiter* in his lavish gold-braided silk clothing was Jan Mendoza in person. Jørgen Daa nodded to one of the attendant musketeers to go over and remove the belt with the pirate's sword.

2

All sources indicate the same thing, directly and indirectly: the victory was Jens Munk's. In the first place, he risked his own person to bring about a surrender through negotiation; and when that failed, it was he who in effect forced a decision by military means. Nor was he without a part in the sequel. The following day he sat once more with Jørgen Daa in the judgment seat on the upper deck of the *Victor*. Before them stood Mendoza and his men, all with their hands tied behind them, and surrounded by armed Danish musketeers. Twenty-four pirates had fallen in the battle; about fifty men remained —a wretched bunch as they stood there in their torn shirts, some carrying their arms in slings, others with dirty rags around their heads.

The court resolved that Mendoza himself, his captain Walther Brahe, and his master Linnert should be taken to Copenhagen in irons and brought before a royal court of justice. The Danish ship's boy, who had informed Mendoza about the caliber of the cannon, was acquitted; but as to the rest of his men, the list of their crimes was a long one. The court rejected their appeal for clemency. Amid deep silence from all present, Jørgen Daa announced that they were to be punished in accordance with the Articles of War, Paragraph 31, sub-clause b. While Mendoza looked on, fifty-four of his men were lashed together two and two, back to back, dragged to the rail of the *Victor* and tipped overboard. The current took hold of the twenty-seven bundles and carried them away like sheaves of straw.

Only the pirate ship remained; it appeared that it would take several weeks' work to get it afloat. Jørgen Daa dared not let His Majesty's ship lie so long at anchor off the open coast, where they would be at the mercy of the breakers in the event of an onshore gale; accordingly they had to abandon their capture. The plundered goods were transferred to the *Victor* and the ship was set ablaze.

In order to collect the ship from the Faroe Islands, Jørgen Daa laid his homeward course via Kildin, and at the same time took the opportunity to inspect those ships which were engaged in whaling from the island. All the masters had their papers in order; but when Daa arrived at Vardøhus on July 6th, the governor, Klavs Bagge, informed him that a number of Basques were hunting whales off the shores of his fief without the royal permit. Jørgen Daa patrolled the fjords in the heavily indented coast and on July 17th found in Tømmerviken, in Laksfjord, two ships whose crews were busy rendering train oil from their whales ashore on the beach. As the *Victor* glided nearer, Jens Munk was able to survey the extensive camp. The work had been broken off at the unexpected appearance of the Danish ships. The Basques had settled on the floor of a sheltered cove; on the beach lay their whales, towed in at high tide and beached now at high-water level, where they occupied almost as much of the landscape as did the two ships lying at anchor farther out. Great sheets of cut blubber were dragged from the whales to the chopping boards, where the crowd of workers still stood with their long knives in their hands. From there the chopped blubber was taken on skids to the copper cauldron over a brick-built furnace, the column of smoke from which had betrayed the position to Jørgen Daa as it rose straight up in the chilly calm of the arctic sky. In the grass on the other side of the cauldron lay some old pinnaces, in which the train oil was cooled, and around them stood the coopers, who had been engaged in making casks to hold the finished product. An acrid smell of train oil hung over the spot, and a host of seafowl fought, amid a great din and screeching, over the hunks of blubber and offal.

The Basques' ship was armed only with a pair of old iron cannon, and in any case their captain, a distinguished gentleman named Jan Haraneder, made no attempt to offer resistance. In return Jørgen Daa let him off with a mild sentence: his catch was confiscated, but he himself and his men were given a safe-conduct. Jens Munk was to remain at the spot with the *Jupiter* and supervise the remaining train-oil extraction, while Jørgen Daa continued his voyage of inspection with the *Victor*. In order to transport the finished train oil to Copenhagen the Danes had to take over the larger of the foreign vessels, while the Basques were given permission to sail away in the smaller boat.

Jens Munk had lost none of his old interest in whaling, even though his activities as a whaler had been short-lived. During the intervening years great numbers of whalers from many countries had discovered the waters where as a young master mariner he had dreamed of taking up whaling. In the ensuing busy days at Tømmerviken he had a chance to learn something about the famed whaling technique of the Basques. On the beach lay the rowboats that the whalers had used during the hunt: three long, slender, and astonishingly frail pinnaces without any great freeboard and built as lightly as possible to achieve the greatest possible speed and maneuverability, with room for the harpooner in the bows, the four rowers, and the coxswain who stood in the stern sheets steering the boat with an oar. Here lay the harpoons, quite short and made of the finest forged steel to give them the greatest possible piercing strength and elasticity, with the barbs in front and with the whale-line bound fast to the rear—first the thin running line of fine and slender rope, then the long heavy line of untarred hemp. Jens Munk knew the prices of train oil, which particularly in these years were rising everywhere in Western Europe, and in the course of the long summer days in Tømmerviken the seamen watched their lieutenant walking around by himself, picking up one tool after the other without a word and examining it long and earnestly.

After two weeks the extraction of the train oil was completed, and the last barrels, their tops awash, were towed out to the ship which the Danes had commandeered. Shortly afterward the three familiar masts of the *Victor* came into view behind the headland, followed by two other ships. Once again Jørgen Daa had been in luck. Some distance farther to the west, in Kjelvik at the mouth of the Porsang, he had got onto the track of two Spanish ships, the *Señora de Rosario* and the *San Pedro*, whose captains had also carried on unlawful whaling and had stolen wood and shot reindeer ashore as well. This time both ships were seized with their crews and their entire catch, which according to Jørgen Daa's report consisted of the train oil from no less than eighteen whales.

By now the two Danish warships could hardly cope with more prizes, and at the beginning of August they set their course for Copenhagen. Jørgen Daa and Jens Munk had repeated their Elfsborg victories, and the home-coming took on the air of a triumph; from the ramparts at Bremerholm the inhabitants of the city saw the *Victor* and the *Jupiter*, still bearing the unmistakable traces of battle, glide into the harbor with no less than four captured ships between them—one of the vessels from the Faroe Islands and the three whaling boats from northern Norway. "No man could recall, that there ever was come to Copenhagen a ship with such great riches," says Jon Olafsson, and that is most probably correct. Apart from the four prizes, and the pirate ship from Vestmanhavn which had already been sent to Copenhagen, Jørgen Daa and Jens Munk had with them the stolen goods taken over from Mendoza's pink and the immense quantity of train oil they had confiscated from the whalers. These were no trifles. As to valuables, Olafsson says that there were nine chests in all, "eight of them filled with all manner of silver coins and so heavy that it needed four men to carry the least of them up to the palace, while the ninth was full of pure gold coins, so that ten men were needed to carry it." The amount of train oil is recorded in Jens Munk's logbooks: in Tømmerviken they took five hundred hogsheads, in Kjelviken the haul amounted to six hundred, which according to the prices current then represented approximately 44,000 guilder, an enormous sum for those times.

And this was, after all, the least part of the triumph. The King's instructions had been carried out and the dreaded Mendoza brought to Copenhagen in chains. Christian IV gave short shrift. Jørgen Daa arrived in Copenhagen on August 26th and by the 29th the three men were hanged outside the East Gate, i.e., near the present Kongens Nytorv. Ship's master Linnert was hanged on an ordinary gallows, while Mendoza and his captain Walther Brahe were given the chance of trying out the new strappado, which had just come to the country from Germany. "And there they hung still, when I came to the city in the autumn of 1615, whole and intact in their silken clothes trimmed with gold braid and gold-embroidered shoes. The which be to all ungodly people a caution and admonition and a conversion from a sinful life," Olafsson says.

Even if the three whaling ships were eventually released—the last two only after lengthy lawsuits—and even though Jon Olafsson certainly exaggerates the number of Mendoza's money chests, it was nevertheless enormous booty which was now to be divided among the victors. According to the biography, the King received one half, but other sources say that he contented himself with a third. Of the remainder, according to current practice, by far the greater part fell to the ship's officers. In the autumn of 1615 Jens Munk was a well-to-do man for the first time in his life.

Yet, exactly as after Elfsborg, the victory was to cost him dear. The large spoils from the arctic had fired the imagination of people both high and low in Copenhagen, and little by little the notion gained ground that this Mendoza was not the only one of his tribe—he must surely have brothers. Soon rumor had it that there were no less than five of them; and it necessarily followed that they, too, must be pirates with ships filled to the rails with treasure. While Mendoza dangled on the strappado outside the East Gate, his brothers were surely avenging themselves from Iceland to North Cape. The thought of the treasure accumulating in their ships exerted a dramatic appeal; and in April, 1616, the King decided that this year, too, an expedition should be mounted.

The year before, when there was still only one Mendoza to be captured and brought to Copenhagen, there had been great difficulties in finding sufficient officers. Only a single nobleman was found willing; only two ships were fitted out. But in the spring of 1616, no fewer than twelve noblemen wanted to join in, and six men-of-war were equipped on Bremerholm.

It was natural that Jørgen Daa should again be appointed commander of the squadron on board the *Victor*, but since so many noblemen had volunteered, Jens Munk could not very well be given his former position. The lords put their heads together; certain episodes from his time as quartermaster were recalled, and it was felt that he had been richly rewarded already. And so things were reorganized. The previous year Munk had acted as vice-admiral for the squadron, second-in-command on the *Victor*, and lieutenant. Now these three positions were taken from him one by one and allocated to noblemen. The vice-admiral of the squadron was the highborn Frans Brockenhuus on the *Lübeck David*. The second-in-command on the *Victor* was the highborn Holger Rosenkrantz. And the lieutenant on the *Victor* was the highborn Lavritz Brems. There were plenty to choose from. In the end there was actually difficulty in finding a place for the victor of the previous year; Jens Munk did not even get a ship for himself like the squadron's only nonaristocratic captain, Peter Nielsen. When all the positions were filled, he was made lieutenant under Frans Brockenhuus, who had been his subordinate at Elfsborg. It was just about the lowest commissioned post in the whole squadron, a plain degradation. It was rumored that Erik Munk's son did not like being humiliated. That was his vulnerable spot. Good—this time the humiliation was total.

3

The important thing now, however, was to deal with Mendoza's brothers. On April 4th the distinguished company set sail from Copenhagen in the name of God, with prayers and blessings. For reasons which will shortly become clear, Jørgen Daa did not submit a report to the King on this occasion, and for similar reasons the biography of 1723 dismisses the voyage with a single line. Our knowledge of these painful events, therefore, would be rather scant were it not for the loquacious Jon Olafsson, this time among the rank and file on board the *Victor*. This stout musketeer took part in the voyage from first to last; it was his first expedition with the King's navy, and he had his eyes open. What did he see?

In the middle of April the six ships reached Flekkerø, where the inhabitants told them that a pirate had been operating along the Norwegian coast. The Danish noblemen felt certain that it must be one of Mendoza's brothers, and gave orders to take up the pursuit. "And we sailed away from Flekkerø then and northward along Norway with our six ships, in and out of many harbors, in order to search for the aforementioned pirate, but without our being successful in finding him," reports Olafsson. The governor at Vardø was perplexed; he had heard nothing about Mendoza's brothers. In the hope of repeating the triumph of the previous year, however, the noble captains set a course toward the White Sea, where they cruised around off Kanin Nos for a fortnight without seeing anything other than the charred remains of Mikkel Vibe's pink. Not even on Kildin could the people remember having seen anything of Mendoza's brothers; but on the other hand there was a visit from a Russian officer, who soon turned out to be just as high-ranking as the Danish noblemen. The party lasted the whole day. Toasts were proposed for the King of Denmark and the Grand Duke of Muscovy and for the distinguished people in Denmark and Muscovy; twelve Russian soldiers brought a number of large speckled salmon, which they presented to the Danish noblemen on their knees; and four and twenty cannon-shots were fired as the Russians finally went ashore in the light night.

On the following day the hunt for Mendoza continued in a mood of exhilaration. The general gaiety persisted all the way to Vardø, where Jon Olafsson and several other musketeers were sent ashore to procure fresh supplies. "Most of our number were somewhat drunk and as the gale grew in force the sea swept in over the boat, but we had nothing wherewith to bail, and it became at last almost filled with water." None of those on board the nearby flagship thought it necessary to lower a boat, and only a long time after was aid forthcoming from one of the more distant ships. "Only five men drowned," says Jon Olafsson.

Not only had the royal squadron now discharged its first cannon-shots, but it had also suffered its first loss of human life; and as the ships continued toward North Cape a few days later, it looked as though the first sea battle was upon them. One morning when an unknown squadron was observed heading toward Russia, a council of war was summoned; and when the distinguished gentlemen learned that the squadron consisted of five ships, they had no doubts at all. Now they had Mendoza's brothers. The Danish vessels were cleared for action, the gear stowed away on the gun deck, the cannon ports opened up, so that the lionheads faced the right way, brandy was issued to the crew, and the admiral's flag was hoisted on the main-truck. Everything was ready to give the five brothers a warm reception.

Meanwhile, one of the ships, the *Unicorn*, had moved into a position astern of the strange ships, and when their commander observed that they were being surrounded, he struck the sails, lowered a boat, and rowed over to the *Victor*, where the Danish noblemen stood in their finely embroidered silken clothes, ready to receive the surrender. The whole thing had moved more quickly than the previous year, and all could see that the spoils, too, would be far greater. Step by step the dreaded pirate climbed up the rope ladder to the deck where everyone was at battle stations. But the man had a piece of paper in his hand. Jørgen Daa scrutinized it carefully. It was a sea pass, and it was in order. They might just as well close the cannon ports again; Mendoza's brother was a peaceful merchant from Hamburg.

Consequently the Danish nobles received the good man politely; his other captains were summoned. From Jon Olafsson we learn that before long everything was just as merry as during the visit of the Russians on Kildin. "The strangers gave us twelve casks of good Hamburg ale; in the evening a great celebration was held for them, and we parted with hearty salutations, cannon-shots, and the playing of trumpets."

Where were Mendoza's brothers? They had been sought in vain from Flekkerø to Kanin Nos, so now it was decided to make for Iceland. At the same latitude as Eyjafjalle Glacier, however, the ships were overtaken by a severe northwest gale, which lasted for a week and increased in force. Meanwhile the ships drifted closer and closer to the dangerous coast, and one evening they came so near that Jon Olafsson could see his fellow countrymen driving home their flocks to be milked. So Jørgen Daa had to go about and head for the Faroe Islands. The ships now had the storm aft, and it took them only a day to reach Thorshavn. But during the passage they lost sight of the *Leopard* and the *Gabriel*, and when after twenty-four hours the two ships still had not arrived at Thorshavn, they were considered lost. At the same time another regrettable affair had to be given attention. On the voyage from Iceland the steward of the *Unicorn* had relieved himself in the breadstore during the gale. All the noble captains took part in the sitting of the court, and as they were vested with the same authority as the previous expedition to give the strictest interpretation to the Articles of War, no leniency was shown. That same evening the sinner was strung up on the ship's bowsprit.

This served as a prelude to the festivities, which lasted for four days. Jon Olafsson gratefully enumerates twelve different kinds of ale in the magistrate's splendid repast. In the early hours of the morning the exhausted guests reeled back to the ships. Beneath the bowsprit of the *Unicorn* the dead steward swung in the wind. There was still no news of the *Leopard* and the *Gabriel*. Be that as it may, the magistrate's civility was now to be returned; and the following day the farmers of the uplands were instructed to come aboard and each supply a sheep and some milk and cheese. The next four days there was merry-making from morning till evening, first on the *Victor*, then on the *Jupiter*, the *Unicorn*, and the *Lübeck David*. The weather was fine and tables were set up on deck, where the officers of the squadron sat down to roast mutton, while the guests were permitted to take their places in a circle around them. Countless toasts were offered to the King, the Council of the Realm, and the Danish nobility; the drummers labored, the trumpeters blew, and according to Olafsson three thousand cannon-shots were fired altogether. And yet there was no loss of life; only a boatswain from the *Unicorn* lost a few fingers during the firing of a cannon, but this was attended to the same evening by the surgeon and six strong men. Also, the cattle ashore were frightened by the many explosions. While one countrywoman was milking her cow, a cannon ball suddenly came rushing through the air and buried itself in the grass near the cow's tethering post, and in its fright the beast overturned the milk-pail and leapt away, while the woman was left lying un-conscious. But the following day she dug up the cannon ball and took it out to the flagship. The noble lords, says Jon Olafsson, "received her most kindly and forthwith gave her a rix-dollar and an old but still serviceable shirt."

Finally the four ships were able to leave the Faroe Islands with a good conscience. At Lindesnes, in Norway, they met up with the *Leopard* and the *Gabriel*; the two ships had not been lost on the passage from Iceland, they had simply not been able to find the Faroe Islands. In the first week of September, 1616, a full squadron was able to put in to Copenhagen, where to the fanfares of trumpets the twelve noblemen disembarked and received the grateful acclamation of the inhabitants. This time, however, there was no report to the King. Perhaps the occasion did not seem to call for it. In the autumn of 1616 the pirates ravaged the shipping from the Westman Islands to North Cape worse than ever before.

Even if Olafsson exaggerates in some details, the facts of the voyage speak for themselves. It is not difficult to imagine Jens Munk's reaction to this parody of a pirate hunt. The previous year he and Jørgen Daa had in the space of three months and with two men-of-war disarmed Mendoza, cap-tured two other pirates, and brought home three whaling ships. This year the expedition had extended over five months and consisted of six men-of-war. In almost double the time and with thrice the force, the noblemen had not even so much as caught sight of the mast of a pirate ship. Was it for such a fiasco that the noble lords had taken his command away from him? He had known the stinging scorn when their decision was made known; but as a naval captain he was compelled to obey orders. The events at Elfsborg had shown long ago that, unlike his father, he stood no chance against his aristocratic opponents: their superiority was too great. He had to swallow the shame, join in the ludicrous expedition, persuade his men to respect decisions and obey commands which both they and he could see were obviously amateurish. That experience and skill should have to yield to an authority based solely on clique, rank, and privilege might perhaps work on dry land, but it could not be tolerated at sea. Munk had to admit that he was finished at Bremerholm. The nobles had proved too strong. Could they not repeat this same treatment at any time? What sort of future could he expect here, where skill was looked upon as provocation, where every service rendered was suspect, every achievement followed by a kick?

A careful study of Jen Munk's activities about the time of the unsuccessful expedition does in fact reveal that in the spring, when the news of his demotion was an established fact, he had already begun to operate a large-scale enterprise entirely unconnected with Bremerholm. The outcome of this enterprise became known throughout Copenhagen when he returned in September from the Norwegian Sea with the twelve noblemen who had not made a skilling out of their expedition. That was his answer to his enemies. The previous year their inconsequential quartermaster had become a well-to-do man for the first time in his life. Admittedly, they were quick to take revenge. But this year the man had more than doubled his profit. People now doffed their hats to him on the street.

14

Ove Giedde

I

It was the year 1616: Shakespeare had died of typhoid in Stratford, Cervantes of dropsy in Madrid, and Burgomaster Frederik Christensen of old age in his stone house with its gable facing the street in Aalborg. Christian IV had chosen Kirsten Munk as "a true companion, with whom he will live and die," and his earlier mistress, Karen Andersdatter, was forced to leave the Court with a nice pension and the isle of Hven in fief. The skilling had fallen again; since the beginning of the Kalmar War it had been rated 74 to the silver dollar, but now it was 80.

With Denmark's entry into the Kalmar War, the King had to shelve all his plans for starting whaling stations in the Norwegian Sea. And while the Danes and the Swedes were busy burning down one another's towns, the English Muscovy Company sent their first whaling boats to Spitsbergen; the following year the Dutch also joined in, and in 1614 no fewer than ten English and eighteen Dutch vessels were whaling in those waters which Christian IV, on his voyage to North Cape, had dreamed of turning into a Danish Sea.

Then the people of Bergen and Copenhagen woke up, and the first Norwegian whaleboats moved out through the islands. In Copenhagen Mikkel Vibe, the burgomaster, formed a consortium with substantial financial backing, and before long the King sent a representative to London to protest

against the encroachments of the Muscovy Company—the
same Dr. Charisius, incidentally, who had drawn his attention
to the whales in these waters on their homeward journey from
North Cape. Mikkel Vibe's first expedition, in 1615, does not
seem to have brought much return; whaling was a complicated
affair, and there was a great lack of experts with a command of
the techniques. Meanwhile, Jørgen Daa and Jens Munk returned home in the late summer from their expedition to the
Norwegian Sea, not only bringing Mikkel Vibe important
news of the pink he had lost to Mendoza, but also displaying
the three whaling ships confiscated in Tømmervik and
Kjelvik, the last two complete with their entire complement of
Basques. Captain Munk could tell him all about harpoons,
whaling lines, and blubber boiling. It must have been obvious
to Mikkel Vibe that if he wanted to keep in business as a
whaler he would have to have this man.

Jens Munk had now received his share of the spoils; at last
he had money to become his own master. A glance through the
accounts of the Sound Dues for this year shows that on April
22nd, eighteen days after Jens Munk had left Copenhagen
with those twelve noblemen on their search for "Mendoza's
brothers," a ship commanded by a master called Hans
Trondhjem had been dispatched by Jens Munk of Copenhagen.
No whaling permit for Hans Trondhjem can be traced; he
was traveling on a Northlands passport, and the later accounts
reveal that he returned in mid-August "with merchandise from
Russia." Nevertheless, a number of circumstances seem to
indicate that his real business was whaling. In the customs
accounts his ship is specifically mentioned as "bound for the
whaling"; this entry immediately follows those for the *Red
Lion* and the *Hunter*, which are shown as chartered for whaling
by Mikkel Vibe. The three ships were probably sailing together. Eight days previously, Mikkel Vibe was given permission to engage in whaling off the Northlands with an
entitlement to take along nine or ten Basques. In 1616 it was
hardly likely that there were any other Basques in Copen-

hagen than those Jens Munk had brought back from the Norwegian fjords the year before.

Other circumstantial evidence makes it clear that by the spring of 1616 Jens Munk and Mikkel Vibe were already collaborating in whaling in the Norwegian Sea. In the biography there is a reference to his largely financing "this fishery," and to the success of the first voyage, which might have been even greater if they had had more casks and barrels with them. The same had happened to them as had often happened to the English in these early experimental years: they caught more whales than they could cope with. By the middle of August, Hans Trondhjem was back in Copenhagen. His expedition had succeeded beyond all expectation; all the barrels on board were full to the brim with train oil, the total value of which was almost certainly greater than Munk's share of the Mendoza spoils.

This news was known to everyone on Amagertorv when Jens Munk and the twelve noblemen returned from their grotesque pirate hunt. It must have startled his enemies— who despite their hopes had gained nothing from their long voyage—to learn that their demoted lieutenant had more than doubled his wealth without lifting a finger. For Munk the news of the great catch, together with the information that there had been more whales than they could handle, meant a real chance of release. Shortly after his return, he resigned his commission as captain in the navy, left Bremerholm, and threw himself heart and soul into a new attempt to realize his old dream of becoming a whaler.

Once again he worked with Mikkel Vibe, who had also had encouraging results that summer. Vibe planned to increase his fleet by two ships the following season, so that he could extend his operations into the tempting whaling grounds off Spitsbergen. This depended upon his being able to sign on extra Basque experts. On October 25th he received a royal permit to send five whaling ships to Spitsbergen and the Northlands, and permission to engage the necessary foreign whalers. In

Whaling in the Norwegian Sea. In the foreground a harpooner about
to cast the harpoon and line at a whale; farther away a whaling party
consisting of three boats each with six men tow a dead whale back to
the mother ship, partly by sail and partly by oars. From a contemporary
woodcut. (*Drie Voyagien*)

November, within three weeks of the issue of the royal con-
cession, Munk left for France to recruit whalers.

Shortly before his departure a family event took place
in his home in Pilestraede. Young Kathrine Adriansdatter
gave birth to her third child, another son. The child was baptized on November 15th in St. Nicholas's Church and was
defiantly given the name Erik Munk. Then Jens Munk left
for France.

As usual he kept a logbook. He left Copenhagen by ship for Amsterdam (a useful center of market information), and from there he went south over land. With his faithful servant Oluf to accompany him, he pressed on day after day in rain and sleet, passing through Antwerp and Bruges, spending his nights in wretched inns, changing horses, then along slushy winter roads, through Flanders, Normandy, and Brittany, to the walled cities of Le Havre and La Rochelle. On and on through the French winter—Poitiers, Angoulême, and Bordeaux, mile after mile on wet, exhausted post horses, with the one aim of finding a handful of men ready to sail beyond the Polar Circle and catch whales. Toward Christmas they reached Saint-Jean-de-Luz on the Bay of Biscay, on the border of the Spanish-Basque region, but had little success here. On December 29th Munk rode north once again to Bordeaux, arriving there on January 15th in the new year 1617. He tried again here, and eventually found a Basque called Jan Lonighem, "and the same did promise to obtain for him eighteen Biscayans who were accustomed to the catching and killing of whales." This number was no arbitrary one. Jens Munk had learned that a whaling team should consist of nine men: three harpooners (*maîtres arponniers*), three linemen (*maîtres de la ligne*), and three boatmasters (*maîtres de chaloupe*). Jan Lonighem's eighteen Basques thus made up two teams.

No sooner was the contract with Lonighem signed, however, than the local authorities got news of the affair and tried to prevent the Basques from being hired in this way; some clerk had probably seen in this a good opportunity of extorting a bribe from the foreigner. The biography states that "the Count of Gramante would not permit them to travel abroad, unless generous gifts were made to him." Jens Munk was not without experience of deals of this kind. He refused Monsieur le

Whalers off Spitsbergen. From a contemporary woodcut. (Aertsz)

Comte; under such conditions he was not interested. He well knew that the Basques were eager to enter Danish service, for they had been worsted in the struggle for the rich whaling grounds off Spitsbergen, where the English and the Dutch had turned against them with armed men-of-war. In the end Jan Lonighem and he agreed to a private arrangement: the eighteen Basques were to make their own way to Amsterdam, while Munk would leave Bordeaux unaccompanied to avoid attracting the Count's attention. He would contact them later in the Dutch capital. It took eight days to negotiate the contracts, and on January 23rd Jens Munk started on his long homeward journey, first by horse to Saint-Martin, then by sea to England, and finally to Amsterdam, which he reached on March 16th. All eighteen Basques had honored their agreement; and a month later, on April 17th, Jens Munk arrived with them in Copenhagen. His journey had taken nearly six months; it was the first time in history that Basque whalers had been brought direct from France to Copenhagen. The foundation was thus laid for the Norwegian-Danish whaling industry, which was to develop during the following decades to a business with a turnover of millions.

Two expeditions were mounted by Mikkel Vibe in the summer of 1617. On June 13th his ships with Munk's Basques on board reached Ice Sound on the west coast of Spitsbergen. One of the captains, Bernt Gundersen, had been in Vibe's service the year before. As neither of the two captains was familiar with conditions in the local waters, an Englishman, James Vaden, who had previously sailed to Spitsbergen, was engaged as navigator.

What is surprising is that Jens Munk's name is not to be found on the ships' lists. He had obtained the Basque whalers, he had had years of experience in navigating under arctic conditions, and he certainly had considerable economic interests in the expedition. For a number of reasons it must be supposed that he stayed in Copenhagen during the summer of 1617, which fact in itself gives some hint as to his new status. It is the first summer he spent in the capital. For nearly twenty years he had spent the summer months at sea; but in 1617 he was his own master.

Nevertheless he would have been useful at Spitsbergen. The armed English whalers would not stand for Bernt Gundersen's being there; they confiscated his whales, attacked his Basque sailors, seized his pinnaces along with their sails and whaling tackle, and harassed him in all possible ways, even though he complained that he was in waters under the suzerainty of the Danish King. Indeed, it was in this connection that Christian IV sent Dr. Charisius to London with protests and claims for compensation. Despite all, however, Gundersen and his Basques succeeded in bringing home an even larger catch than the previous year's. They caught 17 whales, of which the English allowed them to retain 13; these yielded approximately 650 hogsheads of train oil. With the market price in Amsterdam at about 40 guilder per hogshead that year, this totaled 26,000 guilders. If one reckons in the expeditions along northern Norway, the value of which is not precisely known, it is clear that Mikkel Vibe and his company made a handsome profit.

Even though this profit had to be shared among several partners, and Jens Munk's share was one of the most modest ones, there is no doubt that he had made a good deal of money. For three years in succession now he had had an income well in excess of the 200 rix-dollars he had received annually as a naval captain. Not only on Amagertorv did people take their hats off to him; even at Court his prestige rose, and His Majesty once more began to take notice of him. When Christian IV planned a great colonial expedition to the East Indies the following winter, and looked about for a man to command it, his choice fell on Jens Munk. This is well attested, both in the biography and in the Zealand Register. February 20, 1618: Jens Munk was ordered by the King to prepare and command those ships which were to accompany the East India expedition.

This date marks the zenith of Jens Munk's career so far.

After having received the royal appointment, he first invested 300 rix-dollars in the East India Company; then he discussed the future season's whaling with Mikkel Vibe; and finally, one spring day when the weather was right, he donned his short black captain's mantle and set out again along the familiar way from Pilestraede down behind the anchor forge across the city moat, and in through the Bremerholm Gate.

As the chronicler says, one ought to be able to halt the story here: at the vision of Jens Munk returning once more to Bremerholm, selecting three of the King's ships best suited for the great expedition, examining them from keel to masthead, ordering the appropriate modifications and the necessary repairs, picking crew, drawing up lists of equipment, provisions, and supplies, anticipating the long voyage, seeing the tropics once more, the great calm along the equator, the trade wind and Africa, the monsoon and India. One ought to be able to stop here, but that is not possible. For it was not Jens Munk who finally commanded the famous expedition of Danish warships. He attended to the preparations and assumed responsibility for every belaying pin on board, but he did not become admiral of the expedition. He was given no command, nor did he even accompany the expedition. Six months after these events the King thought better of his choice and made over the leadership of the expedition to another man who was only twenty-four years old, who was without any experience at all of a ship's deck and wholly unfamiliar with conditions in the tropics. But he was an aristocrat.

3

Once more it is the incorruptible Zealand Register which provides the requisite documentation: on October 24th the nobleman Ove Giedde received the King's orders to proceed to the East Indies with the ships *Elephant, David, Christian,* and *Copenhagen.* And one month later, on November 29th, the King noted in his diary: "On this day our Indies fleet under

Ove Giedde sailed out of the Sound. May Almighty God grant them good fortune!"

Jens Munk might have been expected to try to compensate for loss and disappointment by concentrating on whaling, thus making the most of the luck he had enjoyed in this enterprise. On the contrary, one discovers that he also had to give up his association with Mikkel Vibe the same autumn—indeed, that he never again resumed that whaling which had cost him so much effort and so much money to organize.

That autumn Jens Munk made his way across Amagertorv practically unnoticed. Two great ambitions had been shattered, and one must ask why. Why did the King withdraw his appointment? Why did Mikkel Vibe discontinue their partnership? This is one of the most puzzling periods of Jens Munk's life. What happened in that short time between February 20th, when the King assigned him command of the ships for India, and October 24th, when the same post was taken over by Ove Giedde?

It is the year 1618. The skilling has fallen again, 84 to the silver dollar against 80 only two years before. In the autumn a great comet appeared over the city; people called it "The Broom,"and uneasily observed it night after night in the northern heavens. They recalled the eclipse of the moon which had heralded the Kalmar War, and knew that ill-starred events were once again imminent.

By this time the East India Company was already two years old. It had been founded in 1616, and in the beginning support lagged; but then a Dutchman, calling himself Marselis de Boshouwer, suddenly turned up in Copenhagen. Boshouwer announced that he had lived for many years in Ceylon and introduced himself to the King as personal adviser to the Emperor of Ceylon, Prince of Migomme, Knight of the Order of the Sun, Supreme Councillor of War to the Emperor and Grand Admiral of his fleet, and much more besides. That would not have gone down so well at home in Holland, but Christian Frederiksen was impressed. He put on his knowledgeable look and studied the beautiful imperial credentials which Boshouwer himself had prepared for the occasion; they were in order. The King would willingly conclude a pact of friendship with his Imperial Highness; Denmark would willingly undertake to send a squadron of the fleet to Ceylon and liberate the country from the Portuguese oppressors, in return for the exclusive rights to trade with the island. The Prince of Migomme assured him that there were whole mountains of spices, pearls, and ivory. Christian IV found him more and more engaging and offered him a position on the company's executive body. The Prince of Migomme reluctantly allowed himself to be persuaded. Finally, the King appointed a president for the whole thing—his son by Kirsten Madsdatter, Christian Ulrik Gyldenløve. The Prince of Migomme thought this an admirable idea. At this point in time the honorable president had just reached the age of five.

So everything was ready to send off the expedition; and, as we have seen, Ove Giedde left Copenhagen in the middle of November with his five ships, one of which carried the good Boshouwer, who had now become a wealthy man. A number of factors in the King's decision require explanation. Ove Giedde was at this time a quite untried man—he had never had command of a ship, he knew nothing about navigation, trade was a closed book to him, he did not possess the requisite knowledge of languages, and his cold, arrogant, and stubborn bearing made this young man incapable of maintaining even a tolerable relationship with his subordinates.

In all these respects Jens Munk was his superior. No one ever saw a seaman deserting one of his ships. Ove Giedde was even to sentence his own officers to disciplinary punishment. The notion of mutiny was unknown on Munk's many voyages; Ove Giedde was to put down an open revolt by armed force. Jens Munk had long experience of trading with colonial territories; he knew the Portuguese from many years of life among them; they, above all, were the people with whom one would have to negotiate on the expedition, and he spoke their language like a native. Time and again Ove Giedde reports his difficulties in obtaining a Portuguese interpreter, and important negotiations came to naught because of language troubles.

Doubtless there were weighty reasons for the King's preferring him to Jens Munk. As so often, the biography of 1723 gives a hint: "As he at last could not get on with the persons concerned, and as the promises made to him were not honored, he afterward felt His Royal Majesty had but loaned him to the company and that he was not bound to serve it. His Majesty was gracious enough to release him from the said voyage." In other words, it was on Munk's own initiative that the collaboration seems to have been broken off. Why, then, did he renounce this unique opportunity? The explanation given in the biography is that he could not get on with the persons concerned, and that the promises made to him had not been kept. There is no mention of financial matters: on an expedition of this scope a few rix-dollars more or less are of no consequence. The promise that had been made to him and not kept was, quite simply, that he should be leader of the expedition. Wise by experience, he had made this a condition. "The persons concerned" can be none other than his old enemies—the nobles who served as the company executive and who had followed his success in the whaling industry with mounting displeasure. It is they who got the King's appointment rescinded so that they could insinuate one of their own kind instead: Ove Giedde. Once more he found himself in the situation which he knew *ad nauseam* from his encounters with the King's diplomats: to have all the expertise and responsibility without having the authority. In 1618, however, he saw through the whole game and foresaw the consequences; this is the reason he withdrew. "His Majesty was gracious enough to release him from the said voyage." One understands that phrase all too well; to use a modern expression, he "resigned." Ove Giedde of Tommerup had won by virtue of the one thing in which he was superior. Had not the King himself said that the trading companies "shall be to Us an honor and to the merchants God willing no detriment"? Before the commercial interest came the representative. It was a matter of showing the flag, of raising the prestige of the Danish King. Here lay Ove Giedde's advantage. He is representative; Jens Munk, the former ship's boy, born out of wedlock, is not.

This was also his status, however, when he received the King's appointment on February 20th. Were there perhaps special circumstances? A glance at Jens Munk's life during this period may provide a clue.

As in the previous year, Jens Munk spent the summer in Copenhagen. It was not necessary for him to go to sea; he was still a member of Mikkel Vibe's consortium, still a whaleship owner. During the winter Dr. Charisius in London had negotiated full Danish participation in whaling operations off Spitsbergen; when summer arrived, Mikkel Vibe and his company fitted out two ships of 100 tons, which were the largest whaling boats to date originating in Copenhagen. They were also the most expensive. On this occasion the two vessels were commanded by the same captains as the year before and bound for Spitsbergen. Jens Munk remained serenely at home and devoted himself to preparing the ships for the East Indies. As usual, he had put everything he owned into Mikkel Vibe's ships, and there was every indication that the catch would even exceed the record of the previous years.

No report is available from Bernt Gundersen for that year, though he does seem to have avoided trouble with the English. The difficulties on this occasion were of another kind. From English accounts we know that enormous masses of ice prevented whaling in all the northerly grounds. From the accounts of the Sound Dues, one notes that the two ships returned on August 29th "with ballast." There was not one cask of train oil on board.

This bitter fact is confirmed by the biography, from which it appears that Jens Munk had to abandon whaling after having lost "over 1000 rix-dollars." At first sight the figure does not seem alarming; but if one thinks that this represents the equivalent of more than five years' salary as a naval captain, one can understand how heavy the loss was. Jens Munk had no reserves like Mikkel Vibe, and no credit. He was ruined, and in consequence had to withdraw from the company; that was the end. He had no occasion to renew the association. The whaling industry, which he had largely founded by bringing in the Basques, continued during the following years with ever-increasing yields; it became one of the country's largest sources of income, but it did so without Jens Munk.

What is striking about the East Indies project is that the King's appointment of Ove Giedde was first considered on October 25th, that is, the very time when the news of Jens Munk's losses had had time to leak out and get talked about. It is impossible not to relate these two things. The aura surrounding Munk after the profitable expedition against Mendoza and his two successful years in whaling had vanished overnight; he was no longer a member of Mikkel Vibe's esteemed company, no longer belonged to the leading circles in the city. He was back where he was before: a former ship's boy, born out of wedlock. The jealous nobles were not slow to exploit his fall, and this time the King was easily persuaded: one really could not associate such a man with a distinguished gentleman like the Prince of Migomme.

So far as Munk was concerned, "His Royal Majesty commanded him to attend again to his old service," as it states in the biography; and Jens Munk had no alternative but to obey orders and return to Bremerholm. He was no longer his own master. On the evening of November 14, 1618, he made his way homeward from the Holm. He had just seen Ove Giedde sail away to the accompaniment of trumpets and kettledrums with the five ships which he himself had made ready, equipped, and manned; and now he went along the familiar way out through the Bremerholm Gate, across the city moat, and home to Pilestraede. Autumn was nearly over, and winter was at hand; it grew dark early in the streets, and up in the northern heavens over the thatched houses was the comet that heralded momentous events. He had, with time, grown accustomed to starting again from the bottom, but never had the situation looked so hopeless. He would never be a whaler, and he would never be an explorer. Everywhere the path was blocked by the nobles—his only inheritance from the prisoner at Dragsholm. But now he was worse off than ever before—his only ally in the old feud, his brother Niels, had died the previous year. He was alone, ruined and ridiculed; as he walked through the twilight, the trumpet fanfares to Ove Giedde still rang in his ears.

During the months when Jens Munk was working on preparations for the Indian voyage, he had studied time and time again the route Ove Giedde had now taken, calculated courses, allowed for variations, and pored over the copperplate sea charts and Portuguese navigational aids. First Ove Giedde was to make his way down through the Channel, then continue to the Cape Verde Islands, cross the equator, and proceed south the whole long way down to the Cape of Good Hope. Yet there he would not be substantially nearer his destination; for in line with the practice of the time, he had to sail back along the east coast of Africa, up through the Mozambique Channel to the Comoro Islands, cross the equator once more, and continue north to an island called Socotra. Only then could he begin to lay a course eastward to India. All his captains were nobles, and if the expedition went in any way like the hunt for Mendoza's brothers, it would clearly be an interminable undertaking. . . .

But what if the way south circling Africa were now the only passage to the Orient? What if those people were right who claimed that there was a passage to the north of America which was only a fifth as long? Ove Giedde would sail south and north and east, but what if one ought in reality to sail *west*? Or as they said in Bahia, *para buscar el levante por el ponente*, seek the sunrise through the sunset. His brother Niels

194

was dead. This sad fact could not be altered; but Jørgen Daa, his old friend and comrade in arms from Elfsborg and Kanin Nos, still lived and was in the best of health. What if he could be prevailed upon? What if it might one day be rumored on Amagertorv that Jens Munk had landed in China long before Ove Giedde of Tommerup had even reached India?

Six months later a round-the-world race was under way. Both captains kept their logbooks carefully during the passage; both logbooks are preserved, and we can still follow their respective positions from day to day. One thing is incontrovertible: four days after Ove Giedde sighted the Cape of Good Hope and began to make his way at snail's pace up into the bright tropical warmth of the Indian Ocean, Jens Munk swept past Cape Farewell under full sail bound for the ice-filled Hudson Bay.

15

Almighty God in Heaven

I

Much suggests that Jens Munk deliberately entered into a race with Ove Giedde. No scholar hitherto has mentioned any connection between the two expeditions, although it has been suggested that the King assented to Munk's project, wishing to compensate him in some measure for being displaced as leader of the expedition to India.

Read in context, the facts chronicled above encourage one to ponder the possibility of a much closer relationship between these two famous expeditions than has hitherto been supposed. Jens Munk had to seek satisfaction for the harm done to him, seek revenge for his slight. It is unlikely that Ove Giedde knew anything about his plans; but he knew about Giedde's. He was in a position to assess Giedde's chances, and he realized that they were not so great as to deny him—Munk—a chance of being first and winning.

This was no wishful thinking. Ove Giedde had by far the greater distance to cover, and he had started out on the interminable voyage at an unfavorable time of the year. He had left Copenhagen on November 14th with his five ships. He himself was on board the *Elephant*, while the *David* carried the distinguished Marselis de Boshouwer. Because of persistent northwesterly winds they were forced to anchor off Elsinore, and only on the night of November 29th were they able to get out of the Sound. In the Skagerrak they met bad weather with gales and sleet; one ship took a severe beating in the heavy seas and began to ship water so that it had to seek shelter below Norway, but the remainder of the fleet rounded the Skaw and reached the Isle of Wight, off southern England, on December 17th. Here they came to anchor in order to wait for the disabled vessel, which turned up a month later, and on January 23, 1619, the entire squadron was able to get under sail once more.

Returning skippers brought news of Ove Giedde's brisk progress to Copenhagen, where Jens Munk was laying his plans. The tidings of his rival's final departure must have worried him, especially as he himself had not advanced a single step with his project in the meantime. For him, too, it was a bad time of the year to prepare for an expedition of this sort, and a number of circumstances combined to make the winter of 1618-19 particularly unsuited. People had other things to think about than voyages of exploration. The skilling had fallen again, unexpectedly and catastrophically: 96 to the silver dollar as against 84 the year before. Since the accession of Christian IV Danish currency had depreciated by over a quarter of its value; inflation, by means of which irresponsible rulers can postpone problems until the morrow, and which usually ends in complete collapse, had been a feature of Danish society for twenty years by then. No wonder that people of substance found the moment inappropriate for a search for the Northwest Passage to China, and at no time could Jens Munk hope to raise private means for the execution of his plan.

Then the plague came to Copenhagen. The jail had to be closed. The King had in great haste to enlist extra seamen in the fleet to replace the sailors who were dying off like flies. In the port of Bremerholm free brandy was distributed to the people "as antidotum in this time of sickness." Under such conditions only a dreamer could imagine men being placed at his disposal for a voyage of exploration. Jens Munk divided his time between work on Bremerholm and his home in Pilestraede, where Kathrine presented him with a little girl

197

who was named for her mother. But nothing else happened. Then something happened which when added to the rest of his difficulties seemed to undermine the very foundations of his plan.

With his brother's death in 1617 Jens Munk had lost his only true ally in his conflict with the nobility. There remained his friend Jørgen Daa, but of course he was a nobleman himself. On the other hand, Daa could for this very reason count on the King's support and good will. Jørgen Daa and Jens Munk had worked together without friction for many years; they owed their greatest triumphs to one another, they enjoyed one another's confidence, and there is much to suggest that they discussed Jens Munk's new plan with a view to placing it before the King. At all events they had ample opportunity for doing that. In February, 1619, the two men made a journey together to the borders of Halland, a journey undoubtedly related to the King's meeting with Gustavus Adolphus, which was at that same time taking place in Halmstad. Jørgen Daa seems to have been quite an adventurer; the possibility of a voyage to China would have aroused his enthusiasm, and he must certainly have been willing to put the matter to the King when they reached Halmstad. However, nothing came of all this. In Eldsberga, a few miles south of Halmstad, Jørgen Daa was suddenly taken ill, perhaps stricken with the plague. A few days later he was dead.

Meanwhile the unsuspecting Ove Giedde was increasing his lead. It is easy to follow him in the logbook. On January 23rd the entire fleet had left southern England. On February 6th they passed Madeira; then on the 10th, Palma and Tenerife. On the 11th they sailed past Gomera and Ferro. Everything was going smoothly. On the 19th they reached Cape Verde, where they captured two pirate ships and destroyed a third by a skilfully executed action. On February 26th they dropped anchor in the approaches to Portudal, on the palmy coast of Senegal, in order to take in supplies of fresh water.

Jørgen Daa's sudden death at Eldsberga had been a hard blow for Jens Munk. He laid out money for his friend's burial and afterward was accused by the heirs of having been extravagant. Daa's death left Munk very much on his own. Yet as so often before, the challenge acted as an additional incentive.

During the two weeks between his friend's burial and the conclusion of the negotiations between the King and Gustavus Adolphus, Munk was probably daily in the presence of the King. There was ample opportunity for meeting; and, as was usual when the King was traveling, this could take place on a far more informal basis than a state audience—that is, in precisely the manner which suited Munk best, which indeed was perhaps the only one open to him after the affair of Ove Giedde. Talks about the Northwest Passage took place in much the same way as when the two men had discussed the Northeast Passage ten years earlier.

Niels Slange claims that the initiative for the new expedition came not from the King but from Jens Munk. This is the earliest statement we have on the matter, and everything does indeed point to Christian IV's historian being right. Not only had Jens Munk strong personal motives for undertaking this voyage, but his technical qualifications were also in order. In the course of ten years' missions in arctic waters he had acquired the necessary knowledge and experience, and like all navigators of his time he believed that a passage to the Pacific Ocean was to be found north of the American mainland. This was called the Anian Strait, which James Hall had already mentioned following his expeditions to Greenland in 1605-7; in his report he attributed the fierce tidal currents in the Davis Strait to the existence of a passage through to the Pacific Ocean, and said that the way through this to China and the East Indies could at most be one fifth the distance of the way around the south of Africa. If Jens Munk had heard about Henry Hudson's discovery of Spitsbergen, while he was in Iceland in 1608, the chances are that he also learned of the

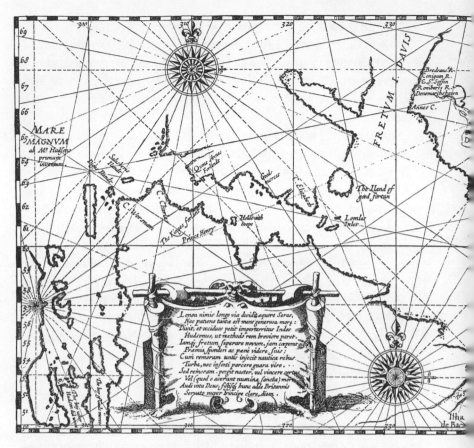

Hessel Gerritszoon's chart, from 1612, of the North Atlantic and
Hudson Bay which Jens Munk certainly had with him when he sailed
from Copenhagen. The little island believed to lie in the waters between
Iceland and Greenland has still not disappeared from the map, but the
situation of Greenland and the Hudson Strait conforms more or less with

catastrophe that subsequently befell the English captain in
those waters that bear his name. As early as the summer of
1612 the Dutchman Hessel Gerritszoon published a chart of
Hudson's discoveries; it appeared in a number of editions in
both Latin and Dutch, and was printed twice in Germany and
once in England. Remembering the close relations existing at

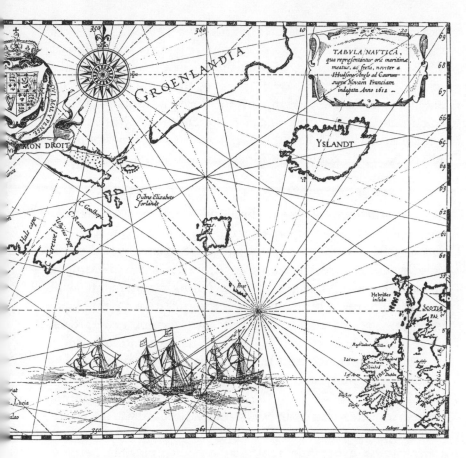

modern maps and corresponds with the specifications in Munk's orders. Hudson Bay is badly drawn, especially in regard to the western shore. The question of the location of the Anian Strait and the existence of the Northwest Passage remains undetermined; the northern sea route to China by America is still a possibility.

this time between Holland and Denmark, it can safely be assumed that this chart reached Copenhagen. One may even suppose that Jens Munk himself possessed a copy, otherwise it would be difficult to explain the fact that he employs the spelling used on this chart every time he mentions little-known geographical names in his logbook. English accounts of

Button's, Bylot's, and Baffin's journeys in Hudson Bay were available in print as early as 1615; and two years later a report of Hudson's expedition was published. Even if all these books had not reached Copenhagen by 1619, the main part of their contents was known. Many of the foreign captains whose acquaintance Jens Munk had had the opportunity of making in these years would have been able to pass on important details. Finally, of course, he himself was in both Amsterdam and London during the winter 1616-17.

Fantastic though it might have sounded, therefore, the great project was no mere flight of fancy but a carefully pondered plan based upon expert appreciation and a sound study of the documented material. There existed a real possibility of finding, to the north of America, a sea passage to China. The King listened to Jens Munk's statements with growing interest. He did not take the initiative in the expedition himself; he could scarcely make yet another approach to the man he had rejected as leader of the expedition to India six months previously; on the other hand, that embarrassing decision may well have left a trace of bad conscience which caused the King to treat the offended captain with rather greater consideration than was strictly necessary. Moreover, any misgivings which might apply to his qualifications as leader of the expedition to India were inapplicable here. A search for the Northwest Passage was in no sense a diplomatic undertaking; it required no particular representative distinction of the person in charge of the mission, and the King would not have to fear any trouble from his nobles if he sent this unpopular naval captain on an expedition among the icebergs of Greenland. Finally, Munk's plans constituted a continuation of the Norwegian Sea project which the King himself had formed after his expedition around North Cape with Dr. Charisius twenty years before. Indeed, it was the only part of the project which had not yet been realized. In 1609 he had himself sent Jens Munk out to find the Northeast Passage. Suzerainty over the Norwegian Sea in the intervening years had been asserted partly through the work of Dr. Charisius in London and partly through countless patrolling expeditions in which Jens Munk, incidentally, had been a most successful participant. Only the third point of the old plan was still not implemented: an exploration to discover whether there was a passage to the northwest. And financially, from the King's point of view, times were good in Denmark. The last brutal devaluation of the skilling had brought about a notable increase in his coffers; a similarly ruthless readjustment of the Sound Dues had doubled his income at Elsinore; and, finally, Gustavus Adolphus had, against all expectation, just shown himself capable of paying the last installment of the ransom for Elfsborg.

All in all, this meant that during the period in question the King had an additional annual revenue of something like one million rix-dollars over and above his usual income. Jens Munk was of the modest opinion that an expedition to find the Northwest Passage could be carried out for 5000 rix-dollars. The King gave his assent. King Christian IV of Denmark and Norway was then approaching his forty-second birthday. It was just before the great catastrophes began to overwhelm him. He still believed in the future.

2

The King arrived at Kronborg on March 3rd; Munk must have returned home at about the same time, and it can be seen from the letter books of the Chancellery that the first engagement for the new expedition was made as early as March 11th, so things were moving quickly. Jens Munk must have felt that he still had a chance of reaching the Orient before Ove Giedde.

His expedition cost only a fraction of his rival's, and in the matter of equipment it was not nearly so comprehensive. While Ove Giedde had five ships and several hundred men at his disposal, Jens Munk had only two ships and sixty-one men assigned to him. It is possible, however, that he did not wish for more. Once again he went in for the old combination of a heavier "mother" ship and a fast sloop, which he had used during the search for the Northeast Passage and which had shown itself to be especially effective during the engagement with Mendoza. From among the idle ships in Krabbeløkke Bay he chose the frigate *Herring Ness* and the sloop *Lamprey*. The *Herring Ness* had been Jørgen Daa's flagship at Elfsborg; Jens Munk knew it inside out. The *Lamprey* was part of the booty which fell to them after the victory. One does not need to be as superstitious as Jens Munk in order to see the fortunate omen which lay in the two names.

However, this propitious combination came to naught. In the course of the spring several naval officers of noble birth suddenly had need of the *Herring Ness*. Perhaps there was still time for malice. At all events it appears from the records that at the very last moment Jens Munk had to exchange Jørgen Daa's flagship for the frigate *Unicorn*. It was a ship he was also familiar with. In all probability he had attended its launching with Niels in 1605; he had been working at Bremerholm when it was lengthened in 1614, and it had accompanied the expedition of the twelve noblemen the year afterward. But there lay no particular promise in its name, and he had never sailed it himself.

Just as important as the ships were the crews who were to man them. Here Munk was delayed by new difficulties. It appears from the Bremerholm accounts that he had to devote the rest of March and all of April to assembling them. Many precious weeks went by, partly because the plague made it difficult to get people, partly because Munk had disposed of his best sailors in manning Ove Giedde's ships, and he did not wish to make do with second-best. A glance at his crew lists indicates the importance he attached to experience and skill. While Ove Giedde's commissioned posts were occupied almost exclusively by nobles, Jens Munk appointed only one nobleman—Movritz Stygge, lieutenant of the *Unicorn*.

But the name Stygge was then not particularly distinguished, and the motives behind the appointment were clearly professional. It was also clear from the beginning that, as lieutenant, he was only to be second-in-command. On that point Munk wasted few words: the command was to be his alone.

Among Ove Giedde's many aristocrats there was none with any knowledge of the waters they were to sail. Both of Munk's chief officers were Englishmen and expert seamen. The first was named William Gordon, the second John Watson. Various circumstances indicate that Watson had accompanied Button's expedition to Hudson Bay; and a William Gordon is known to have taken part in the far-ranging expeditions to Cherry Island and Bear Island, to Pechora south of Novaya Zemlya, to Greenland with James Hall, to Spitsbergen and to Pustozersk in the Barents Sea. This explains the large sum of money which Munk offered him to come along. William Gordon was probably the highest paid of all on board: on March 11th he received an advance of 200 rix-dollars, a whole year's pay for a captain; and two weeks later he was engaged as mate at 50 rix-dollars a month plus a promise from the King of a further 2000 rix-dollars "if he with the help and guidance of God had the good fortune to find the Passage, which we have most graciously commanded him to seek." This corresponded to almost a half of the whole budget for the expedition. William Gordon must have been a very considerable man.

As to the remainder of the crew, Munk followed current practice. Each of the ships was given a boatswain—Jan Olluffsen on the *Unicorn* and Jens Henriksen on the *Lamprey*, two proven Bremerholm men. In addition there were the two Danish second mates who were to assist Gordon and Watson: on the *Unicorn* it was Hans Brok, who had accompanied Munk in 1610 to Kildin on the *Angelibrand*; on the *Lamprey* it was Jan Petersen, likewise an old boatswain from the Norwegian Sea. As was customary, the lieutenant was assigned a servant, a young man named Klaus; and Oluf Andersen, who had been with Jens Munk from North Cape to Biscay, was included. He also took with him a third very young man—the son of his brother Niels, who bore the name of his grandfather. It suited him splendidly to have an Erik Munk with him on the expedition; and apart from this, he felt himself under an obligation to the widow and wanted to assist her boy to a career in the King's service, though this was not destined to be a long one.

The selection of a chaplain and ships' surgeons posed the usual problems; in these respects Bremerholm was seldom well supplied. The plague made it impossible to obtain even an adequately qualified surgeon, for they were all earning lots of money in Copenhagen. Only on April 25th did it prove possible to find a Kasper Kaspersen, of Rothenburg. The King promised "most graciously to provide for him a Surgeon's chest with those requisites which he would need for his trade," and Munk signed him up for the *Unicorn*, while a colleague of his, David Volske, was engaged for the *Lamprey*. Both were Germans and had learned their trade on the battlefields of the mainland; with appropriate assistance they could saw off a leg and do a little patching up on a shattered hand, but this was the extent of their qualifications. They had no knowledge of the use of medicines and compounds; they had never before seen the sea; and that sickness peculiar to sea life, the dreaded scurvy, was for them a mere name.

As chaplain they had to make do with Rasmus Jensen: a sorry figure, unwashed, with a week's growth of stubble on his chin, running eyes, and wheezing voice. But Herr Rasmus was at home in the Scriptures, shuffled around self-effacingly comforting others with God's word and himself with a dram. He received 100 dollars a year—the same as the surgeons and no more than two months' pay for William Gordon.

At the end of April the recruitment of the rest of the crews could start. This took place in the Scrivener's Office at Bremer-

holm. The spacious hall was full of seamen; at a table at one
end sat the two boatswains, Jan Olluffsen and Jens Hendriksen
with their crew lists in front of them. At a long table behind
the boatswains the captain himself could be seen, on his right
hand Movritz Stygge, on his left William Gordon. The Icelander Jon Olafsson, who was also present in the hall that day,
describes him as he sat there: "He was a very wise man," says
the musketeer. "No one understood the art of navigation and
the movement of the stars as he did." Jens Munk sat leaning
back between the officers, the smallest of the three; most of the
time he remained silent and answered their remarks with his
handsome smile, which bared a row of worn teeth. Everyone
could see that the captain was in a good humor, and that raised
their spirits too. It did not occur to him that it was the sight
of them that did him good. For three years he had not been to
sea, and now once more he found himself among the men with
whom he had shared the greater part of his life. Who could
help feeling affection for them as they stood there—the rogues
and heroes of the gun deck, boisterous and impatient, dogged
and devoted, well used to toil and sweat, storm and cold, cards
and tricktrack, with strong arms and weak characters, easily
fired and difficult to control, brutal, thick-skinned, and infinitely sensitive, so courageous and yet so afraid, but without
the slightest envy or calculation, without a spiteful thought
behind their open faces, with their thick lips and bright eyes.
The great, childlike toughs of the Norwegian Sea, sunburned
as dark as Negroes and decked out like cannibals, each with
his amulet around his neck and his arms covered with half-
faded red and blue tattoo decorations, hearts and anchors, oak
leaves and silk ribbons, moons and stars and faith and hope
and love. . . .

The men went up to the boatswains one by one and gave
their names. Apart from one man who stood in the background
and answered all invitations with a shake of his head, everyone
was eager to join. Iver Alsing and Jens Borringholm, Christoffer Opslø and Rasmus Clemmensen, the brothers Jens and

Laurids Helsing. They came from all corners of the realm; many were from Norway, others from Halland, others again from Sønderborg, Marstal, Nyord, Dragør. Dialects from Samsø met with the tongue of Gotland; one inquired in Lolland and was answered in Icelandic. A man from Fyn stepped forward and informed the boatswain that he was called Erik Hansen, adding in his singsong dialect: "That's a rare name in China!"

Laughter resounded; only the boatswains sat serious, scraping away at the paper with their irksome goose quills. Anders Sodens and Oluf Boye, Jens Bødker, Christen Gregersen and Povel Pedersen, and now a man with the awe-inspiring name Ismael Abrahamsen. All sizes and weights were represented; one was small and slight, surely a real monkey at scrambling up and reefing the topsail; another was nearly six feet tall and stood calm, dignified, and condescending in the midst of the general mirth. Anders Stavanger and Lauritz Hansen, Oluf Sundmør and Thor Tønsberg. Vain and dashing-looking fellows as they strode forward under their tilted, extravagantly broad-brimmed Spanish hats, with newly trimmed mustaches, coarse-mouthed and exuberant, lunging out at one another with paws like bears, familiar with every form of dissipation and more pious at heart than any archbishop. Anders Oroust and Hans Bendtsen, Peder Amundsen and Halvord Brønnie, Anders and Morten and Svend from Marstrand . . .

The boatswains had difficulty in keeping up. In a group by themselves stood the three ship's carpenters: Svend Arvedsen, Jens Jørgensen, and Peder Nyborg. The world's oldest and noblest craft reached its highest refinement in them: the art of shipbuilding distinguished them from the others. Calm and erect they stood amidst the din, silent and untattooed pipe-smokers.

Jan Olluffsen and Jens Hendriksen had almost finished their lists. The men were signed on as they were, clad in reefer coats over a pair of home-made woollen trousers tied below the knee. Most of them had a little bundle of clothes and trifles with them, which they were permitted to keep, but they did not take any further extra clothing with them. The point is worth noting: Jens Munk had no leather clothing with him when the ships left Copenhagen. He did not realize what problems this would occasion. He had had trouble before as a result of the crew's inadequate clothing, but that was on a voyage around North Cape. The Anian Strait, he knew, was to be sought to the north of the Skaw—a mere nothing to seamen who were used to the Barents Sea. At that time nothing was known of the meanderings of the Gulf Stream, extending one arm to the White Sea, but not entering Hudson Bay. One timorous soul in the crew was not greatly reassured by the comparison with the Skaw. Suppose in spite of all it really did get cold next winter? But his question was swept away in a burst of laughter. Don't be alarmed, my friend, next winter we shall be in China!

All those present were signed on with the exception of the solitary man in the back row, in the garb of a musketeer with a ruff above the tight-fitting vest and the baggy trousers. The boatswains had repeatedly tried to tempt him with both pay and monthly allowance, and now they even offered to make him able-bodied seaman, but once again the man rejected their offer. It was not a question of money or rank; he simply did not want to join the expedition. The next day, however, he signed up for an expedition to the Norwegian Sea, from whence he came back safe and sound in the late summer.

In his memoirs, Jon Olafsson gives the reason for his refusal: the previous night an angel had appeared to him in a dream and threatened him with the wrath of the Lord if he went on Jens Munk's expedition.

Jens Munk had reason to fear that the many weeks he had devoted to finding crews for his ships had set him further behind Ove Giedde; but if he did, he was wrong. The East Indies expedition had not made very good progress in the meantime; new difficulties had arisen, and before long the new and untried admiral found himself in a very serious situation.

On February 26th, as we have seen, Ove Giedde had anchored off Portudal on the coast of Senegal to take on fresh water. One or two weeks were spent in reloading the goods from the captured pirate ships; and only on March 11th could he go ashore together with Tyge Stygge to investigate the availability of drinking water. He found two springs, the first a hundred paces from the beach, the second a thousand paces farther inland. Because of the danger of attack from the natives, Ove Giedde decided to make use of the first, even though its water was brackish. But both officers and soldiers protested; they all preferred the water from the more distant spring, "asserting that rather would they venture thither than die at sea on account of the salt water." The upshot was that the admiral gave way. Three ensigns and a handful of soldiers were ordered ashore to cover the transportation of water from the farther spring. But when Ove Giedde and Tyge Stygge had rowed out to the ships once more, "that ensign, who commanded the middle troop, forsook his appointed position, and joined his troop to the one which was nearest the beach, and thereupon did not only himself proceed to the beach to bathe, but also permitted his subordinate soldiers to do likewise." The result was immediate. The most distant troop, thus abandoned, was attacked by Negroes. Eight Danes were killed, ten wounded, and twenty-three taken prisoner as hostages, and Ove Giedde was cut off from both springs. A few days later a sounding of the fresh-water tanks in the *David* and the

Christian revealed that the two ships still had ample supplies of fresh water to cover the requirements of the entire fleet during the farther passage. The sacrifice had been pointless. Ove Giedde now had to spend weeks negotiating the ransom of the Negroes' hostages. But this stiff-necked, intransigent young man was a poor negotiator. In spite of the many objects of barter he had with him, he succeeded in obtaining the release of only eleven of the prisoners; and when he finally decided to set sail on April 8th, after a delay of nearly a month, he had to leave the remaining twelve hostages to their fate. It was not a gentle one.

The episode at Portudal had revealed the serious lack of organization and authority in Ove Giedde's squadron. Even during the stay in southern England a number of men had deserted, and it is little to his credit that Ove Giedde's own servant was among the runaways. During the passage down to Africa Giedde complains repeatedly in his diary about the heavy drinking in the officers' mess. Drunkenness and brawls were daily occurrences; again and again he attempted to reduce the brandy ration, but the men saw no reason to take his orders seriously. After the scandal at Portudal, however, it was a matter of urgency for him to assert himself as commander in chief; and in his cold desperation the twenty-four-year-old captain saw no other recourse than a series of summary punitive measures. The captain on one of the pirate ships was subjected to "torture." The boatswain on the *Christian* was relieved of his post and his monthly pay withdrawn. A second mate on the same ship was keel-hauled three times. Two seamen on the *Copenhagen* who had been involved in cases of petty larceny received the same punishment.

And so it went. Ove Giedde's whip struck at random, and it soon became clear that the trouble had far more serious causes than a wretched boatswain and a couple of seamen. It was not in these secondary limbs but in the very heart of the expedition that something was wrong. At Portudal there had been a battle of wills between the two senior commanders, Ove

Giedde and Boshouwer. When the former decided to have the Danish coat of arms painted on the stern of the captured pirate vessels, the Prince of Migomme demanded that the ships should also bear the arms of the Emperor of Ceylon; but Ove Giedde would not agree to this. "I left things as they were, alleging the little space that there was, and caused only the arms of Denmark to be painted thereon." From then on there was a coolness between the two men.

This ludicrous affair was soon followed by a more serious incident. At this stage the whole fleet was steering southeast by east bound for the Cape of Good Hope; but when Ove Giedde came out on deck on the morning of April 29th he observed a most alarming circumstance: the ship *David*, with Boshouwer and a number of the expedition's coffers on board, had disappeared during the night.

Ove Giedde relates that Boshouwer's ship was in the habit of keeping to the leeward a good way astern of the others. When the remainder of the fleet had gone about the previous evening, the *David* had not followed suit, although the lookout on the mainmast must clearly have seen the maneuver of the other ships. Accordingly, Ove Giedde gave orders for the fleet to go about and seek the missing ship on the other tack. At noon they sighted the *David*, but the ship lay so far to the leeward that they had no chance of overhauling it, and the *David* apparently made no effort to fall off before the wind and steer toward them. The captain of the *Elephant* was ordered to increase sail, and all through the night they signaled to one another with lanterns and fires. It made little difference; the next morning only a glimpse of the *David* could be seen from the mainmast of the *Elephant* like a dot on the horizon. Then Ove Giedde gave orders to the master of the fast sloop to do his utmost to reach the *David*, and two days later the sloop succeeded in coming up to it; but even then it was not until the requisitioned and heavily armed pirate ship also arrived on the scene that the *David* was seen to alter course and steer back toward the others.

At this point these puzzling events aroused fearful misgivings in Ove Giedde. Was this great undertaking founded on
lies and fraud? Was the distinguished Marselis de Boshouwer
neither Prince of Migomme nor Knight of the Order of the
Sun, but simply a common traitor? On May 3rd he sent for
the master of the *David* to come over to the *Elephant*. At
first the good fellow tried to prevaricate—they had not seen
the rest of the fleet go about on the evening of April 28th, and
when it had again come into sight the day after they had kept
their distance, believing the fleet to be hostile Portuguese.
All these evasions were wasted on Ove Giedde's icy calm. Soon
the unfortunate master had to come out with the truth. It was
a fact that he had seen the fleet go about on the evening of
April 28th; it was a fact that he had continued on course with
the *David*. But he would take an oath that it was not his fault.
He had acted on orders from Boshouwer.

4

No, Jens Munk had little reason for concern in Copenhagen;
for him the outlook was more promising than ever. During the
time spent in manning the *Unicorn* and the *Lamprey*, Ove
Giedde had only moved a few nautical miles farther south.
On May 3rd he had wrested the fateful confession from the
master of the *David*. Six days later Jens Munk sailed from
Copenhagen.

The last few days had been hectic. The *Unicorn* and the
Lamprey had been moved from Krabbeløkke Bay into the new
Arsenal Harbor behind the Castle for loading. How much
would sixty men consume on a voyage whose duration one
could only guess at? In and out of the Victualing Yard the men
went in a steady stream, up and down the gangways with sacks
on their shoulders, sacks of flour, beans, peas, sugar, barrels
of ship's ale and salt pork, tar and pitch, wax and tow for
calking the ships, bottles of brandy and vinegar, jars of honey
and mustard. Spare compass needles and lanterns, rope

sufficient to replace the longest running halyard on board, planks for the replacement of broken spars—and even for repairing the mast, if things got really bad—fishing nets and hooks, harpoons and muskets, hourglasses and cross-staffs, cannon balls and gunpowder, hundreds of candles, reserves of belaying pins, thimbles, trucks, clip-hooks, slip-hooks, hawse-pipes, buntlines, deadeyes, snatch blocks and shackles. The *Unicorn* resembled a Noah's Ark stuffed to the gunwales not with animals but with things. If all the rest of the world had been inundated, one would still have been able to find on this ship one example of practically every object, every implement, that existed at the time of Christian IV. Pennants, iron tongs, tow rope and pump leather, hammer axes, calking tools, boat's gripes, inside calipers and brace and auger, adzes and gouges, dunnage wood and throat seizings, bodkins, toggles and marlinespikes, needle horns filled with tallow to serve as pin-cushions. And then all the barter wares for trading with the strange peoples—an appalling collection of junk, but effective. Small, cheap mirrors in which simple souls could see their own faces for the first time, bells and gilded armlets, knives and scissors, painted beads and colored glassware, motley scarves and pixie hats, and—more serious—the long, heavy iron bars which in outlandish regions represented a fortune and which because of their weight were stored in the bottom of the ship as ballast.

Munk went around indefatigably with his lists; he knew that where he was going the smallest nail, the most insignifi-cant needle, possessed a value that could be paid for neither in money nor in blood. When the last goods were carried aboard on the evening of May 8th and stowed away and checked off, the expedition's coffer was placed under his supervision under lock and key in the poop. Next he brought his personal navigation instruments, a portable sundial of brass with an inset compass, an hourglass, an astrolabe of wood with the dial engraved on a curved brass plate, a pair of dividers, a collection of goose quills, and a star chart complete with tables and a

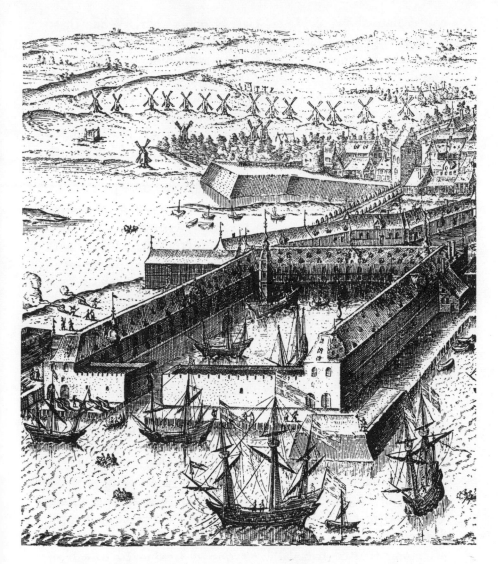

The new Tøjhushavnen, where Christian IV fitted out his men-of-war.
In the foreground a three-masted frigate of the same size as the *Unicorn*;
to the left two new bronze cannon are tested across Kalvebod Strand, in
the background the gallows down near the water and the line of wind-
mills out toward Valby. From this harbor Jens Munk began his "northwesterly voyage." (Van Wick)

copperplate showing Hessel Gerritszoon's chart. When these were arranged, he placed two books on the table beside the chart lantern, the only ones he had with him, one thick and one thin. One was the Bible, the other a small writing book with fifty blank pages stitched together with lightly tarred marline and bound in plain parchment. Across the first page was written in his hand: "A description of Jens Munk's voyage which he began Anno 1619 on the 9th of May to seek China."

The last days had been extremely busy because Jens Munk would not postpone the departure even for a day or two. May 9, 1619, was a Sunday, and no other day would be fitting for the start of such an important undertaking—an ordinary weekday would augur misfortune, shipwreck, and death. Sunday, May 9th, came with glorious weather, sunshine from a clear sky, and without a wind stirring. Jens Munk would probably have preferred a moderate southeaster, which would have brought him clear of Kullen.

In the morning divine service was held in Holm Church for the members of the expedition. It can be noted that, shortly before, the King had sent, as a token of his good will, a missive to Rector Steffensen at Sorø School requesting admission of the captain's two older sons as soon as there were vacancies; and as a further expression of favor he assigned to Jens Munk one of the sites recently parceled out in the new quarter of Christianshavn. Now Christian IV stood face to face with his seamen in Holm Church. The King was grave. The muster clerk had just called out the names, and everyone had taken his oath of loyalty. The King spoke simply, in a low voice, as if among trusted friends. Everyone was exhorted to a God-fearing life, true loyalty, decent conduct, and manly action, for the honor of the Danish realm and in the interest of their own good and honorable names. When the brief address was over, he bared his head; the seamen kneeled down, and the King prayed for God's blessing on all of them, wherever they might fare abroad, on sea or on land, in storm and in calm.

After the service the men walked down to the ships in a body led by the standard-bearer with Christian's naval ensign, which was to be raised on the mainmast of the *Unicorn*. They had been moved by the seriousness of the moment, but now came the exhilarating work of making the ship ready; this took time. Only late in the afternoon could they cast off. The approaching event had long been known in the city, and all Copenhagen was out and about in the fine weather. People stood in groups around the excavation work for the newly begun Exchange building. Even the convicts at Bremerholm came rattling down to the beach in their chains. At last the two ships glided out of the Arsenal Harbor and moved into line ahead. The procession filled nearly the whole channel between Amager and Copenhagen. First of all came the *Lamprey*, drawn by six rowboats, each with eight men at the oars. Behind followed the *Unicorn*, towed by twelve rowboats. There was ample time to observe all the details. Though the men at the oars did their best, the great wooden ships moved slowly through the water. On each of the yards the sailors hung four by four in their royal and topgallant footropes, small patches in the vast pattern of the rigging, ready to slack off the clew lines so that the square sails could unfurl and catch the breeze when the ships were out in the Sound. The rhythmic creaking of the tholepins from the towboats could be heard; otherwise everything was still. But at the very moment the *Unicorn* was level with the Castle, Kathrine Adriansdatter, who stood in the front row with her infant at her breast and the three boys at her skirts, burst into tears, which caused many of the citizens to fold their hands in prayer.

After the service in Holm Church, Jens Munk had shut himself up in his cabin and entrusted the preparations to Jan Olluffsen and Jens Hendriksen. Officers and mates who pushed forward with a thousand questions at the last moment were turned away by Oluf: the captain wished to be alone. But just as the *Unicorn* glided past the Castle, the little man was seen to step out into the sunshine and place himself, bare-headed, on the bridge before the sterncastle. That was the signal: at once the trumpeters raised their newly polished instruments and struck up the hymn tune. The harbor rang with the brassy music, the bluff, swelling tones harmonized with the slow forward motion of the ships, and yet they were marked by the sadness that permeates all music heard across the water. The chronicler hazards a guess that Jens Munk chose the old Reformation hymn for Whitsuntide in praise of life and the Holy Spirit; May 9, 1619, was the Sunday before Whitsunday, so there could not have been many alternatives. Everyone knew it by heart; the melody brought the text to mind, and all the spectators, including the disfigured convicts on Bremerholm, even Jens Munk himself, who stood on the *Unicorn* wishing that he now had Niels and Jørgen at his side —everyone felt that the words were addressed specifically to him.

> Almighty God in Heaven above,
> Praise and honor to his mercy
> Bestowed on us with fatherly love.
> He freed us from sin's sore distress.
> Great joy and peace are now on earth,
> All men may well contented be
> With God's blessing and good will.

Then the boatswain's silver pipes sounded, the sails unfurled, and the *Unicorn* was shaken by three cannon-shots. Astern, the light shone obliquely down as though to show beautiful Copenhagen to the departing men for the last time.

The calm weather lasted a week, and only on May 16th did the ships round Kronborg. Jens Munk entered the important date in the book with the parchment cover; and the King also noted the event in his diary. "This day," wrote Christian IV, "the 'Unicorn' and the 'Lamprey' sailed on the voyage northward, may the Almighty grant them good fortune." The King had made virtually the same entry six months earlier when Ove Giedde had set off for India. The great race had begun; spirits were high among the seamen, eager to be off. Now their way lay west to the Orient, now they were to see the land of the Emperor of China. Fortunately, May 16th was also a Sunday, indeed Whitsunday itself. A better omen for the voyage could not be imagined.

16

The Wintry Road

I

Between western Greenland and the Canadian mainland there lies an archipelago of about the same area as Europe: in the south there is the bleak inland sea, Hudson Bay, in the north the ice masses of the Arctic Ocean, and between the two seas hundreds of islands, large and small, intersected by sounds and straits. Seen on the map, the tortuous and winding channels resemble the legendary labyrinth at Knossos, at the center of which was the terrible Minotaur claiming its annual human sacrifice.

To penetrate these straits is, indeed, every bit as dangerous as finding a way through the Cretan labyrinth. Most of them are shallow; submerged rocks abound, and in many places the tide forms a swirling maelstrom. The magnetic North Pole, in the center of the labyrinth, causes variations of up to 180°, deflecting the compass needle right around to the south, and sometimes spinning it around and around under the influence of the violent magnetic storms that color the sky like blazing discharges of red, yellow, and green phosphorus. Winter lasts for ten months of the year; many of the sounds never become ice-free; temperatures of minus 70° C. are accompanied by howling storms with snow and ice crystals. Darkness reigns in November, December, January, and February; but at the end of April the grouse arrive, the snow sinks imperceptibly, and shiny puddles begin to form on the ice. Spring does not come until June, and a week later it is summer. The spell of the labyrinth is broken, rivulets begin to babble, a riot of flowers covers the gravel-strewn earth, and even on the northern slopes forget-me-nots flower in the midnight sun. Out on the crumbling ice, seals doze in the sun beside their fishing holes; the mountain hare feeds upon moss and bilberries; the caribou moves north from Canada's forests in herds of thousands; at night the ringing sound of their hoofs is heard as they nervously paw the rocks near the fjord. But in August the animals must return; and one autumn day the sun appears for the last time behind the hill crest to the south; all the details merge in the coal-black northern slope, while every stone that lies across the ridge is picked out. A caribou suddenly appears and stands right in the sun like a fly in amber. Then darkness takes over once more; the ice moans as the temperature drops; in all the straits of the labyrinth the white Minotaur lies bellowing again beneath the northern lights.

Jens Munk was not the first or the last navigator to venture into these desperate waters. Here lies the shortest route from east to west, the Northwest Passage. Almost every year for four hundred years frail wooden ships attempted to pioneer a way through this passage.

On June 24, 1497, the navigator and explorer John Cabot, sailing from England with a patent from Henry VII, had to give up at 56° north. Then the Portuguese in their alarm tried to steal a march on the English. Gaspar Corte-Real was stopped by ice at about the same spot as Cabot, but managed to carry home some fifty natives who, according to tradition, were sold in Portugal as slaves. The Portuguese for slaves is *labradores*, and for this reason the new land became "Labrador." Corte-Real made a second attempt with two ships, but he never came back. Sebastian Cabot penetrated some way into Hudson Strait, then the crew lost their nerve and forced him at gunpoint to turn back. In 1527 John Rut sailed from England and did not return. In 1536 John Hore had to give up near Newfoundland. Forty years later Martin Frobisher came to a halt within Frobisher Bay; he found no passage, but he did find some gleaming stones and experts declared that they contained gold. Frobisher went out with fifteen cargo ships and after inhuman toil succeeded in filling them to the rails with the gleaming stones and sailed them to London. The precious lumps of rock might have been suitable for road-works; the "gold" proved to be silicon.

The Northwest Passage still eluded discovery and London merchants increased the pressure. For three years in succession John Davis fumbled his way forward among the icebergs off western Greenland, reached latitude 66° north, and returned home disappointed. No passage to the west. In 1602 the crew forced George Waymouth to turn about off Disko. In 1606 John Knight was shipwrecked on the coast of Labrador and with five survivors was slain by the natives.

Then Henry Hudson determined to enter the labyrinth. In April, 1610, he left the Thames with the *Discovery*, went south of Iceland, south of Greenland, and in through the ice off Hudson Strait. The crew refused to continue and mutinied, but Hudson put down the mutineers and pressed on. He passed the most westerly point of the strait, saw the unbroken horizon of the sea open out toward the west and south, and believed for a few blissful days that he had reached the Pacific Ocean. Then he came face to face with the coast. It was not the Pacific Ocean; it was only Hudson Bay. When the search was discontinued on November 1st, ice blocked the way back and the *Discovery* had to spend the winter there. But the ship was provisioned for only six months, a large part of the crew starved to death, and when spring came the mutiny succeeded. In order to make the last biscuits go as far as possible and get home, the mutineers put Captain Hudson and the sick— nine men, all together—into the ship's boat and left them to their fate. No more was heard of them; but the white Minotaur was satisfied with the sacrifice and permitted the *Discovery* to slip out of the labyrinth with the loss of only four more men. During the hearing at the maritime court in London it was

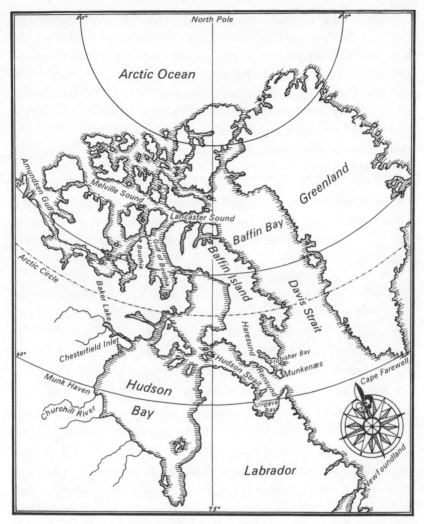

A modern map of the Northwest Passage with Munk's most important landing places marked: Rensund, Haresund, and Munk Haven.

revealed that it was precisely these four who had instigated the mutiny.

The explorations continued. In 1613 Thomas Button had to give up in Hudson Bay; in 1614 Gibbon was trapped for twenty weeks in the ice there; in 1615 Robert Bylot and William Baffin had to discontinue their voyage to the north-west in Hudson Bay. But the merchants in London were insistent: if there was no passage through Hudson Bay, then one must be sought farther north. In 1616 Bylot and Baffin sailed up by western Greenland, reached latitude 75° north, and found an indentation to the west which they called Lancaster Inlet. The name was incorrect—it should have been Lancaster Sound. But the ice mass deceived them, and led them to take the sound for a fjord. On August 30th Bylot and Baffin sailed back to England without realizing that they had discovered the actual approaches to the Northwest Passage. For the next two hundred years that route was not sailed by a single ship.

Once again the old routes were tried. Hawkridge had to give up in Hudson Bay. Luke Fox and Thomas James went out armed with a letter from the King of England to the Emperor of Japan—and had to give up in Hudson Bay. In 1719 Barlow and Vaughan disappeared with the whole of their crew in Hudson Bay. Scroggs set out to search for them but returned home with his mission unaccomplished, and only fifty years later were the skeletons of the tragedy found on Marble Island, where the men had starved to death. In 1741 Christopher Middleton was defeated by the ice in Hudson Bay. The English Parliament offered a reward of £20,000 for the first person to sail through the Northwest Passage, and William Moor confidently set off with two well-equipped ships —and had to give up in Hudson Bay. The same thing happened to Christopher in 1761, to Pickersgill in 1776, and to Duncan in 1791.

But in August, 1818, John Ross and William Edward Parry ran up by western Greenland and reached the waters which Bylot and Baffin, two hundred years before, had mistakenly called Lancaster Inlet. The two captains could not agree. Ross thought that their predecessors had been right in taking the indentation for a fjord. Parry was convinced that here was an inlet to the Arctic Ocean. The following year he returned at the head of a new expedition. Where Ross had believed there were mountains he now saw a wide, ice-free strait opening out, and running before a fresh easterly wind he penetrated the waters which since that day have always been called Lancaster Sound. On September 20th, he reached Melville Island, in the Arctic Ocean, and took up winter quarters. The ships were well furnished with antiscorbutics, and Parry took pains to keep his men occupied during the eighty-four days in which the sun stayed below the horizon. Physical exercises were introduced, a weekly magazine was issued, and amateur theatricals were put on. After ten months' confinement in the ice Parry continued the voyage—westward. Then he was halted anew and had to turn back. But the next year he made a similar wintering in Hudson Bay, and this time reached as far as the Fury and Hecla Strait before he gave up.

His discoveries aroused interest, and the following year one expedition after another was fitted out. Parry himself sailed through Lancaster Sound to Prince Regent Inlet; Lyon sailed into Hudson Bay; Franklin went overland to the mouth of the Mackenzie River; Beechey attempted to make his way from the east through the Bering Strait; George Back spent ten months combating the ice in Hudson Bay. John Ross was compensated for his humiliation in Lancaster Sound by reaching the Magnetic Pole on Boothia Felix and discovering King William Island. After three winterings the provisions ran out and the ship had to be abandoned, but Ross succeeded in finding Parry's depots and thus getting through a fourth wintering. When summer came he hauled the sick by sledge out to Lancaster Sound, where they were taken aboard by a whaling ship which took them back to England after four and a half years in the labyrinth.

Then a catastrophe occurred which shook the civilized world. Just as it seemed that the problem was nearing solution, the white Minotaur claimed its biggest sacrifice. On May 19, 1845, the fifty-nine-year-old Sir John Franklin sailed at the head of an expedition of a hundred and twenty-nine men with two steamships, provisioned for three years. On July 26th of the same year they were observed by a whaling ship in the northern part of Baffin Bay moored to an iceberg, awaiting a passage through the ice. Thereafter, nothing more was seen of the one hundred and thirty men.

After waiting for two years without news from Franklin, the English government became anxious, and the following spring three expeditions were sent out. Moore and Kellett were to go through the Bering Strait, John Ross through Barrow Strait, and Richardson and Rae overland. All three expeditions had received the same brief order: *Find Franklin!* All three returned with the same negative result: no trace of the missing men. A wave of disquiet swept England, the government offered a reward of £20,000, Lady Franklin increased the sum by £3000, and no less than fourteen ships were sent into the labyrinth: *Find Franklin!* Written messages to the missing were laid in cairns equipped with long signal poles, cast overboard in bottles, copper cylinders, and casks fitted with flags, and fastened around the necks of captured foxes, which were afterward released. From the east McClintock advanced to Melville Island, where he met McClure, who came from the west. Only in 1854 did the last of the fourteen ships return home to England, and still there was no trace of Franklin. By that time hundreds of islands in the archipelago had been examined, with one exception: King William Island. All had been forced to abandon their attempts to reach this. It was there that the victims lay.

The government suspended the search, but Lady Franklin would not give up hope. In 1857 she sent out McClintock, and two years later he succeeded in reaching King William Island, where among skeletons and wreckage he found the written accounts of the tragedy: the *Erebus* pressed down by the ice, the *Terror* raised onto the shore, a hundred and thirty men starved and frozen to death, the whole occurring at a time when an ice belt of only a few sea miles prevented Franklin from sailing the Northwest Passage.

And then Theseus entered the labyrinth and slew the Minotaur. He did not have a hundred and thirty men with him like Franklin; he had but five. He did not have two iron ships with steam engines at his disposal, he had only a seventy-two-foot sloop of wood equipped with a petroleum motor engine running on paraffin. Theseus was thirty-one years old, Norwegian, a former medical student, who instead of completing his medical examinations had taken his mate's ticket, who was born at Sarpsborg not far from Fredrikstad, where Jens Munk sailed as a boy. His name was Roald Amundsen. On June 17, 1903, he left Christiania, and during the three ensuing years the *Gjøa* drew in its wake an invisible Ariadne's thread from sunset to sunrise. On October 19, 1906, Captain Amundsen was able to telegraph home from San Francisco: the Anian Strait had been found and the Northwest Passage sailed through, but it would never come to have any practical significance, for its narrow straits were too shallow to permit the passage of vessels of ordinary draught.

Today the air route from Copenhagen to Tokyo goes over the Northwest Passage. In well-heated, pressurized cabins the passengers sit staring down at the labyrinth where Hudson and Franklin disappeared. The dessert on their menu is called "Surprise Pôle Nord."

2

It was toward this deathtrap that Jens Munk steered the *Unicorn* and the *Lamprey* that Whitsunday in 1619, as the crew lightheartedly watched Kronborg sink below the horizon. Their sailing instructions are not preserved but can easily be inferred from the information in Munk's journal. He was to seek out the Hudson Strait at latitude $62\frac{1}{2}°$ north, sail through it, and head southwest in Hudson Bay until he reached the coast to the west and could begin his search for the Anian Strait, where Button and Bylot had given up.

So far all the omens had been auspicious. But in the Kattegat something happened which boded no good: a member of the *Unicorn*'s crew committed suicide. Jens Munk himself witnessed the episode: "In great haste the man leaped full two fathoms outboard, thrusting his head under the water, and yet he could not get under as speedily as it seemed likely; but since the light failed so quickly, no man could save him (the which I had gladly seen), whereupon he went under and was lost."

This ill omen was followed by another incident which must also have given cause for thought. On May 25th, when the two ships were off Lista, in southern Norway, Munk was informed that the *Lamprey* was shipping water. Captain Hendriksen had to keep the pump manned the whole time. Jens Munk hugged the Norwegian coast up past Stavanger and ran in to Karmsund, where the sloop was put on the stocks. It turned out that the leak consisted of three nail holes, which the carpenters on Bremerholm had forgotten to calk. While the damage was being repaired a cooper in the crew died, and, as replacements for him and the Kattegat suicide, Jens Munk took on three men in Skudenaes. The total complement was thus brought up to sixty-five men.

Jens Munk was not disposed to extend the delay in Karmsund more than was absolutely necessary; and when the *Lamprey* was ready, on May 30th, they again put to sea, course west-northwest. They were still in waters which he knew from many earlier voyages, and the passage went according to routine. On June 2nd, the day before the captain's fortieth birthday, they passed the Shetland Islands, and two days later Suderø lay dead ahead. Munk sailed south of the island, using it as a base for his navigational calculations, and set course west by north for Greenland. The weather was calm, and the captain made use of the tranquil days to draw up a complete inventory of the expedition's supplies of victuals and ordered the steward to keep careful records of the casks broached, and to enter the date when they were empty. "I had therewith a true abstract of what had been consumed and what was in store of all kinds of provender and drink," says Munk, who wanted at all times to relate rations to the stocks in hand. He knew all about Henry Hudson's fate.

After sailing for sixteen days they again sighted land, and William Gordon recognized the east coast of Greenland north of Cape Farewell, which he had passed seven years previously together with James Hall. Ice drifts along the coast forced them to go out to sea again; nor did they escape the severe storms common in these waters, and only on June 30th did they sight Cape Farewell once more. "It is a high land, much indented and uneven with lofty, jagged fells," Munk writes in his journal, where he also gives an explanation of the great numbers of icebergs occurring here in all seasons. "Greenland inclines most to the northeast, then more easterly on the eastern shore, so that all the ice that comes from the east drifts southwest. Likewise Greenland inclines most to the northwest in the Fretum Davis and then more northerly with the whole Fretum Davis, whence there comes ice without measure. And this collects off Cape Farewell, which is shaped like a triangle."

Now they faced the last stretch to America. William Gordon knew the powerful, south-flowing Labrador Current in the Davis Strait: if they laid a course due west, the current would bring them too far south in relation to Hudson Strait, which was their immediate objective. After having calculated the compass variation, Munk accordingly set a course west by north, and sailed up into Davis Strait, which with doubtful propriety he renamed Fretum Regis, King's Strait, in honor of Christian IV.

The climate was now the arctic kind Munk knew from the Barents Sea, but with a greater difference between day and night temperatures: "By night there was such fog and great cold that icicles a quarter's length hung in the rigging so that none of the men could protect themselves from the cold. Yet on the same day, before the hour was three after noon, the sun shone in that same place so hot, that the men cast off their smocks and part of their undergarments to boot." All about them the sun shone down on countless icebergs, moving south like an armada of white sails on the blue water; even the sun-bleached Lübeck canvas of the *Unicorn* and the *Lamprey* looked dingy by comparison. Jens Munk estimated the largest of them to be forty fathoms high, "the which would seem scarce credible to one who had not beheld it, and yet so it is in truth." Like many seamen, he shrank from disseminating that sort of information, knowing how easy it was to be accused of boasting. As they were running freely they had no difficulty in avoiding obstacles, and only one week later, thirty-nine days after leaving Norway, they sighted the American coast at latitude $62\frac{1}{2}°$ north.

This was precisely in line with their instructions, and as they made their way through the ice and entered a great bay, both Gordon and Watson were of the opinion that they were in Hudson Strait. Munk was skeptical, for nowhere in the approaches had they found any of the islands which, according to Gerritszoon's map, were situated there. Gordon and Watson were indeed mistaken; they had run into the first of the many blind alleys of the labyrinth, Frobisher Bay, a good way north of Hudson Strait. It was here that Martin Frobisher, forty-one years earlier, had filled his fifteen cargo ships with rubble. After laborious reconnaissance in the ice, Munk discovered that it was a closed stretch of water without an "entering" or approach; then, following his instinct, he sailed south along the coast, until he reached the most southerly cape on what is today called Resolution Island, behind which he found the approaches to the Hudson Strait. This important point, which represented for him the first certain landfall at the approach to the Northwest Passage, he called after himself, giving it the name Munkenaes.

The expedition reached Munkenaes on July 11th, and "at noon, it being fine clear weather and sunshine, we are able to get the correct latitude in which Munkenaes lies, which is 61 degrees, 20 minutes," a position precisely confirmed by the most modern sea chart—where, however, Munkenaes is now called Cape Best, after the Captain Best who sailed with Frobisher. The following day he sent ashore Movritz Stygge and some of the men to find an anchorage and fetch fresh water, while he passed the waiting time on board with a little shooting. "I shot two or three birds with a musket, and in the end this same musket burst asunder and took away the brim before my hat." In the evening the lieutenant returned with water, but they had not found an anchorage where the ships could lie protected from the ice. It now covered the strait as far as they could see, and toward evening on July 13th they had to heave to. The sails were taken in and the *Lamprey* was made fast to the side of the *Unicorn*. "And so we committed ourselves into the hand of God and drifted forth in the ice trusting in God's merciful help."

Their situation was perilously reminiscent of their plight at Kolguev: day by day the pressure from the ice grew; and even though the King's man-of-war was far more solid than the vessel that Jens Munk had bought for himself as a young man, they had to prepare for the worst: "While we drifted hither and thither in the ice, this did strike against a great knee at the one side of the ship, the which stood beneath the head post and was secured with six great iron bolts." This was the heavy, curved stern piece connecting the stem with the underside of the figurehead, in technical jargon called the knee of the head. If that were torn off, obviously the whole prow would be crushed sooner or later. Munk sent all his ship's carpenters outboard to repair the damage, but Svend Arvedsen, Jens Jørgensen, and Peder Nyborg came back with their task unaccomplished; the pressure from the ice was too great. Then

231

he had the idea of turning the ship with the help of the sails, so that the ice pressure would come from the opposite side and force the knee back into place, "the which did occur and as well as if twenty carpenters had been over it to make and mend." It was now a simple matter for Arvedsen to jump down, straighten out the iron bolts, and drive them in again. The *Unicorn* was saved.

Finally on July 15th, "on the morrow at the break of day," the ice eased so much that they were able to set sail and stand in under the northern coast. Here they continued "with small sail" along the land channel to the west into Hudson Strait. Jens Munk renamed it Fretum Christian and noted the enormous tide range of over five fathoms and the consequent fierce tidal current, which is also marked on modern sea charts. The run lasted for only two days, however, then the ice blocked the water in front of them again; and in order not to run the same risk as before, Munk sent the *Lamprey* on ahead to find a sheltered anchorage under the land. On July 17th the two ships anchored behind some rocky islets. As the men who were sent ashore to forage returned with some newly shot reindeer, Jens Munk gave the name Rensund "(Reindeer Sound")" to their new position.

On the evening of the following day he entered in his journal a description of his first encounter with Eskimos:

As we now lay in the shelter of a holm with the ship and the sloop, we remarked that there were people on the southerly side of the haven, wherefore I at once manned my boat and went there in person. When the people of the land perceived that I came to them on shore, they remained motionless and had laid down their weapons with whatever other tackle they had behind some stones. And as I now approached them, whatsoever courtesy I did show them, the same they showed me likewise; but they took no little pains to keep between me and the place where their weapons

A pink in difficulties. The pack ice has suddenly broken up, so that the men who have been working with mattocks and axes have to leave their implements behind and hurriedly scramble aboard or be hauled up by their comrades. From a contemporary copperplate. (Gerrit de Veer)

lay, the which I had carefully remarked and repaired thither and took up their weapons and tackle in my hands and observed them. Then they caused me to understand that rather would they lose all their apparel and be naked than they would lose their weapons and tackle, and pointed to their mouths giving me to understand that with these same weapons and tackle they must seek their food. And when I again laid down their weapons and tackle, they smote their hands together and looked up to heaven and conducted themselves most glad and merrily. Thereafter I presented them with knives and iron fitments of all kind and among other things I gave one of them a mirror. But he did not know what it was, wherefore I took it from him and held it before his face that he might see himself. And when this happened, he gripped the mirror in haste from me and stuck it into his bosom. Thereafter they presented me in like manner of what they had, which was diverse kinds of fowl and seal flesh. And there was one of my company whose face being dark of complexion and his hair black, they did all of them take him in their embrace, surely believing that he was one of their own kind.

Jens Munk did not waste precious time at Rensund. A reconnaissance on July 19th revealed that ice still blocked the strait, and he let the men spend several days washing their things and hunting reindeer. But on the 22nd he was intent upon getting under sail, even though the situation showed no marked improvement. In spite of persistent efforts, he saw no more of his Eskimo friends, whom he very much wanted to consult about sailing conditions along the coast, he writes. On the evening before their departure he went ashore, sought out their fishing gear, "and did lay thereto diverse sorts of our wares, knives, and all manner of iron things." The Eskimos in Rensund were the only strangers Jens Munk was destined to meet during his long voyage, just as Ove Giedde was also to come into close contact with the natives on only one occasion.

What a difference, however, between the encounter at Portudal and the one at Rensund! Ove Giedde had to exchange shots with the natives, Jens Munk was met with embraces; the former left hostages behind him, the latter gifts.

The departure from Rensund on July 22nd was a rash decision that stemmed from Munk's desire to speed up the expedition at all costs. The following day the *Unicorn* and the *Lamprey* were already stuck fast in the ice: "When the day became clear we found ourselves compassed on every side with ice." Once more the ships were made fast to one another and the yards taken down, so that they would not chafe their rigging in the storm. Then the ice took over. On the night of the 23rd the four anchors on the *Lamprey* were shattered and the hull shot up, "so that a man could lay his hand on the keel from stem to stern." On the 24th a storm arose from the southeast, pressing them and the ice in toward the shore. On the 25th the rudder on the *Unicorn* was smashed, and two men who tried to lay out anchors in order to bring up the ships and check their headlong career in the tidal race were nearly drowned in a fissure which suddenly appeared. The same night the ice carried them between some islets and the mainland. And with one of his powerful images Jens Munk writes that "had there been ten helmsmen, who had sailed these waters year after year, then could they in no wise have piloted the ships among these islets better than they now were carried and driven unscathed by the ice and current."

The ice drift ceased on the 26th; on the other hand, the pressure against the ships' sides increased, and the stout oaken balks creaked and groaned. The danger of shipwreck was imminent, and everyone knew that the coming night would be critical. "The whole day the ship lay still, nor did it drift in or out, so that we were at the same time in the greatest need and peril. And we knew now no other good counsel to follow, but committed ourselves into God's hand and prayed to Him most fervently for help and assistance, and the same day we did each give according to our means into the Chaplain's coffer."

Herr Rasmus had spoken his humble words, and now the last rays of the sun were reflected in the ice and by the trumpets on the upper deck, where the crew held evensong.

> As night the earth doth blind,
> And gentle falls the gloom,
> That time us doth remind
> Of Death's own darkling tomb.

Then the temperature fell, and the packing commenced. At short intervals sharp explosive sounds came from the ice below, in comparison with which the *Unicorn*'s twelve-pounder cannon-shots were as nothing. The iron hand closed about the two wooden hulls as about two eggs. Was it Daniel Sinclair's curved oaken frames or the strong arm of the Lord that saved them? When the sun appeared once more the ships were still unscathed. In the daylight Jens Munk observed how the packing of the night had raised the ice to such heights "that it was not possible to go ashore at any place, had one therewith been able to win the whole earth." The men had to pass another day in prayer and psalm singing, another night in dread and terror. But on the morning of the 28th a narrow channel could be seen in the ice, and they succeeded in partly sailing, partly hauling the ships into a little bay behind some islets, where they dropped three anchors and took two cables to the shore. But the anchoring was carried out at low water, and when the tide turned the ice headed for them with such fury that all the sixty-five men had to exert themselves to the utmost to prevent the ships from being smashed against the rock-bound coast. In the middle of all this a nearby iceberg calved, causing a flood-wave so high that the *Lamprey* would have capsized had they not cut away the mooring to the *Unicorn* at the last minute. During the next three days and nights the work of saving the ships continued without a break, and not until the 31st did they manage at high water to get them over some rocks and into a cove, where they could lie without fear of being crushed. "But the men were then so utterly fatigued that they could no longer endure the incredible labor of freeing the ship from the fearsome quantities of ice, likewise the extreme amount of veering and hauling which it fell to them to do."

The following day Jens Munk went ashore with fifteen of the crew. He did not find any Eskimos, as he had hoped to do, but in many places he found traces of their tents. In the rocks were orelike deposits which Munk thought were mica, and just to be sure he had several casks filled with it. The few reindeer they saw were very timid, and as they had no dogs with them, they had to give up the hunt. On the other hand they shot a fair number of hares. Jens Munk called the place Haresund and had a cairn built with the arms and monogram of Christian IV, as had been done at Rensund.

The Danish expedition remained at Haresund for almost a fortnight. For Jens Munk the waiting meant a new and serious delay; a month had now gone by since their first sight of America, and with each day the chances of finding the Anian Strait before winter really set in were diminishing. This discovery was essential if he was to reach the East before Ove Giedde. Each morning the captain made his way out to the tip of the headland to inspect the state of the ice; and as at Rensund, here too he fell a victim to his own impatience. On August 5th, it seemed to him that "the ice began to thin somewhat and drift away," and when he returned from his morning inspection he gave orders for departure. The ships took on extra ballast, the beer was racked, and men were sent ashore for fresh water. Everything proceeded at high speed. While the crew made ready, the officers met in the captain's cabin, where Munk issued new navigation orders and made arrangements as to "what places and latitude we should be found at, should we by reason of the fog be separated."

But once more he had reckoned without his host. On August 6th the ice still imprisoned them in Haresund; on the 7th there was no improvement; and on the 8th they awoke to find the ships covered with deep snow. The same day the boatswain Anders Stavanger died and had to be buried at the side of the King's cairn. But on the 9th, three months after their departure from Copenhagen, Jens Munk could wait no longer and set sail.

The course was laid by William Gordon. The point of departure in his reckonings was Haresund, but unfortunately he had little chance of determining the position of this place with any accuracy. Since leaving Munkenaes they had moved westward on more or less the same degree of latitude, and in those days it was not possible to measure the geographical longitude. Furthermore, it had been extremely difficult to estimate the distance covered during the ship's random movements in the drifting ice. William Gordon was convinced that on their arrival at Haresund, they had traversed the whole of Hudson Strait. By transferring Jens Munk's entries in his journal to a modern chart, it is possible today to fix the position of Haresund due east of the point where North Bay cuts northward inland. The configuration of the coast at this place would thus have supported Gordon in his assumption that they were near the western outlet of Hudson Strait, close to Hudson Bay. This assumption also partially explains Munk's haste. If William Gordon were right, then Haresund was only a few days' sailing from their objective—the southern end of Hudson Bay, where the climate must surely be milder, and where they were to begin their search for the Anian Strait.

According to the King's instructions they were to sail westsouthwest down through Hudson Bay, and that was indeed the course William Gordon set as they left Haresund on August 9th. A fresh northwest wind had come to Munk's

Jens Munk's stay in Rensund and Haresund depicted in the same woodcut in his book *Navigatio Septentrionalis*. The two ships are stereotype, the engraver following traditional forms, and his picture gives no true idea of the *Unicorn* and the *Lamprey*. For one thing, the two vessels were not of equal size. To the left four of the men bring down a reindeer; farther up the meeting with the Eskimos on July 18th. Here, too, the engraver must have been in difficulties: he did not know what Eskimo clothes looked like and therefore chose to represent them as naked.

assistance and during the night had swept the sea clear of ice, but the wind was backing and increased to storm during the day; soon there was "so great and hollow a sea, as neither I nor any other being on board had seen before," Munk writes. No mean words, coming from such a man. But rather hold on with water up to the waist than be held fast in the vise-like grip of the ice. The *Unicorn* and the *Lamprey* raced along, foam flying, at a speed of almost ten knots. At last he had shaken off the iron hand. At this speed it would take only another two days at the most to reach the Anian Strait.

Then, shortly after noon, the captain received a puzzling report from the lookout: land was in sight along the whole horizon ahead! At this stage Jens Munk would, despite all, have preferred to hear of ice. A coastline at this part of Hudson Bay was clearly impossible. Questions crowded in on him and added to the concern he felt at the delay at Haresund. Had the unbelievable happened? Had William Gordon made another mistake? *Were they not in Hudson Bay at all?*

A particularly malicious wave struck the *Unicorn* forward, and the countless tons of water towered up level with the foremast before crashing down on the deck with a roar like an earthquake. For several minutes only the masts were visible, then the hull gave a heave, jets of water two feet long gushed out of the scuppers, the snow-white foam ran in frantic streams from bow to poop. It was as though the ship slowly emerged from the foaming jaws of the sea. Erik Hansen of Fyn rose dejectedly where he had been thrown to the floor when the ship struck the wave.

"That gets the dust out of the corners," was how he put it in his sing-song dialect.

3

While this was happening, Ove Giedde was continuing his voyage on the other side of the world. Since May 3rd, when the young admiral had learned of Boshouwer's attempted flight with the *David*, an uneasy atmosphere reigned in the squadron. Would the Dutchman's behavior end in open mutiny? Would the day come when Danish cannons would have to be trained on Danish ships? Ove Giedde dared not openly affirm his suspicion of Boshouwer by strengthening the watch crew on Boshouwer's ship, and confined himself to keeping careful check on the *David*'s movement from the *Elephant*. Slowly the ships steered south across the gleaming tropical waters of the Gulf of Guinea bound for the Table, as the Cape of Good Hope was called at that time. Then several incidents occurred which did not ease the tense situation. Men lost their footing as they were climbing the rigging and plunged to the deck; tough boatswains fell down in a faint; the strongest man aboard could hardly drag his feet up a ladder. Everyone knew what this meant. The critical moment had arrived; they had now been at sea for six months, and it was known from experience that this was the time required by the invisible enemy to prepare his kind of mutiny. The men had scurvy.

In the general wretchedness Ove Giedde's already fragile authority was further threatened. On June 19th the sloop they had seized at Cape Verde disappeared, and soon they lost sight of the captured privateer; then one of the merchantmen vanished. Because of sickness among the crew, Ove Giedde had to introduce four changes of watch instead of three, but to little avail. Week after week, month after month, they made a snail's progress without any sight of land; for long periods they were not sure where they were. Not until July 4th, four days after Jens Munk had passed Cape Farewell, was Ove Giedde able to note with relief in his journal: "Today with great joy we saw the Table."

In time, the missing ships also came along. Finally the sloop arrived, but it became stranded on the coast, where it had to be left as a wreck. Because of the scurvy the voyage had to be halted for a whole month at the Cape of Good Hope. A camp was set up ashore for the sick, and efforts were made to find them fresh food. But things seem to have been badly organized,

A contemporary map of the Cape of Good Hope with Table Mountain, where Ove Giedde pitched camp for a month. (Israël de Bry)

and Ove Giedde apparently had little notion of how to use the wealth of South African fruits. Indeed, at the end of their stay he contented himself with this laconic note in his journal: "So far we have lost roughly two hundred men of the fleet and still have rather much sickness." At the same time, his quarrel with Boshouwer had flared up anew. As long as the two men remained on their respective ships there was small chance of friction between them, but no sooner did they set foot on land than there were new clashes. On July 21st trouble broke out because Ove Giedde had censored a few letters which Boshouwer was sending to Copenhagen with some English ships. Tyge Stygge and Erik Grubbe attempted to mediate between the angry men; but, Ove Giedde writes, "Greatly impatient, Boshouwer refused to hear them, and poured

242

ill words over them, wherefore they were need to part from him without success." On July 26th he decided to strengthen the watch crew on Boshouwer's ship. This was tantamount to a declaration of hostilities; and realizing this himself, Ove Giedde called the captain of the *David* and gave him orders to hoist a black silk flag on the mainmast "if he perceived any unwarrantable undertaking."

In this uneasy situation the squadron left the Cape of Good Hope on August 5th, the same day as Jens Munk made his decision to sail from Haresund. In spite of all, Ove Giedde looked to the future with a certain degree of confidence. It was true that the health and discipline of his men were not good; true also that he had to be ready for unpleasant surprises from the unreliable Boshouwer. But that was not the most important thing. By reinforcing the watch crew, he considered that he had brought the movements of the *David* under control, and in order to tighten up discipline in the ranks he resorted to a device he had long held in reserve. An example had to be made of somebody. Shortly after their departure he had the privateer captain strung up on the bowsprit of the *Elephant*. The gulls pecked out the eyes of the hanged man, and with the bloody corpse dangling before the bows the ships continued their voyage toward their distant goal. That was the main thing. They had passed the Cape of Good Hope. The way to the East was finally open.

The same could not be said of Jens Munk at this time. While Ove Giedde was sailing the calm Indian Ocean, he was being tossed at full speed into one of the blind alleys of the labyrinth. William Gordon again had made a mistake, and this time the error had more serious consequences than the one in Frobisher Bay. In Haresund they had not, as he had thought, been in the western outlet of the Hudson Strait, but only halfway through it; and when they steered south on August 9th they inevitably struck the opposite coast of the strait. This happened somewhat to the west of the point where Ungava Bay cuts south into the land. The worst thing was that the sight of this bay encouraged Gordon to persist in his error. He mistook Ungava Bay for Hudson Bay and continued steadily southward.

Jens Munk gave Gordon his head, even though he apparently had no faith in his reckonings. Navigation was an affair for the pilots, and Munk did not wish to cause dissension on board by interfering. Clearly time was precious to him now, but he was constantly reminded of Henry Hudson's fate and did not want to pay for his progress with the smallest risk of awakening ill-will among his subordinates, which might be the prelude to later mutiny. He writes in the journal that "on August 10th the pilots set their course southerly, in the opinion that we should be come out in the great bay [Hudson Bay], which however was found to be otherwise." But he knew well enough what his compliance had cost him in terms of delay. On their way to the south they followed a deeply indented coastline, and he observed that "without doubt good harbors were to be found in many places, had they been sought out with diligence, and had there been no lack of time." A few days later, in the middle of Ungava Bay, they passed the island of Akpatok, to whose extreme point Munk gave the name Alkenaes. But after passing this point Gordon still insisted on setting a southwesterly course. In the journal there are now traces of a certain impatience on the captain's part: "After Alkenaes there lay a great bay, stretching due southwest, where we came to low-lying and flat land, and which the English mate thought was like to be the place we sought; but those words and opinions were soon retracted. As time was short, and did not permit us to linger further, we set our course out of the aforementioned southern bay to continue our voyage and make headway." The meaning is clear: Gordon had been gently but firmly made to recognize his blunder; he had gone wrong, but that had no effect upon the good relationships on board. In a friendly manner Jens Munk was able to request him to sail north again, and on August 20th he notes with satisfaction in his journal that "we were once more in our right waters."

It was Hudson Strait, but by then the mistake had cost them ten precious days. Since sailing from Munkenaes six weeks ago, they had in fact only moved a short distance westward. Now there was no margin for further detours, and in the next few days they made rapid headway toward the west. The strait was ice-free, and a week later they reached the western outlet where the two barren, rocky isles, Digges Islands, mark the beginning of Hudson Bay. Jens Munk sacrificed one or two days investigating the islands to compile some reliable information on conditions in this region, which in contrast to the rocky havens in Ungava Bay was an important point in the Northwest Passage. He changed the name of the islands to The Sisters; and though the name did not survive, his advocacy of the northerly route did prevail, for even today it is followed by shipping. A similar survey was made shortly afterward when he discovered low-lying Mansfield Island a little farther to the west.

Now he was in Hudson Bay, which he called Novum Marum; and at last Gordon could set a southwesterly course with a good conscience. The day after they had left Mansfield Island they were overtaken by one of the sudden storms that are so frequent in those waters. Munk tells in his journal of "storm and squall, snowstorm, hail and mist." Then once more he received a disturbing report from the lookout: the *Lamprey* had disappeared. It was pointless to search for the ship in such bad weather, so Munk put his trust in the arrangements about course and rendezvous he had agreed on with Hendriksen and Watson, and continued northwest.

On September 7th he sighted land to the south, a low coastline with sparse forest and a rocky spit jutting into the sea and protecting the narrow approaches to a fjord. In the heavy storm Munk had more need than ever of the *Lamprey* to run ahead and pilot the *Unicorn* through the unknown inlet, but the sloop was still missing, and he was now faced with guiding the heavy frigate in through the heavy breakers to secure anchorage in the fjord. Few incidents in his long career bear such high testimony to his seamanship. Experienced mariners, confronted with the details of the maneuver he executed on September 7th, cannot conceive how he managed it. Even today, when these waters have long since been measured and buoyed, it is regarded as one of the most difficult places of call in the world. No ships enter here without the assistance of tugs and pilots. Indeed, during stormy periods one ship after another can be seen hove to out in the bay awaiting calm weather for the dangerous passage.

On September 7, 1619, the wind at this place was blowing at force 10 from the northwest with snowstorms, hail, and fog. Racing toward the coast with a following wind and foam flying from the bows, Jens Munk's full-rigged frigate suddenly appeared through the gray, foggy weather. During the few minutes available to him, and maneuvering with the sails only, he succeeded in bringing the ship through the cross currents, estimating the tide race and the drift, locating the dangerous submerged rocks which reach out from the eastern spit, and avoiding running aground; then, as soon as he was in the fjord, where he had no idea of depths and bottom conditions, taking the way off the ship, bringing it into the wind, striking the sails, and dropping anchor. The whole thing was over in a moment. Beyond the headland the breakers still thundered; within, the fury of the sea had been reduced to a gentle gurgling alongside the ship. The *Unicorn* was safe.

Now the problem was to warn the *Lamprey*, and scarcely had the necessary anchor bearing been completed when Munk gave orders for his pinnace, brought along in six parts after the manner of the whalers, to be put together and lowered. A party of seamen rowed ashore with fuel, rags, and a barrel of tar, and when darkness fell an enormous fire blazed on the highest of the low, rounded rocks. On the morning of the 8th there was still not a speck to be seen on the troubled sea. Many began to fear for their comrades; the whole day passed in restless waiting, and when night approached once more fresh supplies of fuel had to be taken ashore. The night was long;

one piece of wood after another was cast onto the fire. Out in the dense gloom over the sea not a glint appeared, but at daybreak the watch at the fire caught just a glimpse of rigging, like a half-erased pencil drawing in the sea fog. The ship must have been riding at anchor a good way off the coast, but there was no mistake about it: it was the *Lamprey*.

Now it was the turn of the *Unicorn*'s crew to pilot the sloop through the approaches, and soon the two ships lay moored alongside each other. The men on the smaller boat were exhausted; in some of them Munk detected the symptoms of incipient scurvy. He was familiar with the dreaded illness, of course, but in contrast to Ove Giedde he apparently knew how easy it was to combat it with fresh fruits. What Ove Giedde had found too much for him in a South African paradise, Jens Munk succeeded in doing in the arctic wilderness: "I caused the sick men to be taken ashore from the ship, and there we found still some cloudberries, gooseberries, and others which in Norway are called cowberries and crowberries. And I caused thereto a good fire to be made each day for the sick, whereby they were refreshed, and thereafter they came speedily to health again." A few days later when a polar bear was seen devouring a white whale on the beach, he shot the animal himself and had the meat divided among the men, who after so long on salt provisions were glad to sink their teeth into a piece of fresh roast bear.

The *Lamprey* found the *Unicorn* on September 9th. Exactly three months after their departure from Copenhagen the ships had reached the point where, according to instructions, Jens Munk was to start his search for the Anian Strait. It was rather later than anticipated. The repairs in Karmsund had cost four days, the mistake in Frobisher Bay two. Difficulties with the ice had occasioned five days' delay in Rensund and twelve in Haresund; and finally there were the ten days they had wasted in Ungava Bay, all together a loss of over a month. Furthermore, winter at the southern end of Hudson Bay seemed to be much earlier and far more severe than might have been expected at that latitude. A month earlier they would still have had a chance of finding the coveted passage; now Munk had to admit reluctantly that any hope of taking up the voyage again dwindled with each day. On the 10th and 11th of September there was "such fearsome snow and storm, that nothing could be accomplished"; on the 13th he sent out his two second mates, Hans Brok and Jan Petersen, each in a ship's boat to the west and east along the coast to investigate the possibilities of shelter; on the 16th the latter returned with a negative report. During the following days the frost increased, a new snowstorm arose, and there was anxiety for the fate of Hans Brok in the frail boat. At last Munk could not wait any longer for his return and gathered his officers together for consultation. All were agreed that the severe weather made it impossible for the voyage to continue. That was September 18, 1619. When the meeting was over Jens Munk had to call together the two crews on the upper deck of the *Unicorn* and repeat Henry Hudson's fateful words: "We shall attempt to winter here."

17

Munk Haven

When the decision to winter over was made, Jens Munk had
spent ten days at the new place and formed a rough impression
of the surrounding country. He called it Nova Dania, and at
first sight the landscape around him with its low-lying, distant
horizons was indeed very reminiscent of a desolate Danish
river mouth. Toward the east the view was of endless brown
tundra; from the crow's-nest on the *Unicorn* the fjord was seen
to end in a broad river, which threaded its way through the
dense coniferous forests of the south like a shining ribbon;
and only to the west was the landscape more ruggedly con-
toured. Two promontories consisting of low, polished rocks
protruded into the fjord here with broad inlets between them.
Jens Munk had returned to the tree line; and here, in contrast
to the bare plains of rock at Rensund and Haresund, the landscape bore more evident signs of fertility. Dense thickets of
dwarf willow clambered up the rocky slopes; on the higher-
lying hills inland grew larch and juniper; and every rocky
crevice had a profusion of cloudberries, crowberries, bilberries,
and cowberries. The snow that fell at the beginning of their
stay had melted again, and the fjord lay blue and smiling in the
sunshine, stretching inward in broad curves toward the green
meadows between the promontories. An impression of freshness and peace came across through the clear arctic air. But
this was only at high water; when low water came the landscape changed character and revealed the other side of its

nature. In less than an hour the fjord would retreat from cove and promontory, until it was scarcely wider than the muddy river bed; and where the choppy swell had glinted in the light a short while before, there now stretched endless mudbanks studded with thousands of large stones. The strong shadows cast by the sun accentuated the contours of this dreary chaos; the sense of freshness and peace was transformed into one of hostile desolation; and instead of being reminded of some sheltered Danish fjord mouth, one might have imagined that the two ships were anchored close to that distant shore where once the Cyclops Polyphemus had hurled his stones in rage and pain after the fleeing Odysseus.

This interplay was repeated twice a day, and the tidal current which caused it soon made the fjord mouth unsuitable as an anchorage. On the same day as Munk made known the decision to winter over, the two ships were sailed farther in and anchored off the more southerly of the two promontories on the west coast. Already the night frost was severe, and the next morning Munk could see that "the new drift ice had cut a good two finger-breadths into both sides of the ship and sloop." There was now great activity on board. If the ships were to be saved, they must be taken out of the domain of the ice as quickly as possible. At high water they managed to get the *Lamprey* over the stones to the south side of the promontory. A ringbolt fitted with tackle was fixed into the rock, fifty men began to haul, and soon the *Lamprey* lay secure in a depression shielded from the northwest wind by the promontory and just at the side of some high ground which also lay in the lee of the rock slope, but which nevertheless had an unrestricted view to all sides.

It was far more difficult to get the frigate over the mudbanks, which at this point were more than 900 fathoms, or more than a mile, across. Although Munk had marked the largest of the rocks with buoys at low water, he could not prevent "the ship hanging on a rock and getting holed so badly that it was as much as all the carpenters could do to

patch it at lowest water, before the flood returned once more."
After struggling for four days, the crew finally got the ship so
far in that it was protected against the drift ice. The *Unicorn*
now stood only 120 fathoms from the spot to which the
Lamprey had been hauled. At low water one could walk dry-
shod from one ship to the other; at high tide the water rose
about four feet around the sides of the frigate but was not
sufficient to float it. In great haste a number of ringbolts were
let into the nearest stones and secured with lead calking for the
moorings. So that the structure should not suffer from the fact
that the heavy frigate rested on its keel alone, Munk had the
latter buried in the ground; in addition clay and sand were
thrown in between the fjord bottom and the sides of the ship.
Most of this work had to be done all over again four days
later, however, for a heavy ice drift shifted the vessel in its
dock and caused such leaking that it took two thousand swings
of the pump to empty it again. The men were then sent inland
to cut timber, and Svend Arvedsen, Jens Jørgensen, and Peder
Nyborg set to work constructing six caissons, rectangular con-
structions of heavy logs filled up with stones, which they laid
around the ship on the side where the ice drift was strongest.
On October 15th the ice shifted one of these caissons, once
more disturbing the ship in its dock; but the damage was repaired, and as the fjord froze over completely shortly afterward the *Unicorn* did not suffer any further harm.

During the labor of putting the ship in winter dock Hans
Brok returned. His expedition to the east had had the same
result as Jan Petersen's to the west: no natural harbors were
to be found on that part of the coast. The mission had been a
hard one, however. Hans Brok and his boat crew were surprised by a northeast storm in open sea on September 16th;
they had attempted to anchor the frail ship's boat to an ice
floe, but the cable had snapped, and for several days they had
struggled at the oars to prevent the dinghy from drifting into
the surf. After an absence of ten days they managed to get
back to Munk Haven. The oars had held—it was the men who

were broken, worst of all Hans Brok himself. He had looked death in the face for too long; with each day his condition worsened, and soon the once sturdy mate from Kildin was reduced to a shadow of what he had been.

Hans Brok's plight acted as a warning. With his usual care, Munk set about organizing the wintering for his crews. He transferred the crew of the *Lamprey* to the *Unicorn*, so that they would require only one galley in the future, and gave the cook and the steward orders about mealtimes and rations. The frigate's cannon were dismounted and lowered into the hold, where the heavy bronze pieces could not damage the wooden structure of the beached ship; and this made it possible to reorganize the gun deck, which was to be the men's habitat in the coming months. The cannon ports were nailed up and calked, all superfluous equipment was taken ashore, "shirts, shoes, and boots" were issued to the men, and three large fireplaces were constructed, one before the mast, one behind it, and the third on the afterdeck. The crew was divided into three watches of about twenty men each and allotted an area near the fireplaces. Munk realized how important it was to keep everyone occupied and "drew up rosters for watch duties, wood carrying, and charcoal burning, and who should melt snow for water by day, so that everyone knew what he was to do, and how he should conduct himself."

The *Unicorn* and the *Lamprey* in Munk Haven. A comparison with a modern map on page 223 reveals that the shorelines of the inlet are more or less accurate, just as the depiction of the crew at work felling trees, burning charcoal, and hunting polar bears and reindeer closely follows the description in the journal. The ships are lying roughly in the right place, but they are far too large in relation to the surrounding landscape, and once more it is a stereotyped representation. The deciduous trees fit in badly with the region's true growth of conifers, and the two strange buildings correspond neither in appearance, situation, nor fenestration to reality. Apart from a few "hides" in the forest for the use of the hunters, Munk erected one or two wooden huts at the most, and they lay on the raised ground ashore, concealed here behind the ships. (*Navigatio*)

The wine on board was rationed, but he did not put restrictions on the ale. He knew, as did all the seafarers of his time, that ale has a prophylactic effect on scurvy, a fact supported by modern research, although it has also been shown that it is effective for just a few months after it is first brewed.

The new arrangements were introduced at the beginning of October. In the course of that month the winter harbor was completed, and the crew protected as far as possible against the cold, which every day grew worse. At length Munk was able to take a day off and devote himself to something that continued to engage his interest: contact with the natives of the country. "The 7th of October was a fine day. Accordingly I journeyed up the river, with the object of ascertaining how far I could reach with a boat. But about a mile and a half [i.e., six English miles] up the same river there was such measure of stones that I could not go farther and must turn back again. And I had at this time all manner of small wares with me, having that intention and meaning, should I chance upon any of the folk of the land, to give them something as a gift, in order that I might make their acquaintance." Munk had to turn back at the fjord near the present-day Mosquito Point. He did not see any natives, but he found several traces of their summer camps along the banks. The same happened when he attempted a new expedition, this time overland. Together with twenty members of the crew, he traveled three (Danish) miles from the winter harbor. "But whereas a great snow arose, and was too heavy to advance in, we had to turn back again. Had we but skis, such as are used in Norway, and men who could run thereon, then perchance we could have come so far as to fall in with other folk. Else there is little prospect in such places of making headway in the winter."

On this occasion, too, he had failed to catch a glimpse of the natives, but the trip had demonstrated that the lack of skis, combined with the lack of leather clothing, was to have the most serious consequences. Then a little incident occurred which indicated that the natives Munk was looking for could not be far away: "On the 14th of November in the night a great, black hound came to the ship over the ice. Then one of the men on watch became aware of it and knew not otherwise than that it was a black fox, wherefore he straightaway shot it and proceeded to drag it into the cabin joyful in the belief that he had gained a great prize. But on the morrow we beheld a large hound before us and without doubt one trained in hunting; for he had been bound about the nose with narrow bands, so that the hairs had chafed away there, and he was cleft in the right ear, and it was like that his owner had not gladly lost him. And for my part I had gladly seen him taken alive. Then had I made a peddler of him and let him run thither, whence he was come, with small wares." If the Danes had no luck in making contact with the natives, it was not because there were none. Even then the region was frequented by both Eskimos and Indians; the warlike people of the Chipewyan and Cree tribes lived in this very neighborhood; and one must assume that they observed from concealed positions the movements of the Danes around the great ships, which could be seen for miles around. They simply did not venture to approach any nearer. Later it was to be otherwise.

Meanwhile the winter had become so severe that Munk had to abandon any further exploration. Instead, he threw his energies into other matters, observed and noted the relationship between the spring tide and the position of the moon, took measurements of the thickness of the ice, investigated ice drift, speculated about the formation of icebergs on the basis of surveys he had made in Davis Strait. On December 10th an eclipse of the moon kept him busy with his cross-staff, well aware that an accurate measurement of the eclipse could later form the basis for calculating their degree of longitude. According to Munk, "half past the hour of seven, when the first eclipsing began, the moon was $15\frac{1}{2}$ degrees above the eastern horizon, but when the eclipse came to an end the moon was 47 degrees over my southern horizon, and it was ten of the clock." It is obvious that, with the primitive instruments at his disposal and lacking an accurate chronometer, he had no chance of making these difficult observations with the necessary precision; and indeed a calculation based on his figures gives a longitude appreciably farther west than his actual position. But he took all the blame for the uncertain result upon himself: "This is my brief and simple description of the aforementioned Eclipse, which I have seen and observed at the aforementioned place, hoping that the gentle reader, having understanding of these things, will judge my intentions to be of the best, even though I am far from describing each circumstance in the detail it deserves." Overconfidence was never one of his faults.

While the captain strove hard in his role of scientist, the men passed their time in felling trees, burning charcoal, and hunting. The desolate landscape began to bear the signs of human occupation. In every direction men showed as black dots in the snow; between the *Unicorn* and the high ground they had worn a broad path, which was crowded with people all day long, walking to and fro with their tools on their shoulders or dragging sledges with wood and charcoal. From on land there sounded the regular and musical strokes of cutting axes, blended now and then with a sudden musket-shot from the hunters farther away. All through the autumn, hunting yielded a good return. The men discovered animal tracks and set traps or built small hide-outs in the forest, laid out bait and lay in wait for the game; and nearly every day they came home with fresh grouse, mountain hares, cross foxes, and sables as a welcome supplement to the cook's everlasting salt provisions. Anything extra was hung in the rigging and saved for festive occasions. In his younger days Jens Munk had known at first hand something of the unappetizing life of the gun deck, so he knew how important it was to introduce some variation in the men's daily round. They had to be kept occupied from morning till evening; but occasionally they also needed a chance of letting themselves go, of thinking about something else. Each Sunday was marked by divine service, a few pious words by Herr Rasmus, and an extra ration of brandy. And when Martinmas Eve arrived, on November 10th, Munk gratefully seized the opportunity for a celebration on board: "The men had shot a number of grouse, with which we had to content ourselves in the absence of St. Martin's goose. And I caused the men in each watch to be given a pot of Spanish wine over and above that which was otherwise daily prescribed, wherewith the whole ship's crew was well satisfied, thereto merry and glad, and of ship's ale was given to them as much as they desired." The clay pipes were brought out, Erik Hansen told stories in the dialect of Fyn, song and laughter rumbled under the deck planks, and doubtless one or two ship's boys suddenly began to feel that the *Unicorn* rose and fell alarmingly, as though the ice had set it free and sent it out again to the open sea. The captain went the rounds, joining first this group and then that, and all must have had the impression that he felt at home among them. No one sensed that even at the height of the jollifications he was still anxious to assure himself that everything was properly organized. He knew that the ale on the *Unicorn* had been frozen in the casks, and had therefore asked that it be reboiled after being thawed out. But he also knew that most of the ale which the men now sat pouring down themselves had only been thawed out and not reboiled. "Nevertheless I let them have their own will in this, because the common man is so minded, that whatsoever is forbidden him, that will he do out of very contrariness by stealth, and will in no wise consider whether or not it might benefit or injure him."

So far the winter had passed better than expected. Both ships were secure and could easily be refloated when the spring returned. Hunting provided ample food; there was no shortage of wood in the forest; and the men were in a cheerful and good-humored mood. Even so, it could be remarked that winter was slowly tightening its grip on Nova Dania and its tiny

257

population of sixty-four people. They had several days of
snowstorm from the northwest; all outdoor work had to be
suspended, and the air was so thick with whistling ice crystals
that visibility dropped to less than one yard. When the storm
died down and the weather cleared again, the temperature
sank to a level no one on board had believed possible. Even
the game seemed to have been driven from their known haunts.
But worst of all was the fact that because they lacked all leather
clothing, the hunters could not endure the cold for long periods.
Similarly, since they had no skis they were forced little by little
to give up tending their traps, let alone frequenting the more
distant hide-outs in the forest.

In the middle of all this something happened which seriously alarmed Munk. On November 21st, only ten days after
the big celebration of Martinmas Eve, one of the *Unicorn*'s
boatswains died. The ship's carpenter made a coffin and a
wooden cross for the dead man, who was buried on the piece
of high ground. This event caused sorrow but not consterna-
tion; after all, they had lost men in Karmsund and Haresund,
too. Only Jens Munk brooded on the cause of this death,
which occurred exactly six months after their departure. But,
mindful of morale on board, he chose to keep his anxieties to
himself. They would have to wait and see. Perhaps the death
of the boatswain was only an isolated case. Perhaps there were
no grounds for alarm.

The day after the burial the temperature dropped once more.
"The 27th of November there was so deep a frost that all the
glass bottles we had on board did freeze asunder." On December 3rd Jens Munk measured the thickness of the ice in the
middle of the fjord, where the tidal current was strongest, at
seven Zealand quarters, or more than four feet. As he turned
for home at sunset, the whole western horizon was ablaze
behind the ice-covered rigging of the *Unicorn*. Redder and
redder the frosty sky flared over the white fjord; nearly an
hour went by before the darkness came with flickering northern
lights and a cold which seemed to freeze even the stars in the

firmament. Out in the fjord the Minotaur howled, and sharp-ridged snowdrifts lay like white dolphins around the prow of the *Unicorn*. But the dolphins had frozen stiff in the middle of their leap. They were not alive; nothing lived here. It was as if the forces of nature could unfold themselves more splendidly, more freely here than anywhere else. Flames and ice formed a single concept, and Man himself was but a passing error.

A week later David Volske, surgeon aboard the *Lamprey*, died.

2

It was December, 1619. The tropical sun beat down with a fierce glare above the calm sea, where every ray of light seemed to splinter into thousands of smaller rays, a diamond dust of sparks that blinded the eye and wearied the brain. From the yards of the mainmast the sails hung limp in the heat; the pitch bubbled between the deck planks; you could fry an egg on the deckhouse roof; and the rusted anchor at the prow was so hot that it left burns if inadvertently gripped with bare hands.

Everywhere that offered any trace of shade on the ship the victims of scurvy lay groaning. Only a few men were able to stand; wrists and ankles were swollen to twice their normal size; the sores spread up from their very fingertips, where the nails had loosened and come off; spongy gums hung in folds over their teeth, so that they could not shut their mouths. At long last evening came. The mainmast lost itself beyond human reach up beneath the Southern Cross; the half-moon lay horizontal, sailing like a bolt across the purple night sky; phosphorescence glowed in the wake of the ship. Wherever the gaze turned the sea stretched desolate in the moonlight; the other ships of the squadron had vanished; no one on board knew anything of their fate, and, what was worse, no one on board, not even the admiral, knew at that moment where they themselves were on that interminable ocean.

Since their departure from the Cape of Good Hope every-thing had gone wrong for Ove Giedde. They were out only a few weeks when Boshouwer had managed to elude them and make off. "The 30th of August the ship 'David' fell away from the fleet, though we were only under our mainsail. On the morning of the 31st we saw him northwest of us, but at the stroke of two of the clock in the afternoon, he gradually ran out of our sight."

Why had the Dutchman made off? What surprises could they expect from him? Ove Giedde had ample time to think about this, for they made only slow progress, and not until they had been fifty days at sea did they sight land at Mozam-bique. That represents an average speed of less than one and a half knots, not a quarter of Jens Munk's speed across the North Atlantic. Ove Giedde was reluctant to anchor off the open coast, but the crew's need of fresh water was so great that they refused to obey his orders and sent a boat ashore. The dinghy capsized in the surf, and six men were drowned. The voyage then proceeded north, and on October 6th they reached the Comoro archipelago between Madagascar and the African mainland, and anchored close to the island of Mohéli. The anchorage was protected by coral reefs; on the white beach palm trees stood tall and slender in clusters of two and three, their tousled heads touching, and great turtles lurched out toward the clear blue water, where the native boats with their woven sails glided past against the red sun.

On this occasion Ove Giedde managed to avoid a clash with the local population. He presented the black queen of the islands with a roll of red silk and received in return oxen and fresh water. No doubt the sick also had an opportunity of fortifying themselves with fruits from the island. As usual, Ove Giedde is silent on this important point; on the other hand, it is clear from the journal that the state of health among the men continued to be very poor—indeed, not even the officers, who were far better provisioned, got off scot-free. So far during the voyage, Lauritz Willomsen, captain of the

Copenhagen, had died of scurvy; and on Mohéli they had to bury the captain of the merchantman *Christian*, Jens Hvid. This was the man whom Jens Munk had had with him as his companion when he had tried his fortune as a merchant skipper in the Barents Sea in his salad days.

After more than a month's stay on the Comoros, Ove Giedde set course for the north once more on November 4th. Just as he had done on leaving the Cape of Good Hope, he began the voyage by setting a few examples as a deterrent to his crew, and again the prisoners from Cape Verde were the victims. This time two men were hanged from the bowsprit of the *Elephant*, while three others were chained to the mainmast. On November 10th Ove Giedde states laconically in his journal that one of the latter "had died in the irons."

But this death-dealing discipline imposed by the young admiral no longer had any effect. Sailors were flogged, penalties rained down upon mates and chief boatswains, but these punishments fell on men already plagued by a worse scourge. The ships had hardly been at sea a month when scurvy again made itself master of the gun deck. In the early stages they tried to fight the disease with the old "remedy"—painting the gums with a mixture of flour, salt, and tobacco ash—but that did not stop the bleeding. The trouble grew worse; the slightest movement caused excruciating pains in the elbow and knee joints; the sick grew apathetic and feeble; it was impossible to force any food down, their mouths became open sores, and the slimy water from the ship's tanks smelled so badly that even the healthy men had to steel themselves before each sip. A few boxes of oranges from the Comoros could have halted and overcome this misery. The remedy was known and used even at that time by experienced skippers, but the Danish squadron was led by a man who was not a sailor but a jurist; he had more confidence in regulations than in oranges. As they approached the equator, and the temperature rose daily, the condition of the sick grew worse. The *Elephant*, the *Copenhagen*, and the *Patientia* resembled those grim *tumbeiros* which came sailing into Bahia with slaves from Africa. An unbearable stench came from the gun deck; scurvy was an executioner who did not give his victims a speedy end, but let them slowly putrefy. The hale, too, were left to their own devices. Ove Giedde had no contact with his men and did not understand how to introduce those little variations from time to time which might have diverted them and taken their minds away from their wretched surroundings. He does not mention the approach of Christmas by so much as a word. But in the midst of the misery there was nevertheless time to hold a court-martial and to sentence three members of the crew to a conditional fine of six months' pay "for their stubbornness."

It became more and more difficult to get even the healthy men to carry out their duties. The working of the sails was done without care, haphazardly; everyone did virtually as he pleased; time after time they lost sight of the other ships. Even navigation was neglected. It appears from Ove Giedde's journal that he drifted around for months at the mercy of the monsoon. One day his readings show a northerly latitude, fourteen days later a southerly latitude, eight days later a northerly latitude again, and so on. In the end he had to instruct the captain of the *Elephant* to attempt to overhaul any ship that might appear on the horizon so that its captain could tell them where they were.

3

When David Volske, the ship's surgeon, died on December 12th, it was so cold in Munk Haven that no one could leave the ship to bury him. Not until two days later could the burial take place. Once again the ship's carpenter made a coffin and a wooden cross; once again the little group went over the ice from the *Unicorn* to the high ground ashore; once again Herr Rasmus read a prayer. But the ceremony was brief, and the last few verses of the psalm had to be dropped. "So fierce a cold was it," writes Munk, "that blisters rose on the noses and cheeks of the men, where their bare faces came into contact with the wind."

That was on December 14th. In ten days it would be Christmas Eve. Most of the men were made uneasy by this latest death, occurring so soon after the first; and Munk seized on the approaching festival as a welcome opportunity of diverting them. He set the Christmas preparations in motion; the gun deck was made ready; and as December 20th turned out to be a day of mild and sunny weather, he sent all hands ashore, "one part of the company for wood and charcoal, one part on a shoot, in order that we could have something fresh for the forthcoming Christmas holy days." Once more the ring of axes sounded from the shore, broken by the more distant musket-shots. Once again the sledge carried in firewood across the ice. And as the sun went down, the hunters came home with "a whole collection of grouse and a hare." The days passed in ceaseless activity and high spirits. There seemed to be no end to the men's ingenuity and energy; even if the ale had frozen, there was no difficulty in lugging up the heavy casks from the hold and reboiling the contents. At the conclusion of this work, Munk took the opportunity of conducting one of his experiments: "I caused a Rostock cask to be filled with water, and on the morrow, when they loosened all the hoops of the cask it was quite frozen solid and altogether ice."

Before they knew it, it was the 24th. The officers were unusually sociable; the cook, quite unapproachable; the steward, near to nervous breakdown; and the boatswains, agitated and preoccupied. There was just time to wash behind the ears, shave, drag a fairly clean blouse out of the ditty bag, and give one's neighbor a quick hair trim. And that was that. The blaze along the western horizon died; the stars froze in the sky; the moon shone on the white dolphins by the bows. No church bells rang; not a breath of wind in the rigging. It was as if the cold had reduced the whole globe to silence, when Herr Rasmus rose and read in a voice thick with brandy of the days when Cyrenius was governor and all the world was to be taxed. Then the priest shut the book, and it was Christmas Eve in Munk Haven.

"Behold a rose is growing, out of the frozen earth, in midst of coldest winter." The hymn was worded somewhat differently in 1619, but the melody was the same. The tune woke memories of many past Christmases in the sailors, which mingled with their fears for the future. "After the sermon we all made offerings to the priest in accord with ancient custom, each after his means, and though there were little riches among the men, albeit they gave of what they had. A deal of them gave white fox-skins, with which the priest might line a kirtle; he was not, however, ordained a life long enough to allow him to wear it out," Jens Munk writes.

The service was over, and now the steward appeared with an appetizing roast of hare accompanied by tasty grouse; and the captain himself went around to make sure that the tankards were kept well charged. "I gave the company wine and strong ale, so that they waxed merry and were in fine humor, nor did any ill word pass between them," he writes in his journal. He expresses himself briefly, yet the words reflect the affection he felt for his men. There they were, sitting with crossed legs on the gun deck and stuffing themselves with good things. Iver Alsing and Jens Borringholm, Christoffer Opslø and Rasmus Clemmensen, the brothers Jens and Laurids Helsing. Chatter and laughter resounded in the room, where there was scarcely space to stand. Among the platters and the tankards were the candles, all at that slight oblique angle that marked the list the *Unicorn* had taken when the ice last moved the ship in its dock. In order better to heat the room, Munk had ordered some four-foot-long ballast irons to be heated red-hot in the furnace and then dragged out with smith's tongs onto a base of large stones; from here the red-hot iron now spread its glowing heat, which would last for a long time. The steady glare lit up the men's faces: Anders Sodens and Oluf Boye, Christen Gregersen and Povel Pedersen, Morten Nielsen and Ismael Abraham-

sen. The cold and the snow, their fears and their sadness, were
drowned in the strong ale; and there they sat, newly washed
and flushed, with their big bodies, heavy wrists, thick lips,
and blue eyes, replete and good-humored, full of good will
toward one another, enjoying themselves in the Christmas
spirit, their minds far away, and talking of other things—
Danes! How different they were from those southern peoples
among whom Jens Munk lived in the far-off years of his youth,
when he last spent Christmas in the New World. Slow-moving
and simple, where the others had been quick and calculating;
born to the demands a harsh climate makes on one's powers of
endurance, where others accept their paradise unthinkingly as
a gift from the gods; cool and appraising connoisseurs of
reality, where others are inclined to turn their back on it.

The captain knew from much experience at sea that when
scurvy had once claimed its first victim, it was rarely long before
a second one followed. His second-in-command, Movritz
Stygge, had been complaining of fatigue for some time; Jan
Olluffsen had been bedridden since the beginning of November; things were getting steadily worse with Hans Brok; Povel
Pedersen was ill, four other boatswains lay sick, and even the
cook was quite unable to sink his loose teeth into the appetizing
roast hare which he had prepared for the others. Two dead and
nine ill: how to ensure that the rest of the crew were not
attacked? On their arrival in September he had saved the crew
of the *Lamprey* by giving the sick members cloudberries,
cowberries, and crowberries from the land, but even if the frost
had preserved the berries, the snow now lay so deep everywhere that it would be a hopeless task to dig down to them.
Everything depended on the weather. Already they had had
several days of severe cold and snowstorm, so fierce that no
one could leave the ship. January and February still lay ahead.
If the cold intensified it would be necessary to prepare for the
day when their fuel was used up, and when the hunters could
not seek fresh supplies of meat because they lacked leather
clothing and skis, so that everybody on board, sick and healthy

alike, would have to be content with the pernicious salt provisions. In order to hold the disease at bay it was essential to keep the men occupied, keep them moving about. But how to find them work? Sixty men confined month after month to this gun deck, where one could hardly stand upright, without fuel or fresh provisions, without anything to do but . . . No, the captain dared not think further.

Christmas Eve was coming to an end. The men huddled together to make the most of the last warmth from the iron bars. The celebration had been a success. It had not been difficult to divert them, and for once reality had been put to flight.

More than three hundred years have passed since that Christmas Eve in Munk Haven; the captain and his men are gone and their ships long since lost. But in the summer of 1964 the "Jens Munk Memorial Expedition" was able to locate and survey the site at the head of the fjord to the south of the promontory where the *Unicorn* had lain in winter dock 345 years previously; and one Sunday afternoon during the survey work, on August 9th at 15.55 hours, just as the sun's low position in the west produced that oblique lighting with its wealth of contrasts which is so favorable for observation, there was found a bar of cast iron, 3.2 inches square and 40 inches long, half buried in the mud, at map reference 1382/534. From the complete agreement between these measurements and the precise details in the contemporary sources, one had to conclude that the object in question was one of Jens Munk's ballast irons. The sun kept shining; the mud remained mud; it was still August 9, 1964, and one still stood there in rubber boots with red soles; but the encounter was with a fragment of a distant Christmas Eve, when the sun was not shining and the fjord was not free of ice. That iron bar was in all probability one of those which had lain glowing red on the stones, while Herr Rasmus read the Christmas gospel. Here it lay now—cold, heavy, mute, but real. Just as real at this moment as it was when Christian IV sent Ove Giedde to the Gulf of Trincomalee and Jens Munk to the Anian Strait. While it was still glowing, the final phase of the great drama in which these three characters played the leading roles was imminent. During the months that followed, all three men kept regular journals, and all three journals are preserved. We can set them before us on the table and open them; they are just as concrete and tangible as the iron bar which lay at map reference 1382/534, but they are not mute. If their account is brutal and direct, almost unbearably so, if there seems to be no meaning in it—so be it, none other exists. Such was the reality, the only reality the people who lived at that time had to huddle up to and warm themselves by.

Christmas Eve in Munk Haven was at an end, but the captain allowed the men to continue their festivities during the following days with services and further celebrations. "Throughout all the holy days the weather was fair and mild, and so that the time should not be heavy on our hands, the men practiced diverse games, and whosoever was best able to invent pastimes, he was best accepted, so that the folk then had all sorts of distractions and diversions, and in such wise we did while away the holy days with that merriment, which was then afoot." Once more Munk had succeeded in cheering up his men. But at last the festivities had to end. Reality and the ordinary round returned; in Munk Haven, on the Indian Ocean, and in Copenhagen it was now Anno Domini 1620.

18

The Days Grow Longer

I

From the journal of Jens Munk:
The 1st of January being New Year's Day, there was a fearsome
sharp frost, and I caused the men to be given two jars of wine
to each watch over their daily allowance, so that they might
make merry therewith. And there was that same day clear
sunshine, and the most severe frost came always from the
northwest. In these days we had the sharpest frost it had been
during the whole winter, and that same cruel frost did then
reduce us utterly.

The 8th of January and all the past days the fearsome frost
lasted, and the weather was from the northwest and clear sunshine. This same day died one of my boatswains.

The 9th of January the men began once more to catch some
foxes and sables.

The 10th of January the ship's chaplain, Herr Rasmus Jensen,
and the ship's surgeon, Master Kasper Kaspersen, took to
their beds after having been sick for some time past, and henceforth violent sickness day by day gained the upper hand among
the company. And this same day my best cook died.

The 18th of January. All these days the weather was as mild
as could sometimes chance at this season in Denmark. On
this account all those men who were in good health were em-

ployed in the forest according to their skills, but especially in shooting, that they might shoot some grouse for the sick.

The 21st of January it was fair, clear weather and sunshine, and there was then to be found among us thirteen persons who were affected by sickness. And then, as often before, I inquired of the ship's surgeon, the aforementioned Master Kasper Kaspersen, who also lay sick unto death at this time, if he knew of any good *remedium* which might be found in his chest and which might come to the relief and assistance of the men and himself, and desired that he should reveal this to me. Thereunto he answered that he had already made use of all the many *remediis* which he had with him, and this to the best of his knowledge and as far as seemed most advisable to him, and that if God were not willing, then he knew not any other means to use to succor them.

The 23rd of January my one mate Hans Brok by name died, who toward five months' time had lain sick. That same day it was fine, fair weather and bright sunshine. Then the priest sat up in his berth and preached a sermon for the men, and that was the last sermon he made in this world.

The 25th of January. When I caused the body of my aforementioned mate, Hans Brok, to be buried, I commanded two falconets to be fired, which was the last honor I could show him at this time. Then the trunnion flew off both falconets, and he who fired them had near lost both his legs, so sore brittle was the iron from the sharp and severe frost.

The 27th of January Jens Helsing, boatswain, died. That same day my lieutenant, Movritz Stygge of gentle birth, took wholly to his bed after having been taken for some time by weakness. The same day the men had observed the tracks of five reindeer, which were harassed by a wolf, whereof the spore could also be seen, whereupon I did send a party of men after the same reindeer and wolf, with the intention to take some of them. But by reason of a great snowstorm which overtook the men, they were no longer capable of tracking the aforesaid beasts; wherefore did they return once more and got nothing.

The 2nd of February there was severe frost. Then the men who were ashore got two grouse, which were most welcome to the sick.

The 5th of February died a boatswain, Laurids Bergen by name. That same day I again sent word to the ship's surgeon, the same Master Kasper Kaspersen, with the serious exhortation that if he did know of any *remedia* and good counsel, then he should for the sake of God exert his greatest diligence, and insofar as he was himself extremely sick and weak, he should then reveal to me which means and remedies I could in any manner use for the men; whereunto he did answer now as aforesaid, that if God would not help, then he might in no wise offer counsel and assistance.

The 6th of February I went with three of the men out to the inlet, by which we had entered, to observe the condition of the ice in the sea; though we could not at this time see open water and returned to the ship in the evening.

The 10th of February. During these days the weather was somewhat mild, but there was much sickness and weakness among the men. That same day died two men, who for long had lain upon their sickbeds.

The 12th of February we caught two grouse, which were right welcome to us for the sick.

The 13th of February I did command that to every man should be given at each meal by day a gill of wine and in the mornings a whole measure of brandy over and above the ordinary allotment.

The 16th of February. All these days there was nothing save sickness and infirmity, and each day the number of sick increased apace, so that on this day there were no more than seven hale people who could fetch wood and water and do whatsoever work there fell to do aboard the ship. This same day a boatswain died, who had lain sick during the whole voyage, and truth to tell as unclean as a worthless beast.

The 17th of February died one of my people, Rasmus by name, and there were then of the men twenty persons dead. That same day we caught a hare, which was right welcome to us.

The 20th of February in the evening died the ship's chaplain, the said Herr Rasmus Jensen, who by this time had long lain sick.

The 25th day of February. In all these days occurred nothing of moment excepting the death of the lieutenant's boy, Claus by name, who had lain sick a long time. During this night the bottom of the cauldron burst asunder which was used by day to melt water, and by reason of a little water being left therein the evening beforehand, the which did freeze.

The 29th of February was so severe a frost that no one could get ashore for the purpose of fetching water or wood, but the cook had this day to take for fuel whatsoever he could obtain. Yet toward evening I put a man ashore to fetch wood. And I had this same day to attend to the galley myself, else had we nothing for food this day; for my boy had also become sick and wholly taken to his bed.

The 1st of March Jens Borringholm and Hans Skudenes died, and whereas sickness now had gained the upper hand, so that all the company for the most part lay sick, then did we experience the utmost difficulty in burying the dead.

The 4th of March the weather was mild. This day we caught five grouse out in the land, which were sore welcome to us. These I had boiled with soup and divided among the sick. Yet they could dispatch nought of the flesh, by reason of the fact that their mouths were corrupted inside by the scurvy.

271

The 8th of March died Oluf Boye, who had lain sick for nine weeks, and his corpse was buried without delay.

The 11th of March the sun entered Aries, and it was then *aequinoctium vernum*, the spring equinox, day and night of like length, and the sun rose in those parts in east-southeast and went down in west-northwest at the stroke of seven in the evening, though it was in truth not more than six o'clock by reason of the variation. That same day it was fair and mild weather; then I had all the snow cast overboard from the upper deck of the ship and all made orderly and clean. At that time I had but few to choose from who could so work.

The 21st of March. All these days the weather was changeable, sometimes fair and gentle and sometimes harsh and severe, so that it cannot readily be described. But having regard to the men, then they did all lie for the most part sick (alas), so that it was a great wretchedness and distress to see or hear them. That same day died the ship's surgeon, the aforementioned Master Kasper, and Povel Pedersen, who had lain sick for the most part since Christmas. Henceforth the sickness waxed more fierce each day, so that we who were left, suffered great hardships, before we could consign the dead to the earth.

The 24th of March. All these days it was fair and mild weather and with no frost, so that we now had fair promise that thereafter the weather would mend. Thereto was one of the men ashore, who clambered up on a high rock and saw the open water beyond the inlet, which gave us good confidence.

The 25th of March Captain Jan Olluffsen died who had lain sick for nineteen weeks. That same day it was fine weather, so that I was myself ashore and did search under the new-melted snow for cowberries (as they are called in Norway) which remained as fresh where the snow had gone as they had been during the autumn time. Yet it was needful to pluck them without delay, else did they wither at once.

The 26*th of March* it was fine weather yet again; I was ashore then and did collect a goodly quantity of berries, which I divided among the men and which were most acceptable to them and pleased them not ill.

The 27*th of March* I inspected the surgeon's chest, and what there was therein; for inasmuch as I now had no ship's surgeon, I must now manage as best I might. Yet was it a matter of no little neglect and error that there lacked some simple inventory of *medicis,* whereunto such *medicamenta* were serviceable, and how they might be employed. And I am full sure, and would venture my life thereon, that there were to be found diverse species in the aforementioned surgeon's chest which mine own surgeon knew not. Even less did he understand their application or their employment. For all the names were written in Latin, of which he had but little while alive; but whenever he desired to inspect any bottle or receptacle while he was alive, then must the chaplain read for him the inscription thereon.

The 29*th of March.* All these days the weather was full mild, and that same day died Ismael Abrahamsen and Christen Gregersen, whose dead bodies were also buried that same day, as well as did permit those conditions and abilities, which were then to hand.

The 30*th of March* there was a sharp frost. The same day died Svend Arvedsen, ship's carpenter. At this time my greatest distress and misery began, and I was then like a wild and forlorn bird. Now had I myself to run about in the ship and give the sick to drink and to prepare drinks for them and procure for them what did seem most beneficial, which I was not wont to do and had thereof but scant understanding.

The 31*st of March* died my second mate Johan Petersen, who had lain sick for a long time.

The 1*st of April* my poor nephew, Erik Munk, died. And

273

Johan Petersen's and his bodies were placed together in one grave.

The 3rd of April was a fearsome frost, so that none of us could expose ourselves for the cold. Nor had I anyone to dispose over, for now did they all lie under the hand of God, so that a great distress and misery was upon us. The same day Iver Alsing died.

The 4th of April. Now it was such severe and hard weather, nor was it possible for any man to come ashore and dig a grave for the bodies of the dead which were then on the ship.

The 5th of April died Christoffer Opslø and Rasmus Clemmensen, my master gunner and his mate. The same day toward evening my chief boatswain, Lauritz Hansen by name, died. And there was now so small a number of healthy folk, that we were scarce able to bury the bodies of the dead.

The 8th of April died William Gordon, my best pilot, who for long had lain sick. The same day toward evening Anders Sodens died; and his and the aforesaid William Gordon's bodies were buried together in one grave, which we who still were in life did bring about only with the utmost difficulty by reason of the grievous weakness which was among us. Nor was there anyone with such vigor and strength, that they could go into the forest and collect wood, by reason whereof we were in need in these days to seek out in the ship as much wood as might be found, and when that was burned up, we had need to take our cutter for burning.

The 10th of April died the honorable and well-born Movritz Stygge, my lieutenant, who had long been sick. And I took of mine own linen and wrapped him in the best I could. And it was only with great difficulty that I could make a coffin for him.

The 12th of April it was fine sunshine with some rain, then it had not rained in this land for seven months. That same day we did convey the lieutenant's body onto the land and with that opportunity which was then to hand was it well placed in the earth.

The 13th of April I took a bath in a wine butt, which I had made ready therefor, and used therein all manner of herbs, which we found in the surgeon's chest and might be serviceable. Thereafter were my men also in the bath, as many of them as could stir themselves somewhat and were not too much weak, which bath did please sore well, God be praised, and myself best of all.

The 14th of April was a sharp frost, and that same day there were but four besides myself, who could suffer to sit upright and then to hear the Good Friday sermon.

The 16th of April, being Easter Day. Then Anders Oroust and Jens Bødker died, who had long lain sick, and as the weather now was somewhat mild, I did get their bodies buried. That same day I made my boatswain to captain, though he was sick, so that he might help me somewhat, as much as his strength allowed. For I was then myself so wretched and so forsaken by the whole world, as any man might suppose. Thereafter in the night died Hans Bendtsen.

The 17th of April died my boy Oluf Andersen, who had served me well and true during seven years.

The 19th of April died Peder Amundsen, who had long lain sick and was quite wasted away.

The 20th of April was fine sunshine weather, wherefore a part of the sick crept up from their berths that they might warm themselves against the sun. But by reason that they were so very feeble, some of them did swoon, so that it became them but ill. And I had sufficient to do with them before I could get each to his berth again. That same day toward evening we did get two black grouse, which were extremely needful to us, that we might obtain something fresh to sustain ourselves with, which sustenance happened by the particular providence of God, for of the salt food they could dispatch but little, excepting alone the soup.

The 22nd of April in the afternoon I caused a bath to be prepared, wherein we all as many as were in possession of such strength that we could stir us, bathed ourselves, and it became us well.

The 24th of April died Oluf Sundmør, who was the boatswain's mate.

The 25th of April the gray geese began to arrive, which caused us to rejoice, in the hope that summer was now near to hand. But in this hope we were mistaken, for the cold lasted much longer.

The 27th of April there was a sharp night frost and southerly wind. The cold which came in these days did reduce us utterly and caused us great injury and infirmity. The same day died Halvord Brønnie, who had lain sick more than two months, and I buried his corpse only with great labor.

The 28th of April Morten Nielsen and Thor Tønsberg died. And it was with great difficulty that we four persons, who were still astir, could bury their bodies.

The 3rd and 4th of May. During all these days no one came out of his berth excepting me and the undercook, who were still some little able. On the last aforementioned day died Anders Marstrand and Morten Marstrand, who had long lain sick.

The 6th of May John Watson, the English mate, died, who was the fourth mate I had. These bodies lay for some days, because it was such a severe and sharp frost that none of us three poor humans, who were yet able, could help to inter their corpses.

The 7th of May the weather turned somewhat milder. Then we did succeed in burying the bodies of the dead. Yet by reason of our great infirmity it was so difficult for us that we could not otherwise consign the dead bodies to the earth, than by dragging them on a little sled, which was otherwise used to drag wood with in winter.

The 10th of May. During the past days there was indeed most severe cold and frost, which occasioned us thereto the most extreme debilitation and hurt; but on this day it was fine, mild weather, and then did the geese come again, full many. And we caught one of them, wherein we had sufficient for two meals. At this time we were eleven persons alive.

The 11th of May it was most severe cold, so that we on this day all lay still in our berths. For by reason of our extreme weakness we could in no wise endure the cold, so utterly were our members reduced and broken by it.

The 12th of May Jens Jørgensen, carpenter, and Svend Marstrand died. Only God may know what misery we suffered before we buried their bodies. And these were the last to be buried in the earth.

The 16th of May it was a fearsome cold. Then died Captain Jens Hendriksen, and his corpse must needs lie unburied.

The 19th of May Erik Hansen died, who had been most industrious and active throughout the whole voyage, nor had he incurred the wrath of the humblest person or been deserving of any punishment. And he had then digged so many graves for other persons, and now was there no man who could help him to earth, but he must lie unburied.

The 20th of May it was fair, mild weather and south wind, and it was for us a sore affliction, that there was such surfeit of God's gifts of diverse birds, and yet was none of our number so strong as could go out in the land to shoot any of them.

The 21st of May was clear and fine sunshine, and it was with extreme labor that I with three others went ashore and built a fire and smeared our joints with bear-fat, and I came ashore again in the evening with one other.

The 22nd of May it was such fair and warm sunshine, as could be desired of God. And by the providence of God there came a goose close by the ship, whereof the leg had been shot off three or four days before. This we did seize and cook, whereof we had sustenance for two days. Concerning the birds which are in this region, there were come in the course of eight days all kinds, and in particular all manner of geese, swans, ducks, terns, lapwings from the south, swallows, snipe, which are good and edible birds, gulls, falcons, ravens, grouse, and eagles.

The 28th of May. During these days there was little of moment to record, save that we seven wretched persons who still remained alive, observed one another with distress and awaited each day that the snow should be thawed and the ice gone. Having regard to the *symptomata* and condition wherewith we were afflicted, it was a strange and remarkable sickness; for all the members and joints were shrunken so sorrowfully, with great spasms in the loins, as were a thousand knives stuck through them, and the body was as blue and brown as a bruised eye, and the whole form was utterly without strength. And the condition of the mouth was ill and wretched, for all the teeth were loose, so that we could not dispatch any *victualis*. During the days when we lay so sick in bed, Peder Nyborg, carpenter, Knud Lauritzen, boatswain, and Jørgen, cook's boy, died, who all remained lying in the poop, for there was no one who could bury their corpses or cast them overboard.

The 4th of June being Whitsunday there were but three others and myself now alive, and the one lay and could not help the other. The stomach was ready and had appetite for victuals; but the teeth could not dispatch it, nor was there any of us so strong as could go out into the hold for to fetch us a drink of wine. The cook's boy lay dead beside my berth, and three men lay dead in the poop, and two men were on the land, who desired to be in the ship again; but it was not possible for them to come inboard, for they had not strength sufficient in their limbs to help themselves up into the ship. Both they and I lay languishing, by reason we had now since four whole days received naught for the sustenance of the body, so that I awaited nothing more than that God would make an end to my wretchedness and take me unto His Kingdom. And believing this to be the last which I should write in this world, I set down the following document:

> Since I no longer have any hopes of living, I can only pray to God that we may be found by some good Christians and that for God's sake they will cause my poor corpse together with the others to be buried in the earth, receiving their reward from God in Heaven, and that this my account be given unto my Gracious Lord and King (for every word herein is altogether true), so that some good may arise unto my poor wife and children out of my great hardship and sorry departure. Herewith, I say good-bye to the world and give my soul into God's keeping.
>
> JENS MUNK

2

From the journal of Ove Giedde for the same period:

The 5th of January we perceived the mainland of Africa, wherefor we changed course and headed for open sea.

The 10th of January it was ordained that each man be given four pounds of bread per week and one and a half quarter-pounds of dried cod per day, and that in accordance with the navigator's opinion we should run with a southeasterly and south-southeasterly course 150 miles by sea.

The 7th February it was ordained that no one might gamble or play doubles either within or without the quarters under forfeiture of three months' pay. And whosoever was found wholly or part drunk, then to lose one month's pay, and in addition thereto to lose his ration for eight days.

The 13th of February. Some few of the petty officers from the "Copenhagen" were transferred to the other ships, by reason of the ship's council's assertion, accusing them of revolt.

The 7th of March it was ordained that whosoever was found asleep on watch should forfeit his ration for three days and be flogged by the men of the watch, and whosoever neglected his whole watch should lose a month's pay and be flogged by the whole ship's company.

The 9th of March it was publicly proclaimed on the ship "Elephant" that all, both petty officers and ratings, should obey the ship's officers without question.

The 10th of March we perceived a sailing ship, which we pursued as best we could, but he escaped in the dark. The cause of this our seeking after him was that a part of our navigators believed us to be off the coast of Abyssinia, a part off Manales, and a part off Cape Comorin, and we hoped to obtain thereby certain knowledge from the aforesaid sailing ship.

The 13th of March it was ordained that whichsoever of us did discover any ships in the sea, should make after them and bring them to the Admiral.

The 27th of March it was ordained that Herman Rosenkrantz should defend himself against the judge-advocate's accusations and produce his accounts, and that all the presidents and the ship's counsellors should observe the regulations with diligence.

The 30th of March we sighted the island of Socotra.

The 31st of March in the morning we lost contact with the ship "Copenhagen," but at nine of the clock in the evening it came to the fleet again.

The 1st of April the ship "Christian" was far from us, wherefor I sailed toward him, in order to assemble the fleet. But the "Copenhagen" and the "Patientia" had meanwhile changed course for land without signal. Wherefor did I signal at nine of the clock that they should come to the Admiral, which order the "Patientia" obeyed and changed course, but the "Copenhagen" sailed landward letting the fleet out of sight thereby without any command.

The 3rd of April. After we had recovered the ship "Christian" it was commanded that whosoever of the ship's counsellors remarked during their watch that any of the ships had happened to depart from the fleet, they should then notify their ship's council thereof, and should cause to be recorded in the book in the aforesaid place, the reason wherefor this did. occur.

The 20th April it was ordained that if any ship be observed in the sea, then should the "Patientia" employ the utmost energy to overhaul it.

The 9th of May we sighted a frigate with schuit sail, the which did come wholly near to us, whereupon I caused the white flag to be run up, that it should come to us. But thereupon it ran from us, wherefor I caused a piece to be fired after it. Later there came another vessel, keeping the wind aft and sailing toward the "Patientia," which ship was a little ahead. And when he was come quite near, as he would talk with him, he fired two pieces and showed a white cloth. But when he had passed the ship, he showed a red cloth and went his way. And when I saw that they had the advantage of us in sailing, we went our way again.

The 10th of May we found the bottom at 50 fathoms off the coast of Malabar, though we did not remain there.

The 16th of May IN THE MORNING WE PERCEIVED WITH GREAT JOY THE PROMISED LAND OF CEYLON.

The 18th of May in the evening we anchored off Ceylon in bad weather, at a place which the inhabitants call Panva.

The 20th of May I issued an order that all, whosoever they might be in the fleet, high or low, should regulate themselves in every wise in accordance with the Ordinances of His Royal Majesty, and that the officers should permit neither themselves nor others to depart from the ships, unless they be so commanded, and should transgress no such command, as had happened hitherto to sufficiency, under forfeiture of life and honor.

The 22nd of May there came three black people on board who would take us below Palligame, off which we anchored for the night.

The 23rd of May we sent three boats ashore to negotiate the supply of nuts and fresh provisions for the fleet.

The 24th of May the mate of the "Copenhagen" came to us and related (1) that both the "David" and the "Copenhagen" lay but three miles distant, which we could well enough see, and which were come together in the sea off Ceylon. (2) That Marselis de Boshouwer and his son had departed hence by death eight months ago, in Stephen von Hagen's Bay, where the "David" had taken on fresh supplies.

The 2nd of June we anchored with the fleet off the King of Cotiaram's Land, where we dispatched one of our company on land without delay, there to seek the mate of the sloop who was believed to be there on the land.

The 4th of June (Whitsunday) the mate of the sloop came with three letters, which informed us of the Naik's good affection, of the state of trade in Ceylon, and that a bar of pepper, which is 480 pounds, can be bought for 24 dollars.

The 5th of June it was ordained that we should sail with the first wind into the Gulf of Trincomalee.

Contemporary map of Ceylon with the goal of Ove Giedde's expedition, the Gulf of Trincomalee. (*Die orientalische Indien*)

282

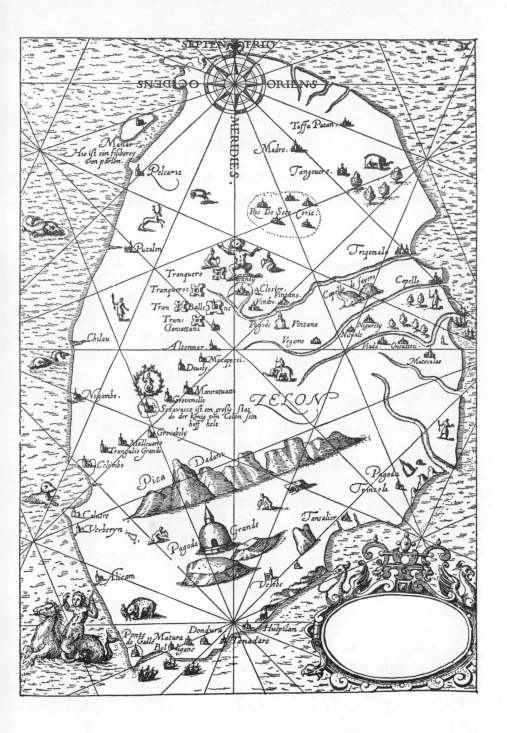

SEPTENTRIO

OCCIDENS

ORIENS

MERIDIES

Manar
Hie ist ein fischerey
von parlen.

Taffe Patan.

Madre.

Pelcare.

Tangouere.

Res De Sete Corie.

Putalon.

Trigomal.

Tranquero.
Tranqueros.
Tran: Balle nc
Tran: Caniattani

Cindo.
Closter.
Vintano.
Vendro.

Capello de Sayero.

Capello.

Pagode Vintano.

Chilau.

Altonner.

Vegame.

Negurety.
Nilgale.
Viada.
Oncattoti.

Matecalao.

Macappti.
Druely.

Neŋombo.

Manratuatto.
Grovenelle.
Sytavacco ist ein grosse stat,
do der König von Celon sein
hoff helt.

ZELON

Grovabely.
Malcuato.
Trangulio Grando.
Colombo.

Pica

Dadare.

Pagoda Trinpola.

Cakare.
Verberyn.

Pagoda Grande

Tansalier.

Alicam.

Velebe.

Ponte de Galle.
Matura
Bellilganc

Dondura.
Tanadare.

Hulpilan.

19

The Lamprey

The great race was at an end, and the noblemen had won. The day after Jens Munk wrote his testament, Ove Giedde sailed into the Gulf of Trincomalee, Ceylon. At the same time Christian IV sat at home in South Jutland gambling away the future of his country over a game of double with Robert Anstruther, the English plenipotentiary instructed to persuade him to join in the wars of religion, a mission which he accomplished to perfection. June 4, 1620, was a fateful Whitsunday morning.

Although the Council of the Realm had rejected the King's war plans, he felt himself sufficiently strong to prepare for an intervention in Germany; likewise he was convinced that his expeditions aimed at world-wide colonization had succeeded. He had read Ove Giedde's account of the successful outcome of the battle with pirates at Cape Verde; and from the letters brought by English ships to Copenhagen he might infer that the squadron had long since rounded the Cape of Good Hope. It was only a question of time before his admiral reached Ceylon and established a monopoly over the mountains of spices, pearls, and ivory which Boshouwer had spoken about.

That Captain Munk had discovered and sailed through the Anian Strait, and was now bound for China under full sail— this also the King regarded as assured. Had things been otherwise, he reflected, then the *Unicorn* and the *Lamprey* would have returned to Copenhagen long ago. As spring went by and Munk did not appear, the conjecture that he had made the great discovery turned into official fact. On April 24th, the day after Robert Anstruther had dined with the King, an experienced English observer, John Chamberlain, wrote to Sir Dudley Carleton at The Hague: "There is speach here that the King of Denmark hath discouered the North-West Passage by the meane of an English pilote."

There is also speech that the Danish King has concluded a pact of friendship with the Emperor of Ceylon. There is speech that the Danish King will crush the Catholic Emperor in Germany. There is so much speech and for so long that it is finally believed; and it is believed for so long that it finally becomes fact; and it is the King himself who says, believes, and knows it all before anyone else. Christian IV is the greatest King in the north, and on this Whitsunday morning fortune smiles down upon him in the east, in the west, and in the south. He can well give a rose noble to his parish priest, for has not the Lord already promised him the whole round earth? He believed in the future, but the future did not believe in him. He allowed Anstruther to lead him by the nose, and the road to the south ended at the massacre of Lutter am Barenberge. He allowed Boshouwer to lead him by the nose, and the roads to the east and west also had bloody endings.

Things went best for Ove Giedde. He had suffered enormous losses, but his ships had reached Ceylon. Even the two deserters of the voyage—the *Copenhagen*, which Erik Grubbe had sailed to Socotra, and the *David*, which had disappeared off Madagascar—now lay rocking in the Gulf of Trincomalee; and to cap it all there was news of Boshouwer's death. Soon, however, it became clear that the envoy's version of conditions on the island bore no relation to reality. The Emperor had long since made his peace with the Portuguese, whose position was now so dominant that Ove Giedde had no possible chance of success. The Emperor declared that Boshouwer's "authority" was nothing more than a forgery and declined to recognize the

Christian den Fjerdes haandskrift. (Rigsarkivet).

Christian IV's handwriting. (National Archives)

"treaty of friendship" that the swindler had signed in his name. Finally Ove Giedde was compelled to give way and transfer his attention to the mainland, where another Dutchman, Crappé, had discovered a tiny principality on the Coromandel Coast that desired to engage in trade with Denmark. Here an agreement was successfully concluded with the local prince which gave the Danes the right to establish a fortress on the spot. In the nick of time. Already Ove Giedde and Crappé were deadly enemies, and the former had completely lost control over his company. Men deserted every day; there were repeated mutinies, and valuable cargoes and a whole ship were lost. The East India Company had secured a foothold in India, but almost a hundred years were to elapse before the trade down there paid its way. No matter how large the sums of money the King pumped into the undertaking, it could not compete with the Dutch; goods shipped home by the company could always be bought more cheaply in Hamburg. After fifteen years the organization went bankrupt; there were corruption and fraud, the accounts were in disorder, and everything was in a state of confusion.

The Danish colony Ove Giedde had founded was certainly no empire, nor were there mountains of spices, pearls, and ivory to be found. In fact it consisted of one dirty little fishing village, and as this was situated near a heavy line of breakers, the Indians had given it the name "Place of the Breakers," which in Tamil is called "Taragambadi." But this was too difficult to pronounce back in Copenhagen; there they just said "Tranquebar."

Though the result of Ove Giedde's year of effort might seem poor, his disappointment was as nothing in comparison with what was happening at Hudson Bay.

2

The Whitsuntide sun settled matters. As the captain sat in the cabin aft on the *Unicorn* writing his farewell message to the world, the snow on the southern side of the promontory was melting. During the night the frost returned, and a dying wail escaped the white Minotaur; but this was as naught compared with the roars which had sounded out there in the long winter nights, as the fissures raced across from shore to shore. The wind now veered to south; there were days with drizzle and fog, the air was filled with the smell of earth, the ice took on a glazed look like the eyes of dead sailors, and when the sun broke through again it shone down upon a landscape glistening with moisture and turning green under the clear sky.

In the midst of all this splendor Munk Haven lay forsaken. Not a soul was to be seen near the two ships; but gradually as the snow melted away, traces of the winter events were revealed. All around on the ice and ashore, scattered items of equipment came into view: a broken cask and a mildewed awning, a piece of cordage, a shoe, a rusty knife. The sun shone warm; on the high ground a sled with firewood stood casually stranded, its runners on the green earth. New formations of wild geese flew over the spot; seen from their viewpoint, it must have resembled a vast playground, where the children had hurriedly cast everything aside to run off somewhere else. The rigging on the ships hung in tatters after the winter storms; the polar bears had rooted in the graves of the dead. As long as the frost persisted the corpses had been as hard as stone; now they too thawed. Spring had come.

Jens Munk's journal contains no entries for the days immediately after June 4th. The captain lay in his berth with the fur rug over him; the sailmaker was dying; everything was at an end. He had nothing more to write. In this way Monday passed, then Tuesday, then Wednesday. On the morning of Thursday, June 8th, however, he took out the book with the parchment cover once more: "As I could no longer bear the stench and evil odors from the dead bodies, which had long lain in the ship, I took myself as best I could out of the berth, for there was no longer doubt that God in His fatherly beneficence would continue to spare my life, and being of the opinion, that it mattered but little where or on which spot I died, whether it be among the others who lay dead without, or whether I remain lying in my berth. And when I therefore was come out of the cabin with God's help, I made shift on the upper deck that night with the clothes of the dead."

Jens Munk had been ashore previously on May 21st, when

he had had three men with him. On their return two of them had been too weak to clamber aboard the *Unicorn* and had had to drag themselves back to the shore instead. Now nearly three weeks had passed, and for some time the captain had given them up for lost. But this was not so; they were still alive. And when on June 9th they saw someone moving about on the deck of the *Unicorn* hope revived within them and they staggered out. Jens Munk writes: "The day following, when the two men who were on the shore saw me, saw that I still lived, they made their way out on the ice toward the ship and helped me off the ship and into the land with the clothes which I cast down to them. And on the shore under a bush we had our dwelling place for a time and made a fire for ourselves by day. And at last we crept all about, wherever we saw the slightest green growing and coming out of the earth, which we digged up and sucked the very root thereof."

Starting again from the very bottom, crawling around on all fours like an animal, rooting about in the earth with nailless fingers to find roots—in this way the days passed. In the course of the winter Jens Munk had seen strong men faint and burst into tears, but the three survivors ashore did not weep; they scarcely spoke to one another. They, as Hans Brok before them, had seen too much, the cat-and-mouse game had been played with them for too long. Their mouths looked as if they had drunk corrosive acid; but also their feelings, even their self-pity, had been eaten away. They had reached the absolute bottom, that firm ground of reality which spurs life on, the original basis of existence, unalloyed suffering.

Munk had felt that spur on the many occasions when he had found himself at the bottom of the ladder, only to throw himself into new enterprises. Now the same thing was happening on the little hill at Munk Haven. His idea of combating scurvy with the aid of fresh green plants again produced results. In spite of their apathy, things began to look up for the three survivors. There were certainly not many bilberries and cowberries, but he got the men to suck at plant roots, "and thereafter we began to feel well," he writes in his journal, "and the warmth commenced to increase apace, so that it began to be better with us."

These are the first words in the journal indicative of progress. Ten days now passed without any new entries. But on June 18th the ice broke up in the fjord, the tide returned, and once more the landscape lay there, changing mood beneath the sun and the stars. The three men on the hummock had now regained their strength to such an extent that they could more or less keep upright, and Jens Munk had perceived at once the potentialities of the new situation: "As the ice left the ship, we procured a flounder net in the sloop; then we went dry-shod to the water and set it at one quarter ebb tide. And when the tide now came again, God gave us six sea trout, which I cooked myself, and the other two went into the 'Lamprey' to fetch wine, which we had not now tried for a long time, for the reason that none of us had had the appetite therefor."

The sun shone, smoke rose into the air from the captain's fire, the trout simmered in the iron pot, and up the hill came the other two with a wine cask between them. Fish soup and white wine—it sounded almost like a banquet, and the guest was Life, who had returned once more: "As we thus caught fresh fish daily now, and it was well cooked, for we could eat naught of the fish saving soup, and drank wine thereto, it refreshed us, so that little by little things improved with us. And later we got a musket ashore and shot birds and arrived at so good a state of refreshment, that we daily grew stronger and day by day our condition became somewhat more tolerable."

As their strength gradually returned, Munk reviewed the situation. He could see how serious it was. What was the good of having saved themselves if they could not get away from the place? The summer was short, and a new winter meant certain death. They were in the midst of a barren, unknown continent, and any thought of relief was out of the question. They had to leave. It must be done quickly, and with their own resources.

They still had two ships, but the *Unicorn* must be discounted at once, for three people had no earthly chance of hauling the large frigate from the dry ground, let alone maneuvering it in the open sea. But the *Lamprey* was a different proposition; if they unloaded the goods and ballast from it, they might refloat the ship with the aid of the tide and a cable out to the *Unicorn*. When they had first sailed, it was manned by sixteen men, who were in pretty poor shape when they arrived in September. Now there were only three poor specimens; one only had to look at their hands, devastated by scurvy and frostbite, and try to imagine them gripping the wet ropework, month after month in the ice of Hudson Bay and the North Atlantic storms. Munk realized that their chances of reaching home were slender, but they had no alternative. On June 26th, eight days after the ice had broken up, he quietly informed the other two of his intention to put to sea in the *Lamprey* and sail to Copenhagen.

"In the name of Jesus, after prayers and calling upon God for fortune and good counsel, we commenced to bring the 'Lamprey' alongside the 'Unicorn' and make ourselves seaworthy, as diligently as we could. Yet it seemed to us a great torment, and our affliction was great, for the 'Lamprey' was set high on the shore by the winter tide, wherefore we must first of all discharge everything which was within, and then bide our time for a high spring tide, that we might succeed in getting it out."

The work lasted for more than two weeks. The three men, who shortly before could scarcely stand on their feet, dragged crates, cannon balls, anchors, and ballast stones up from the hold, laid out planks, dug tree trunks under the keel as rollers, toiled with levers, and hauled for their very lives on the taut lines. Their toil was in vain, however; the heavy wooden ship did not move an inch nearer the water, and there was no other hope than that the sea itself would come and fetch it. The captain suspended the work and impatiently followed the waxing of the moon. Finally, one evening, it hung like a great red lantern above the low rocks near the inlet; and the spring tide came. During the days it lasted, the three men worked like madmen, day and night, with bloody hands and in mud up to the knees. Finally, on the afternoon of the third day the *Lamprey* began to float. Suddenly the ship appeared weightless; a push with the shoulder sufficed. Now it was as light and restless and graceful as it had been awkward and immovable a few minutes before. For the first time in all those many months the men heard again that gurgling sound along the water line, which is the same on all ships, at all times, and in all four quarters of the world, the alluring song of freedom: The world is yours, if you dare!

Now it was a small matter to restow the ballast and anchor the ship. In good spirits Jens Munk went around apportioning the tasks. From the moment he set foot on the ship's deck, the little man was no longer "a wild and forsaken bird"; his authority and grasp of events had returned. Hundreds of details caught his attention: the sails were dragged out and laid to dry in the sun and repaired with the sailmaker's needle; ropework was renewed and spliced, rigging overhauled in all details. And when all running and fixed rigging had been put in the best possible order, he went around contriving such modifications as would make the ship easier to handle for the small crew. Summertime came and the season of departure; the slate-gray shadows of the clouds glided over the fjord, the salt-water breeze from the sea reached the crew, who sat barefoot on the plank deck, working amid the smell of sun-warmed canvas and tarred ropes. "At this time it was as warm on land as might be in Denmark, and the cloudberries were in bud, and there was such a host of midges that it was scarce possible to expose oneself when the weather was still," it says in the journal.

But when the ship was ready to sail a week later, there still remained one task which had been consistently shelved from day to day. When the winter mooring had been established the previous autumn, the supplies in the *Lamprey* had been transferred to the *Unicorn*; and in order to have provender for the voyage a great deal of these stores now had to be brought back. That this had not been done long ago was not due solely to the fact that they had food enough with their sea trout and wild geese. None of them had the courage to go on board the big ship, standing grim and lifeless in its dock with its sorry list and dangling rigging. Out there still lay the six dead, whom no one had had the strength to bury: Captain Jens Hendriksen, Erik Hansen of Fyn, the carpenter Peder Nyborg, the boatswain Knud Lauritzen, the cook's boy and the sailmaker. The first of these had died on May 16th, almost two months ago. They had all looked grim enough while still alive, and the thought of the sight which awaited the survivors in the abandoned ship was sufficient to make them postpone the victualing until the last moment.

The work had to be done, however, and Munk was an honest man; nor could he neglect to describe in the journal how it was done. "Whereas we must finally remove from the 'Unicorn' and into the 'Lamprey' such *victualia* and other necessities, whereover we three persons could dispose and regulate, to assist our passage across the sea, we brought the 'Lamprey' alongside the 'Unicorn.' And when we were come into the 'Unicorn,' we could not stir ourselves to execute our work therein on account of ill-smell and stench, but we must first cast out the dead bodies, which then were quite putrefied." Afterward, at low tide, Munk went down to the bed of the fjord and bored three holes in the side of the ship. He hoped that the water which would fill the ship at high tide would hold it firm in the dock, when the winter ice-drift began once more. Nevertheless, this was also a piece of work he had put off until the last moment. He had just saved one of the ships, now he was scuttling the other.

Then everything was ready, with the sails furled and the ship's dog piped on board. The only thing left to wait for was Sunday. And finally this came, too, but how different it was from the Sunday when they had left Copenhagen! There were no spectators, no trumpeters; the three men stood on deck with bared heads and sang a psalm. Then the anchor was weighed: "The 16th of July, which fell on a Sunday, in the afternoon, we sailed from there, and I have called this Haven after myself."

That name was their farewell. With the captain himself at the helm and the dinghy from the *Unicorn* in tow, the *Lamprey* slid out toward the mouth of the fjord. A westerly afternoon breeze filled the sails, the landscape was in its most benevolent mood; they sailed at high water, and the blue fjord stretched right up to the piece of high ground where the men lay buried. Nothing remained of them but the long streaks in the grass at the foot of the wooden crosses. The sun was low in the west, and when the *Lamprey* rounded the promontory it looked for a moment as if the many parallel shadows reached out toward the water with one final burst of strength. But then they disappeared behind the promontory. Jens Munk reached the mouth of the fjord and stood out in Hudson Bay.

3

Astern in the sunset lay Nova Dania. Although the land was colonized only by the dead, who were never relieved, it remained under their dominion in a certain sense for over a hundred years. The frigate *Unicorn* was soon lost; the water which Munk let into it on his departure had the opposite of the desired effect; the freezing process during the following winter caused the ship's hull to split, and when summer returned the tidal waters twice a day levered away every piece of wood and carried it off with the current. For a long time the Indian tribes were held at a distance from the rich booty by the sight of so many corpses, and when they finally got up courage and broke into the carpenter's wooden hut, they happened to ignite some gunpowder stored there, so that the whole building went up in the air. Many years later there was still fierce internecine strife over the possession of the precious

294

iron objects. The dead inhabitants of Nova Dania continued to defend their territory. When the Frenchman Nicolas Jérémie, one of the first white men after Jens Munk to come to these parts approximately a century later, heard these stories from the Indians, he also learned that the natives called the river Manoteousibi, "The Strangers' River." He himself dubbed it "Rivière Danoise," Danish River, a name which, like Nova Dania or Nova Dacia, was preserved on the map well into the eighteenth century, whereupon it was succeeded by "Rivière Monk" or "Munk River." When in 1717 James Knight chose to site the Hudson Bay Company's new trading post on the stretch of high ground where Jens Munk had buried his dead, he kept a journal in which his precursors are mentioned on nearly every page. The hard-bitten captain was visibly appalled by the traces of disaster that still marked the landscape even a hundred years later: "It is a poor and miserable spot," he writes on August 21st. "Fort York is bad, but this is ten times worse, for here is neither fish, fowl, nor game. Given time it will, I believe, prove to be advantageous for the Company, but it will never be good for those of its servants who must live here. We are compelled to build in a place where we cannot keep ourselves warm, for there is only lee on a sixth of the compass. Yet can I find no better place. The many graves and bones from the folk who lie buried here are a revelation of that which awaits us if we do not lay in supplies before the winter sets in. For although they were Danes and very hardy people, almost 130 of them lie buried here, and a great part of their graves lie under our building. I pray that the Lord may protect and preserve us." The Lord did not do so; what the pious Englishman saw in Munk Haven was only a forecast of the fate awaiting him. Two years later, during an attempt to find the Northwest Passage, Captain Knight ran aground on Marble Island a few hundred nautical miles to the north, and he and his crew there starved to death.

Knight's journal was never published, and after he had established the English trading station the Danish names and the site of Munk Haven gradually passed into oblivion. A town grew up on the opposite shore of the fjord and was given the name Churchill, and Danish River became Churchill River. Yet on the easterly point outside this town, where Munk never went ashore—and more than six miles from the winter harbor—there now stands a cairn with a copperplate commemorating the Danish captain. The inscription is riddled with holes and partly illegible, for some soldiers from a nearby military camp used to while away their time with shooting practice, using the copperplate as their target.

Time was to show that even after so many years Captain Munk was capable of returning the compliment in coin of somewhat larger caliber. In the summer of 1964 the Danish Memorial Expedition succeeded, as we have seen, in locating the knoll where he had buried the dead, and the anchorage on the bed of the fjord bottom where the *Unicorn* met its end: Munk Haven had been found again. During the excavations ashore many fragments of clay pipes, glass, bottles, clothes, and weapons were brought to light, though it was not possible to date them with accuracy in the majority of cases. The finds at the anchorage, however, were unambiguous: apart from the iron bar already mentioned, five of the *Unicorn*'s mooring stones and two twelve-pound cannon balls from the time of Christian IV lay here. That was Jens Munk's final salute. The finds were packed in crates, and there only remained to ship the goods out of the labyrinth and home to Denmark, a journey that did not pass off without delay, for the white Minotaur was not completely silenced.

Jens Munk's own map of his voyage. The names are written in such a way that the north faces downward. The division into degrees of latitude is lacking. In comparison with Gerritszoon's chart (cf. pp. 200-201) Hudson Bay has broadened out, the western and northern coast is outlined, but the badly overdimensioned representation of the winter haven in the south makes one dubious about the detail of the coastline, and the opening to the west represents only a last pious hope of finding the Anian Strait. (*Navigatio*)

All this, however, still belonged to the distant future that July evening when Jens Munk stood out in Hudson Bay. What were the names of the two others he had with him? His muster rolls have been lost, and we are obliged to reconstruct them with the aid of the names of the men who died at Munk Haven, and who are for the most part mentioned in the journal. So far, Jens Munk's companions on the *Lamprey* have remained unidentified. However, it ought to be possible to identify *one* of them. In his description of the recruitment of the crew at Bremerholm, Jon Olafsson mentions an able-bodied seaman by the name of Niels Skoster as one who joined Munk's expedition. As this name does not appear on the list of the dead, it may be assumed that Niels Skoster was with the *Lamprey* when the ship left Munk Haven. "A splendid man," Olafsson calls him, and he must indeed have been a splendid man to have played a third part in the ensuing story.

As soon as the day after their departure they met ice. Munk went about on another tack to try to clear it, but as is often the case there was fog near the ice, and before long they were hopelessly stuck. The *Unicorn*'s dinghy had to be abandoned and the sails taken in. The loss of the dinghy was serious; from now on they had no means of getting ashore, either in emergency or to get fresh provisions and water. Days followed without any change. On the 20th they saw a polar bear close to the stern; the ship's dog chased it but got lost in the fog and could not find its way back. "For two days thereafter we could hear him howling still," said Munk. On the 22nd gales sprang up: "The ship drifted most bitterly, and each time it hit the ice it was as if it had run against a rock. At the same time the ice smote my rudder asunder, and had I not succeeded in dropping an anchor onto a great piece of ice, so that I could turn the ship, then had both it and we been lost that same day." It took four days for the storm to disperse the ice masses so that Munk could get free and make to the east along the coast in the hope of finding a passage. However, just as once at Kildin, the ice-free margin was constantly shrinking, the lead showed ever shallower depths of water, and on the 29th he had to turn back to avoid running aground. The next day he was ice-bound again; the fog was so dense that he could not see the ship's bowsprit from his stand at the tiller. Once more a storm arose, and this saved them. Coming on August 1st, it soon blew so strong that they had to take in the foresail and drift under reefed mainsail. This time Munk sailed north along the west coast. At this point the waters are very shallow at a great distance from land; while the *Lamprey* stood to the north the lead revealed dangerously shallow water, but on this occasion Munk carried on regardless of the risk of stranding. To escape the tyranny of the ice, he would have to stake everything on one gamble. "The 5th of August in the night the ice pressed me so hard that I had to go into 12 fathoms before I could get by the hook."

Everything went well, and the next morning they had rounded the vast ice barrier which for the greater part of the summer blocks the southern part of Hudson Bay. Jens Munk now had forty-five fathoms beneath his keel and open water the whole horizon ahead. He laid his course east-northeast; the wind was westerly. On the first day they covered forty miles, the following thirty-eight, and on August 11th they saw the southern tip of Goats Island. Munk called it Cold Hook and fixed its position as 62° 30′ north, with a margin of error of only 10′. From Goats Island he continued east-northeast before a fresh breeze, and two days later they saw the northern point of Mansfield Island. As the waters here were again blocked by ice, Munk sailed to the south of the island under the foresail only and kept to the coast where the ice was thinnest. On the opposite side of the island they came out into open water once more and the same afternoon saw the Digges Islands. Here, too, the ice forced them to the south and up into the narrow waters between the islands and the mainland. The last week had brought a return of the cold and the sea was covered with new ice, but with the aid of ice anchors and poles they got the ship through. On August 16th, says Jens Munk, "I chanced into Fretum Christian or the Hudson Strait."

It sounds simple. All traces of uncertainty which had beset the navigation on the outward voyage when William Gordon was responsible were gone. An old hand in the art of navigation had taken over, with only two men at his command, and with a damaged rudder. Continually forced off course by the ice, he had guided the *Lamprey* through unfamiliar waters and found the strait which led out of the labyrinth. All his calculations of course, compass variation, drift, and distance covered had been meticulously correct; he had sighted the right islands in the right positions in the right sequence, and now he could fall off before the wind and turn into the Hudson Strait like a pedestrian turning a street corner.

It was high time. By now a month had elapsed since their departure from Munk Haven, and winter was again at hand. "There came snow, and the gray geese began to fly southward," states an entry in the logbook. Fortunately, they got the wind abaft the beam and the passage of the Hudson Strait, which the year before had occasioned them months of delay, took only two days. On August 18th they had Munkenaes to port and sailed southeast toward Cape Farewell; on the 19th they got "a strong west wind" and covered forty miles; the next day they covered thirty miles, then twenty, then thirty-six, then twenty-seven. As on the outward journey, the waters were filled with icebergs; there were strong winds, and ceaseless use of the pump was causing it to leak. In the ships of that time the pump barrel consisted only of a hollowed-out tree trunk which was difficult to repair once it had cracked. Munk had a lashing put around it, so that it became largely watertight, and in this way they succeeded in reaching a position south of Cape Farewell on the evening of August 24th. But just at this point, when they were about to leave the Northwest Passage and run into the Atlantic Ocean, it was as if the white Minotaur stretched out an arm after them and held them back. The wind dropped, and soon there was dead calm.

While the mainsail flapped idly, the three men got a few days' rest. After a month at sea, living on salt provisions and with their clothes frozen stiff, scurvy had returned; their gums and fingertips had begun to bleed again; they got little sleep, no warm food, and after a while they felt too fatigued to go on working the sheets and sails. They lay down on the deck of the *Lamprey* and licked their wounds; after the dry arctic climate of the Northwest Passage the damp air of the Atlantic seemed like an unexpected reminder of home. The sea lay peaceful in the haze, with not a ripple on the water; the smooth swell rose and fell like billowing gray silk; to the north Cape Farewell showed indistinctly like a ragged ruin at the end of a barren plain. Everything was still—a mood that extended even to the entries in the captain's logbook. On August 25th dead calm. On August 26th dead calm. On August 27th dead calm. Tradition has it that it takes three days. Next morning the hurricane struck them.

4

A long time after these events, in the night between September 15th and 16th, 1964, another Danish vessel, the cargo boat *Vinland* of Copenhagen, sailed from Munk Haven. The lights of the ship slid over the bell buoy lying in the ink-black water to the starboard and marking the submerged rocks in the entrance to the fjord. Then two blasts were sounded on the ship's siren and were echoed a couple of notes higher by the tug; the pilot disembarked, and the *Vinland* steamed into Hudson Bay.

They were on the *Lamprey* course, but the vessel was not the *Lamprey*. The *Lamprey* did not have a double radar installation, and Decca gyrocompass; it did not have a plant that converted sea water to fresh water at the rate of ten tons a day; it did not consume Diesel oil to the value of $600 every twenty-four hours, and it had neither library, recreation room, nor movies for the crew. And yet history establishes a con-

301

nection between the two ships. Apart from 18,700 tons of Canadian wheat, the *Vinland* also had on board the crates of the Danish Memorial Expedition with the finds from Munk Haven. After a lapse of 344 years, Jens Munk's cannon balls were being sailed home under the Danish flag.

The weather was calm and the fairway free of ice. On the 17th at noon Mansfield Island suddenly appeared ahead—flat, clay-colored, without a blade of grass, without a bird. A few hours later the Digges Islands lay to starboard with snow on the slopes of the high rocks whose peaks were hidden in cloud. Then the automatic pilot was adjusted slightly and the *Vinland* glided into Hudson Strait. Next day the first icebergs floated on the water like distant, solitary cathedrals illuminated by the sun. "Behind them howl the wolves," it said on the crew's notice board, but this was no reference to the white Minotaur; it was only the title of the evening's movie. When the performance was over at midnight, and one went up into the wheelhouse, where the third mate stood alone in the dark with his pipe and his coffee cup, Resolution Island was to port. The moon was up, but the water lay covered by a low sea fog, so that the island could not be seen by the naked eye. When the radar was tuned in, however, the island came through clearly. Indeed, in this case it was as though this wonderful instrument could see not only through the fog but also some way back into the past. Each time the white streak of light swept like a second hand over the screen and outlined the island, one could clearly see a sharply delineated point to the southeast; this was Munkenaes.

Two days later in the afternoon we sighted Greenland at Cape Farewell. It was September 20th. Jens Munk lay off here with the *Lamprey* on August 27th, but if one takes account of the difference of ten days in the calendar, it is not unreasonable to suppose that the two ships left the Northwest Passage on about the same date. The icebergs had now become less numerous, though there were many flat ice floes, particularly dangerous at night since the radar cannot detect them.

During the day the barometer had fallen from 1020 to 1003 millibars, and the gale warning on the evening weather forecast surprised no one. After sunset the wind shifted to northeast and increased to force 11 in the course of a few hours. The seas struck the bows before the beam, and soon it was as if the whole Arctic Ocean were on the move down through Denmark Strait with the sole objective of casting itself upon the lonely ship. The *Vinland* reared up with its 18,700 tons of wheat, as if it were taking off from this earth for good and all, and then finally descended, endlessly, through empty space, until there was an ear-splitting crash, as though it had struck a rock bed.

A heavy sea filled the wing of the bridge on the port side fifty feet above the water line, flung open the sliding door, gushed into the wheelhouse, soaked the second mate, and went on through the charthouse and down the vinyl-covered stairs. The ship shuddered violently from stem to stern, the hurricane howled an extra note higher, the air was thick with foam, and wave after wave came rolling along at masthead height and tossed itself over the hatches. The patent log was lost; the spare log was streamed and lost. Massive, bolted iron plates, intended to protect the valves of the automatically operated hatches, were bent like cardboard and torn off. Like a waterlogged plank, the long steel ship lay awash in the seas. Below this mountainous seascape lay the motorship *Hans Hedtoft* of Copenhagen, a brand-new ship fully equipped with modern aids, which had disappeared with ninety-five souls on board. And here, many years earlier, but in the same position and in a similar hurricane, there wallowed a slender, single-masted, and partly open wooden ship, without wheelhouse, without technical aids beyond a split pump, manned by three men weakened by scurvy—and came through.

How did it happen? The information in Munk's logbook is laconic, and with good reason. To start with, the calm weather on August 29th was followed by a fresh northwest wind, so they were able to set a course east by north. But after some hours' sailing the wind veered to the north and increased to such force that they had to take in the sails. At the same time the pump sprang a leak again, and for two days the men worked in water up to their waists to keep the ship afloat. On the 31st they tried to set a storm sail, but it had to be taken down again. The hurricane continued to grow in fury; the men could no longer keep upright on deck and lashed themselves fast to avoid being washed overboard. All deck cargo was cut adrift and chests and bedding went floating by. A topcoat was swept away across the sea with outspread arms like a drowned sailor. The hurricane lasted for seven days and six nights; only on the evening of September 4th did the wind begin to drop, after the rain had lashed down the whole day. But now the three men were too exhausted to resume sailing. "For the reason that we were full spent from the pumping, we drifted the whole night without sail, in order that we might find some repose," writes Munk briefly in the logbook.

The storm was weathered; and at daybreak when the captain crawled stiffly up on deck, the ocean stretched out calm in the keen morning air. Every trace of the storm had gone; the foam on the surface had disappeared like snow melted in the sun. Out over the horizon the sky took on those delicate tints of pink and yellow found inside a sea shell. The sea forgets quickly, but the *Lamprey* remembered all. Its appearance was not prepossessing. Tangled rigging; fretted yards and tattered sail; bulwarks stove in; both anchors gone, chains and all. It was pitiful to see. And yet never had the captain regarded his ship with greater affection. The clean-washed deck tilted gently in the swell, gleaming like a naked blade turned in the sun; a golden streak ran up the wet mast, and under the boom the salt water had collected in heavy drops like the clear dew of morning. Wherever his eyes fell on the ship, it gleamed appreciatively at him, the only kind of praise he would think of accepting; and for a moment it was as though he had brought not three, but four, living beings safely through the hurricane.

A bearing on the sun at noon revealed that the storm had driven them off course to latitude 58° 59′ north, but now they steered sharply to the east before a steady westerly breeze. Hour after hour, day after day, with reefed mainsail and foresail the *Lamprey* flew along on a gently undulating sea which did not take the wind from the sails in the troughs. The majestic, thundering rollers overhauled them slowly from the stern, rushed past at deck height with seething foam, and lost themselves ahead with a final roar; the tiny ship just had time to dip its bowsprit into their spume, then it slipped down into the smooth, bottle-green trough between, where the horizon was concealed, until the ship was raised once more by the next wave. In the stern the short gray man stooped over the tiller, deaf to all entreaties, implacable, a permanent feature of the deck fittings. The friendly slipstream from the mainsail brushed down over his tired face; his eyes were swollen and painful, for he had held vigil for so long now that it was difficult for him to shut them. Drenched to the skin, he stood clutching at the tiller; the ship lay in his hand, as he himself lay in the hand of the Almighty, and he well knew that neither of the parties could manage with a lesser captain at this moment. On September 8th his readings had told him latitude 60° 19′ north; this meant that they were not very far from the semipermanent low-pressure region south of Iceland, and once more they must prepare themselves for the worst.

When the storm overtook them three days later, however, it came so suddenly that they had no time to take the sails in. The foresail tore, "and we three had our work cut out, and by the time we got it in, the ship was half full of water." In spite of this threat, Munk was forced to continue the frantic passage, for the other two had not sufficient strength left to take in the mainsail, and they had moreover to relieve each other at the pump without respite. All of them thought this was to be their last night. Behind the ragged clouds they saw the moon racing backward across the sky, straight for the storm; and at the same time the *Lamprey* flew on at breakneck pace in the

305

Seaman making his way out along the bowsprit in rough seas. Detail of the picture on pages 116-117. (The Print Collection)

opposite direction. Havoc followed now, one blow after another. First the topsail sheet tore, so that the square sail was lashed to shreds with a deafening noise. After that the topmast halyard went, and that seemed to spell their death sentence. Almost at the same time the mast was carried away.

"And it was a full anxious labor for all three of us," writes Munk quietly in the logbook. The *Lamprey* resembled an overturned load of hay with its tangled ropework and the broken spars; torn to ribbons, the sails lashed in the storm with the noise of rifle-shots. Frantically the men crawled up into that part of the rigging that remained, recklessly stepping out onto the rocking yard to cut away the fouled tackle. The roar from the seas beneath them sounded like noises from another world.

But the captain held steady, and when the sun rose they had managed to rig up a jury-sail by which the ship could be maneuvered to a certain extent. Then it seemed as though all their efforts were to be rewarded: "We perceived a ship, and when we were come so near to it, that we could shout to the people on board, I asked for assistance and I yawed twice and came alongside them. But for the reason that it blew so strongly, they could in no wise help me." The strange ship quickly disappeared into the drizzle, and dejectedly the three men on the *Lamprey* resumed their course eastward. It was September 13th, and according to Munk's calculations they should be at about the latitude of the Shetlands. For nearly two months they had not set foot on land, and now they were only a few hundred nautical miles from the Norwegian coast. Had they really come so far in vain? The *Lamprey* drove before the weather at reduced speed. Hour after hour, day after day, the same refrain attended each change of watch: Course due east. Course due east. Jens Munk had never reached China, and yet it was as though he constantly pursued the receding sunrise. On September 15th the outlying skerries of the Orkney Islands lay due south; slowly they were making progress, but on the 18th the storm overtook them for the third time. With what bits of sail still remained Munk succeeded in keeping the vessel's head to wind. For two days they lay hove-to, taking turns at the pump, and only on the third day were they able to fall off before the wind and continue: Course toward sunrise. It was September 20th. Jens Munk had kept to brief entries in the logbook, for there was no reason to dramatize their situation; nor was there any change on September 20th. That was the day of the greatest event of the whole voyage, though it received the smallest entry in the journal, a mere half line: "The 20th of September we sighted Norway."

And so silently they sailed in toward the land, gazing upon

it, adoring it as it rose up before them. It was the island of Alden, north of Sognefjord. Munk knew the waters from his voyages to North Cape, and on the 21st he ran to the south of the island, took the ship in through the breakers, and came within the shelter of the skerries near Dalsfjord. But they were still not saved, for even in here the waves broke against the rocks with fearful force, and they had only half an anchor and no dinghy. The whole day Munk tacked to and fro in the mouth of the fjord without finding a place where he could get a line ashore. The storm continued, and then the sun began to set. Soon it would be dark. If they continued in this fashion through the night, they were lost. Munk ran into a small bay, hauled the sails down, and dropped the half anchor. It could not hold the ship, but there was nothing else they could do. A little later they saw a farmer approaching through the twilight in a rowboat. Jens Munk hailed him from the *Lamprey*, but when the man turned and discovered the strangers he was seized with terror and began to row away. It was now or never. Munk rushed down below, fetched a musket and a pouch of dry powder, and lit the slow match. The warning shot passed right over the farmer's head. That changed the complexion of things: the Norwegian turned back, rowed their lines ashore, and soon the *Lamprey* lay securely moored among the rocks. The three men crawled down into the rowboat and sat on the thwarts. Their faces were gray with fatigue; the dark circles beneath their eyes extended to their ears. They were long-haired and toothless, had great cakes of salt in their wildly disheveled beards, and as they grasped the gunwales of the boat the farmer observed with horror their torn, ravaged fingers. They were like animals. Not one of them uttered a word; but then the farmer saw that tears were streaming down their cheeks. Great, wild animals silently weeping. Em-

The harbor at Bergen as it appeared when Jens Munk arrived there in 1620. In the background to the left the residence of Knud Gyldenstjerne, Bergenhus. (Braunius)

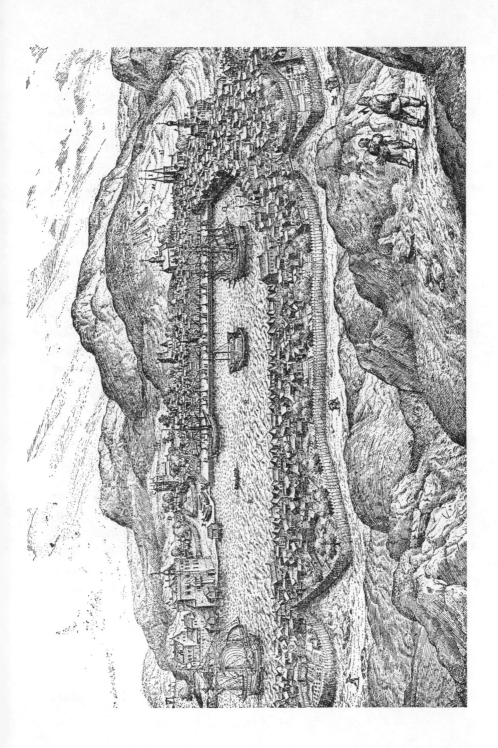

barrassed, the farmer shipped his oars. The keel scraped on the sand. The voyage was at an end. For the first time in sixty-seven days the three men set foot on firm ground. "And having the ship now intact and being come to a Christian land once more, then did we poor humans weep in great joy and thanked God, for having mercifully vouchsafed us this good fortune," Jens Munk writes.

Developments followed quickly. The next morning Jens Munk went alone with the farmer by boat to the royal bailiff of the district, called Sunnfjord, and got him to send men and "fresh victuals" down to the others. When this was arranged, he continued overland to Bergen, arriving there on September 25th. Immediately he visited a doctor, asked him to prepare "drink and medicine" and have it "conveyed to the two of my company," together with a ship's master, and instructions to bring the *Lamprey* in to Bergen. A few days later the ship lay at anchor in the harbor and the other two survivors went ashore. They were still like wild beasts, and had not yet adjusted to civilized conditions. One of them became involved in a brawl in a pothouse, stabbed a man with his knife, and fled. According to the law, the captain is responsible for his crew in such a situation, and the following day Jens Munk reported to the lord lieutenant at Bergenhus.

The official at Bergenhus was Knud Gyldenstjerne. The two men knew each other well. Knud Gyldenstjerne was one of the noblemen who had taken part in the voyage to Archangel six years earlier, which ended with Jens Munk's giving up his appointment as quartermaster. In his present state Munk had no thought for those events. He stood in the presence of this powerful official, racked with scurvy, with watery eyes and shaking hands, still not recovered after the sixty-seven-day nightmare. He found the whole situation incomprehensible. He simply wanted some sort of arrangement made for his seaman, so that he could get home again and lie down. But Knud Gyldenstjerne had a very distinct recollection of that little quartermaster who once imagined he was a nobleman like his father. He had also heard of his ludicrous attempt to reach the East before Ove Giedde. Why had this bastard always to push himself forward? Why did he try to assert himself among respectable people? And what was the result of it all? He had thrown away one of the King's best frigates, and he had lost most of his company. But he had, of course, saved himself together with two other scoundrels, one of whom had already been accused of attempted murder. This was more than enough to add fuel to old hatreds. The position was clear; now this little man would be made to realize that Knud Gyldenstjerne, and not Erik Munk, was the King's representative in Norway. He gave a curt order to one of the men standing by, then he turned frigidly toward Munk and put on his official manner. He very much regretted that nothing could be done. Law and justice must prevail in the realm. His Majesty's commands must be enforced. Formalities required that . . .

Jens Munk gave up trying to comprehend; it was years since he had heard so many words at one time; and when the soldiers entered, he stood there half blind and still not understanding a word of it all. Then his father's fate struck him down, too. Scarcely a week after his return Jens Munk was in prison at Bergenhus.

20

The Captain and the King

I

Jens Munk had been imprisoned on the *Lamprey* for sixty-seven days. The various dates quoted in the sources show that Knud Gyldenstjerne kept him a prisoner in Bergenhus even longer.

After sentence had been passed, salvation could come only from the King; and Christian IV seems to have received details of these events fairly quickly. On September 27th Munk wrote in his logbook that he had sent a letter that same day to the King in Denmark to report his arrival in Bergen. That was shortly before he was imprisoned by Gyldenstjerne; but one can presume that the bearer of his letter was also able to tell His Majesty about this later event. Gyldenstjerne's action could not but cause a stir. During October, therefore, the King received, first the report of the catastrophe in Hudson Bay and, second, the intimation that Captain Munk had been imprisoned in Bergenhus immediately upon his return. Some evidence suggests that in his indignation at the first information, Christian IV forgot to respond to the second. In any event he took his time. More than a month passed before he took measures to redress the injustices of his representative; but when he finally wrote to him on November 30th, his orders were unambiguous: "It appears to Us most strange, that thou has caused Our commissioned Captain and ship thus to be detained. And We pray thee and require, that thou permit the aforesaid Jens Munk, with whatsoever people he has brought under his command to Norway, to make his way hither without delay."

In other words, Jens Munk was imprisoned in Bergenhus throughout the month of September, the whole of October, the whole of November, and a large part of December, before Knud Gyldenstjerne was compelled to release him. This accords with the biography of 1723, which tells us that he returned to Copenhagen only on Christmas Eve, 1620.

He cut no heroic figure as he made his way along Pilestraede in the darkness that day, to the peal of the Christmas bells from the churches of Our Lady and St. Nicholas. The long confinement had further undermined his health. White-haired, bent with rheumatism, and stiff as an eighty-year-old, he suddenly reappeared in these familiar surroundings. He had made a special effort to reach home in time for Christmas Eve, and had no inkling of what awaited him; fate had long since dragged him down so far that he could not conceive of further humiliation. He was come home like Ulysses, who knocked at the back door of his home in Ithaca disguised as a beggar. But at this point the comparison ceases, for Pile-straede was no Ithaca, and Kathrine Adriansdatter certainly no Penelope. She had given up hope long ago of seeing her husband again; at all events, the day had come when she felt that she could not be expected to wait any longer. Though the house was not exactly filled with suitors, she did have one, and that was sufficient. He was a Copenhagen weaver named Rasmus Skult. It appears from the extant documents that his involvement with the manufacture of cloth did not prevent Kathrine from making him a present of those of her husband's clothes which she happened to have.

It cannot have taken the captain long to grasp exactly how things stood with the wife whom he had named in his testament at Munk Haven. His clothes were gone; the whole street was talking; and Kathrine's joy at his return must have appeared somewhat strained. She seems to have gone a good way already toward establishing herself in her new situation. It appears that on May 20th she bought the house in Pilestraede, which until then they had rented. To obtain money for the transaction she had approached the heirs of Jørgen Daa for the return of the sum which Munk had once loaned for his friend's funeral. There was even a lawsuit about it. The ward of the heirs considered her claim excessive. Munk, he asserted, had made more of the funeral than was necessary, and he refused to pay. Taking due account of Munk's weak financial position at the time of his departure, it is difficult to see how Kathrine was able to acquire her property without contracting debts.

That was on Christmas Eve, and in his wretched condition the captain appears to have put the problems out of his mind for the time being. At any rate, he had first to make his report to the King. There is no written evidence of the meeting between the two men, but we know that it took place, probably in January. In all probability it did not pass off quietly. The catastrophe at Hudson Bay was the first of the great disappointments that now began to overwhelm Christian IV. He was a bad loser, and Munk's miraculous homeward voyage was scarcely sufficient to overshadow in his mind the events preceding it. Where is my frigate? Where are my sailors? That these were the principal remarks at their meeting may be deduced from its result. It was merciless. The King commanded Jens Munk to fit out a new expedition without delay and sail back to Munk Haven to save the *Unicorn* and to initiate the colonization of Nova Dania.

This resolution must have been taken in anger. It must have been obvious to the King that this wreck of a man had little chance of surviving a new expedition. Conditions in Hudson Bay being what they were, his orders were virtually a sentence of death; and Munk did try to mollify him by referring to his wretched state of health. In the National Archives a list of the expedition's requirements is preserved, which he worked out shortly afterward at the King's request. He calls it "A register

314

Christian IV's command to Munk to return to the winter haven roused
sufficient attention to provoke an echo in contemporary fly sheets. Here
is a Dutch engraver's naïve impression of the situation involving the King
and the captain. (*Drie Voyagien*)

of all that which I now in haste can conceive and which may be serviceable and highly needful to this voyage." With the first items on the list he corrects the errors made in the equipment of the first expedition: they were to take with them "good medicaments and in particular for scurvy"; they were to have ample green vegetables, smoked meat instead of salt, a complete supply of leather clothing, and above all "skis to walk on in the snow." Then he referred once more to the King's haste; his inventory was not perfect, "as such a voyage has many needful demands the which cannot be called to mind in haste." And finally, he added these personal lines:

I for my part, submissive and loyal, ready with life and blood to serve His Royal Majesty, My Gracious Lord, wheresoever and whensoever I am commanded, cherish the hope that I, unhappy man, my spouse and children may be granted provision and subsistence, and likewise I pray that my Lord Chancellor may cause Peter Paynck or some other Doctor to be instructed to examine me, that I might once more come to my rightful state of health. May God reward Your stern purpose.

These brief words give a clear picture of him after the bitter experiences of Bergen and Copenhagen. He was in a very dispirited state; his inventory was at the same time a petition, whose choice of words conjures up disquieting reminders of the one his father sent from Dragsholm. Translated into straightforward terms, his letter says: he knows well enough that he owes the King obedience, and that in his debt-ridden situation he dare not risk the loss of his livelihood; but he cannot sail to Munk Haven, for he is too ill to take on command of the new expedition. Scholars are of the opinion that the King did indeed relent and release him from the mission; but that is not borne out by the facts. The evidence consists of a letter which the King sent on March 11th to his representative in Aalborg, Manderup Parsberg. The herring fishing in the Kattegat was on the decline, and many fishermen had no employment; however, during the previous year the King through his appointed captain had sought and found a new land, and Manderup Parsberg was now to inquire among the King's subjects in Nibe, Skagen, and other fishing villages in the district whether any men and women desired to accompany the ship which the King proposed to send thither, and settle there. If Manderup Parsberg encountered any such people he was to have them conveyed to Copenhagen by ship, where they would be met by the King's captain, Jens Munk, and receive fitting hospitality.

A glance through the Bremerholm accounts shows that as late as July 7th Jens Munk acknowledged the receipt of ship's ale "for a voyage he was to make in the frigate 'Trost'." Lindenow's old Greenland ship was again destined for an expedition into arctic waters; the crew's wages were agreed on; the Chancellery appointed traders for the supply of provisions, and new preparations were in full swing.

That was in 1621, a year during which there was great difficulty in enlisting men at Bremerholm, and the King had to organize recruiting drives abroad. This was why, in spite of his haste, the fitting out of the *Trost* took such an inordinately long time. The pay lists also show that it proved impossible to find additional crew for the *Trost*. Apart from the general shortage of seamen, there was also popular resistance. Everyone knew of the misfortune that had struck the first expedition, and no one had any particular desire to risk life and limb in a new attempt. The reports seem to have reached even as far as northern Jutland. Manderup Parsberg's efforts were in vain: not a single would-be emigrant applied.

This proved to be Munk's salvation. Without settlers and without a crew to man the *Trost* there was little point in dispatching a new expedition. Furthermore, as the King elaborated his war plans he must have realized that he would need all available manpower in the future; the expedition was abandoned. This last-minute decision on the part of the King cannot, however, absolve him; it was not consideration for Munk, but entirely different motives, that caused him to shelve his plans. Although all the earlier biographical works on Munk maintain that cordial relations prevailed between him and the King during the latter years of his life, with one writer even suggesting that Munk "enjoyed his King's confidence and favor right up to his death," this hardly accords with events during the spring of 1621. Nor does it in any way accord with the events that were now to follow.

After Munk's receipt for ship's ale on July 7th, his name disappeared from the archives. He probably lay ill in Pilestraede all through the summer. Only late in the autumn does he seem to have recovered, and on November 5th he was sent to Holland to recruit sailors. The King's need of sailors was so desperate by this time that he issued an amnesty for deserters and runaway criminals; but for the qualities Jens Munk had displayed there was no amnesty. The brutish, degrading job of recruiting officer was good enough for the man who had just revealed himself a genius in the art of navigation. Munk's trip to Holland cannot be thought of as an exception in an emergency, for scarcely had he got back home when he was sent out again on a similar mission, this time to Bergen. It must have been a comfort to the mighty lord of that city to see his old enemy appear in this lowly role. Knud Gyldenstjerne realized that there was, after all, some justice in the world.

In the Norwegian winter the work was both laborious and time-consuming, and Munk did not get back until Easter, 1622. But even then there was no respite in Copenhagen. A few days later he had to set off as captain of the *Nettle Leaf* to escort the East Indiaman *Vaterhunden* ("Water Dog") down to the Cape Verde Islands. Again after this voyage there was no rest period in Copenhagen; on the homeward trip the King at the head of five ships met him en route for the Council of Nobles in Bergen. Munk was ordered to join the squadron, and only at the end of August did he get home once more. He had been away by then for nearly a year, and again it seems to have been too long for Kathrine. But on this occasion the captain had also had enough. He had the weaver arrested, and arranged for the two eldest boys to attend Sorø School, the promise the King had given him before the departure for Hudson Bay being at long last fulfilled. The divorce proceedings dragged on; on April 12, 1623, the magistrate was instructed to decide the lawsuit between Jens Munk and Rasmus Skult, Rasmus having committed adultery with the wife, and several items of Munk's clothing having been found in his possession. On September 4th the burgomasters and council of Copenhagen were called upon to hear witnesses to the suit; but not until the following year, April 20, 1623, could they "pronounce judgment between Jens Munk and his former wife Kathrine Adriansdatter." Repercussions from this judgment lasted until 1626, when Kathrine complained that Munk was not paying her the annual 100 dollars to which he was committed. The Admiral of the Holm, Sten Villumsen Rosenvinge of Torshof, ordered him thereafter to pay a larger amount.

It is most likely that Kathrine's claim was prompted by real negligence on his part. Her complaint was not the only lawsuit he had to contend with at this time. But in 1626 she may have had particularly good grounds for bitterness. Jens Munk had married again. His new wife was called Margrethe Tagesdatter. She was Norwegian, and her father had been castle scribe at Akershus for a number of years before being appointed judge in Oslo. It is not known when Margrethe was born, but she did not die until 1651; and if we take into consideration the low life expectancy at that time, she was undoubtedly very young when she married the forty-seven-year-old sea captain. If there was no Penelope in this story, at least a Nausicaa was to appear, albeit at the last moment. In this narrative, too, the young girl makes the entry only when utter ruination is an accomplished fact.

This is how it came about. During the years when the divorce was pending, Jens Munk had again been out on far-ranging expeditions. In 1623 he led an expedition to the Kola

Peninsula, where the Russians had begun to collect dues illegally. The following year he commanded three ships on a search for pirates in the same waters. These two appointments have been interpreted as evidence that he still enjoyed the King's favor. But he led similar missions when he was thirty-one years old, so it can hardly be considered a "favor" if he is assigned the same kind of command after thirteen years. Furthermore, he had repeatedly had to accept minor commissions between these expeditions. Again we find him as recruiting officer; he drew up long inventories of equipment at Bremerholm; he traveled about the country acting as a marine surveyor. A glance at his life during the first half of 1624 reveals just how harassed he was. On February 9th he was sent to Pomerania to recruit shipwrights; the King requested him to get at least sixty, and in consequence he did not reach home again until "eight days before Easter." But there was no question of his spending the holidays in Copenhagen; scarcely had he presented his accounts and reports when he was sent on Palm Sunday to Bützow, south of Rostock, to deliver a sum of money to the King's brother, Duke Ulrik, on the Rühn estate. Yet again he barely succeeded in setting foot on the quayside in Copenhagen when he was sent out on April 20th on the above-mentioned pirate hunt.

Munk did not enjoy any favors. He was submissive, ready to serve with life and blood, wheresoever and whensoever he was commanded, and he did so because he had no alternative. He was less himself, less his own master, than ever. True, his Hudson Bay journal when it was published that autumn contained a lengthy dedication to the King, but one cannot take this as evidence of cordial relations between the two. Stylistically, there is an enormous gulf between Munk's terse, concrete prose and the Germanic turgidity of the florid dedication. He did not write a word of it. It was composed by the publisher of the book, the German Heinrich Waldkirch, as the printer's routine homage to the King. By contrast, *Navigatio Septentrionalis* does not contain any of the prefaces which were also an established feature of publications in those years, and in which scholars gave an account of the author's life in Latin or Danish, in prose or in verse, and eulogized his accomplishments. Anything of that nature was out of the question in this case. In 1624 there was no one who found it profitable to enlarge upon Munk's accomplishments; and the story of his career is so painful that a century was to pass before it could be printed in Denmark.

Reference is also made to the fact that he received an increase in salary the following year. At last firm evidence of the King's favor. But the amount was not remarkably high, and it was the first time his salary had been increased since he entered the King's service fifteen years before. It goes up to 300 dollars; by comparison, Johan Braem received 500 dollars for simply inspecting the King's whaling. Finally, the accounts show quite clearly that in this year there was a general increase in wages at Bremerholm, which makes it difficult to regard Munk's raise as a special mark of favor.

One thing at least seems clear: the money fell on stony ground. It is pretty obvious that Munk was hard up in those years immediately after his return. Both in the testament from Munk Haven and in the document relating to the newly contemplated expedition, he referred to himself as "I poor unhappy man." Even though the expression was conventional, there had to be some substance in it if one wished it to be believed. The collapse of the whaling enterprise, followed by Kathrine's activities during his absence, may well have meant a considerable debt. Even before all this, he owed the King 300 rix-dollars, and quite clearly he found it difficult to pay his divorced wife her maintenance allowance. Was he also driven to the brink of even more serious misdemeanor, and does this in part explain the King's displeasure? There was an awkward business with a Dutchman named Peiter Isakson, who complained that Munk had wrongfully confiscated some of his goods on the journey to Kildin in 1623. Admiralty judgment was pronounced in the case; we do not know whether the findings upheld Munk, or whether he simply refused to comply with them. At all events the matter was kept going by Isakson's heirs even after his death; and they must have had a strong case because the court at Bremerholm allowed their complaint. As a commander of the Crown, of course, Munk received a share of captured ships and confiscated goods. That was how he became a wealthy man after the expedition against Mendoza. Was he a little too greedy on that particular occasion? It is noteworthy that when he was sent out on a new expedition in the same waters the following year, his instructions contained repeated warnings against committing injustice against innocent parties; he must "under no circumstances" start any offensive action against the Russians; he must not "do them any injustice" as long as they let him go in peace; he "shall conduct himself in a friendly manner toward all nations," when they have proper papers and documents; and he must "not attack or condemn anyone without reason." When the suit with Isakson's heirs was about to be resumed in 1625, he himself attempted—perhaps in anticipation of its outcome—to bring another lawsuit to secure the resources he so obviously lacked. In January an official at Halmstad, Palle Rosenkrantz, was given instructions to assist Jens Munk to recover certain sums which he believed were owing to him in Halland, "so that he may discharge his affairs without long-drawn proceedings and delay." On this occasion something more important was involved than the old matter of Jørgen Daa's burial at Ildsberg. Evidently Jens Munk was attempting to press his claim to the Hiørne estate near the Viska River, which had belonged in its time to his grandfather Niels. The method was uncomfortably reminiscent of Erik Munk. To protect himself in one lawsuit he started another. But Jens Munk was not cut out to play that sort of game: he had none of the brazen skill and ready brutality of his father; he was soon brought low by papers and regulations. The outcome of the suit in Halland is not known, but everything suggests that he failed. In the first place, any event so sensational as the acquisition of an estate would inevitably have left traces in the biography of 1723; yet this does not contain a word on the matter. Secondly, it appears that Niels Munk had already bequeathed his property to Bente and Anna Christensen, daughters of Burgomaster Frederik Christensen of the stone house with the gable turned toward the street in Aalborg.

In 1625 Jens Munk foresaw his case against the Dutchmen failing, with no great resources to cover the loss. He stood at the edge of an abyss. Shortly afterward, when the chance of a little quick profit presented itself again, Erik Munk's son seems to have succumbed to temptation.

His increase in salary at Bremerholm during 1625 probably had a quite prosaic explanation. In that year Christian IV finally entered the Thirty Years' War. The warnings of the Council of the Realm were swept aside; Anstruther had his way. In such a situation there is nothing remarkable in the King's attempting to stimulate flagging recruitment with promises of higher pay. He needed men.

The mobilization order reached Munk at Nakskov, where he was supervising the construction of a new ship. It was dated August 10th, signed by the Chancellor, and dispatched from Roskilde, where the government had its seat because of the plague in Copenhagen. Jens Munk was to proceed thither without delay, traveling day and night, where there would be committed to his care a number of ships of war that the King desired to be fitted out. Concerning the plague, he need have no fears, for the ships were to be manned by new, fresh companies.

Munk rode at once to Roskilde. In command of five men-of-war, he was to set out for the mouth of the Weser to sever the Imperial communications to Bremen. A month later he had the squadron ready to sail. Among the five ships he selected at Bremerholm was the sloop *Lamprey*, which was not so remarkable since he loved this ship. He had never been rewarded; he had never been promoted; this ship was the only tangible evidence of his abilities. It was to accompany him to the Weser; if all else foundered around him, one thing was certain: the *Lamprey* would remain afloat.

However, his mission did not entail any great risk. As at Elfsborg, he was to form a blockade, but the operation on the Weser was much simpler; there was no enemy fortress ashore, and he need not fear the sorties of foreign warships. All he had to do was to screen the merchantmen sailing to Bremen. But Jens Munk did not execute this simple assignment to the King's satisfaction. In the spring of 1626 he was deluged with dispatches from the royal headquarters at Wolfenbüttel, and from letter to letter the tone grew sharper. It began on April 21st, on a matter of pure formality. The burgomasters of Bremen complained that Munk had refused permission for their men-of-war to fly their colors on the Weser. The King could not afford trouble with Bremen just then, so he revoked Munk's decision and made him withdraw his orders.

That was the end of that. Five days later, however, the letters from Wolfenbüttel referred to more serious matters. It had been reported to the King that Jens Munk had unlawfully confiscated diverse victuals belonging to Gert and Ebel Mayer together with 900 cheeses for Jost van Willem; and he demanded that the wares "should be surrendered without delay." On May 28th there was further trouble. This time Munk was required to explain to the King the confiscation of five casks of butter for Harlingen. Then there was trouble over some rye for Danzig. Then the five casks of butter made their reappearance.

It must be conceded that Christian's concern for trifles rose to triumphal heights; and it is remarkable to observe that while Tilly and Wallenstein marched north, and Christian himself, at the head of a motley crew of mercenaries, was preparing for a confrontation with the combined military potential of Central Europe, the King still had time to count up cheeses and casks of butter. On the other hand, of course, his concern had some basis of fact. Something *was* wrong on the Weser. Compared with the unproven transgressions at Kildin, these new matters spoke their own clear language. Jens Munk had gone too far. Since his return home and Gyldenstjerne's act of vengeance he had been a broken man. From that point in time his career declined steeply, and in the spring of 1626 he stood with his back to the wall. He knew about the claim for damages awaiting him in Copenhagen; his desperate suit in Halland had proved abortive; he had never paid Kathrine; he owed the King money; he was surrounded by debts. And then it chanced that some merchantmen came sailing down the river with provisions, cheeses, butter, and rye. . . .

At the end of the summer the King sent him home from the Weser; and it is understandable that this was the last time the King used this captain as the commander of a squadron. Jens Munk was to return to Copenhagen with all possible speed, leaving only two small vessels in the waters near Bremen. The King's orders were sent at the very last moment from the headquarters in Nordten on August 8th. For now Christian IV of Denmark and Norway had other things on his mind than casks of butter. Eight days later, on the morning of August 17th, General Tilly opened the attack at Lutter am Barenberge.

Meanwhile Jens Munk sailed north with the remaining ships from the Weser. He himself was on board the frigate *Nettle Leaf*. In the Skagerrak they ran into a heavy storm which forced the squadron to lie hove-to. One of the smaller ships got into difficulties, and its captain could not cope with the rough seas. From the poop of the *Nettle Leaf* Jens Munk saw the ship disappear beneath the waves "lock, stock, and barrel," as he later said. For the superstitious captain this sight was a fearful omen: What lay in store for him now? The ship which sank before his very eyes was the sloop *Lamprey*.

2

Now he was truly alone: in disfavor with the King, without friends, in debt and in disgrace, and bereft of the only tangible evidence of his true stature. The navigation records show that he did not reach Bremerholm until September 7th. That was rather a long time for a voyage from the Weser to Copenhagen. Did the storm drive him up to Norway? Did he have to run in to Oslo to have the damage repaired? All we know is that the judge's daughter was called Margrethe, and that this young woman answered "yes." The captain, gray and careworn, had not many teeth left in his head. But perhaps some goddess straightened up the stranger's figure, gave his manner some charm. In brief, Ulysses and Nausicaa were united before the altar in Holmen Church, Copenhagen.

But the wedding was only a respite. The suit brought by Peiter Isakson's heirs continued to be pressed at Bremerholm; Kathrine Adriansdatter advanced her claim for a share of their common property and the payment of several years' maintenance; and now the King called in his loan of 300 rix-dollars with principal and interest. The war had left Christian IV short of money, and he called in a whole series of loans. This was not specially aimed at Munk, but the reorganization of the Weser squadron in 1627 was. There had been too much that was questionable; the patrol had to be trustworthy; he needed another man in that position. On April 11th, when Jens Munk sailed to Bremen for the third time, he was only second-in-command of the squadron. The admiral was now Henrik Vind of Klarupgaard. This was the situation in the year 1628. Munk had been south to Cape Verde for the last time; he had rounded North Cape for the last time. Now he had been demoted to make way for a nobleman. But that was also for the last time, for 1628 was the year of Jens Munk's death.

Here we must move with caution. Hitherto the particulars of his death have been shrouded in almost impenetrable mystery, and not even the exact date is certain. According to the biographical work of 1723, it is "set down by the brother of Margrethe Tagesdatter that he has, mercifully, died in the Lord on June 3rd." But that does not accord with the information in the Bremerholm archives, which say that "his wife

Margrethe Tagesdatter received his pension until St. John's Day, when he died." There is much to suggest that this information is more reliable than that of the brother-in-law. St. John's Day is June 24th, and according to the funeral register of St. Nicholas's Church Jens Munk was buried there on July 3rd. However, that does not resolve the mystery; on the contrary. Why does this otherwise so meticulously accurate biographer commit so gross an error as to have Jens Munk die a month before he is buried? Dare he not divulge the correct date? He is also silent on the matter of the period in prison at Bergenhus. Did he realize that the publication of this date might rouse suspicion that not everything was as it should be?

As to the cause of death, he reports what is repeated in all the accounts of Jens Munk: the captain died from wounds received during the battles off southern Jutland. But these battles took place as early as mid-March; and remembering the standard of ship's surgeons and hospital conditions of that time, it is somewhat mysterious that a man could be mortally wounded and yet remain alive for more than three months. By advancing the date of death the biographer reduces this period by almost a month, making the adduced cause of death more plausible, although still not convincing. For on May 13th, i.e., a few weeks before his alleged death—the court at Bremerholm was instructed to summon him in connection with the lawsuit of Peiter Isakson's successors. No matter how one twists and turns it, it seems a remarkable thing to do to a badly wounded sea captain, lying at the point of death.

From here on the mystery deepens. At most burials it was customary to sum up the deceased's life in a final eulogy. In the case of people of some consequence, the priest's sermon was subsequently printed. This was done for persons much less notable than Jens Munk; indeed, these sermons now constitute a main source for personal biographies of the time. In Jens Munk's case, however, no funeral sermon has been preserved; and nowhere is there evidence to suggest that one ever existed. Tradition has it that he was given a sepulchral monu-

327

ment in St. Nicholas's Church; but unfortunately this also was lost when the church burned down in 1795. We are asked to accept that his tombstone went up in flames. However, in his research on the history of Copenhagen, Dr. O. Nielsen has been able to establish the names of those people who had epitaphs in St. Nicholas's. His list does not include Jens Munk, however. Dr. Nielsen also lists the names of those persons who had a simple tombstone. Jens Munk is not among them, either.

In such circumstances it is clear that no contemporary evidence relating to Jens Munk's death can be ignored, no matter how dubiously it has been regarded in the past. For such material exists.

Isaac de la Peyrère, a Frenchman, was a resident in Denmark from 1644 to 1645, as secretary to the French ambassador, Monsieur de la Thuillerie. He took a lively interest in the latest Danish explorations in the arctic. For a number of years he gathered information, corresponding, among others, with the eminent Professor Ole Worm, whose foster son and succcessor, Thomas Bartholin, was married to a daughter of Jens Munk's second wife, Margrethe Tagesdatter. With the help of these friends, he compiled a book on the subject that so absorbed him, calling it *Relation du Groenland*. Though not a work of impeccable scholarship, it makes lucid and pleasant reading. Among the sources Peyrère studied was naturally Jens Munk's journal, and here, for the first time, it is copiously quoted in a major language. While Munk's journal was quickly forgotten in Denmark, where it was reprinted only twice in the three centuries after his death, *Relation du Groen-*

Peyrère's account of the conflict between Christian IV and Jens Munk excited the imagination of the fly-sheet illustrators. Together with the picture on page 315, this is the only extant "portrait" of Jens Munk, but one can assume with certainty that the likeness in his case is no greater than it is between Christian IV and the medieval monarch depicted here. (*Drie Voyagien*)

land was an instant success. Thanks to Peyrère, Jens Munk was becoming known to the world at large as rapidly as he was forgotten in Denmark. Peyrère's book was translated into a number of languages and reissued in various editions. Shortly after its first appearance, one notes four editions in France, three in Germany, two in Holland, three in England. Eighty-five years after its first publication it was even translated into Danish.

Peyrère was not only interested in Jens Munk's life, he also gave his opinion on the cause of his death. Here is what he writes about it:

> Upon his return Captain Munk made a report of his voyage to his lord, the King, who received him as one receives a person believed to be long since lost. This seemed to be the end of this captain's misfortunes, but his story is remarkable and deserves to be better known. He lived in Denmark for several years, and after thinking long about the mistakes he made on the voyage because of his ignorance of the region and of the conditions there, and about the possibility of finding the passage to the Orient he had sought for, he felt impelled to make the journey again. But as he had not the means to undertake the task alone, he prevailed upon some prominent Danish noblemen and burghers to form a company and equip two ships for a long voyage under his command. He had now taken precautions against all the misfortunes and accidents that had befallen him on the first voyage, and was on the point of sailing for the second time, when on the very day of departure the King of Denmark sent for him and in the course of their conversation reproached him with having by dint of his inadequate leadership of the first expedition thrown away the lives of the seamen with which the King had entrusted him. When the captain gave him a truculent answer, the King became enraged and permitted himself to prod him in the chest with his staff. Deeply embittered over this

affront, the captain withdrew, made his way home, and took to his bed, where he died ten days later of grief and hunger.

Our thanks to Monsieur Peyrère! His contribution contains new information, even if it is evident that he confuses two events: the new expedition to Hudson Bay and Jens Munk's death, which were in reality separated by seven years. In Denmark, however, the whole of his story was rejected as pure fabrication: it was not true that Munk was on the point of undertaking a new expedition, and it was not true that he had fallen foul of the King. But researches in the National Archives brought documents to light that prove quite clearly that in 1621 extensive preparations for a new expedition were being made. On that point, consequently, the Frenchman had been right after all. He was mistaken only about the date and the person who took the initiative.

As to his mention that immediately prior to Jens Munk's death there had been a dramatic clash between him and the King, his evidence here was rather damning for Christian IV. He implied that Munk's death should be viewed as a kind of suicide, caused by the King's brutal behavior. That this interpretation was resisted is understandable. It was somewhat difficult to make it accord with the general notion that Munk "enjoyed his King's confidence and favor right up to his death." Yet the possibility must not be discounted that the Frenchman was correctly informed on this point as well. Isaac de la Peyrère satisfies the most important demand that must be made of any historical source; and it is no accident that Holberg quotes him in his *History of Denmark*: he is virtually contemporaneous with the events he describes. When he collected his information, only sixteen years had elapsed since Jens Munk's death. At the Court he met several people who knew the captain, and who also knew the King. He had listened to all kinds of rumors about the remarkable affair, and he also had to keep in mind that his account would be read by his informants. He could not permit his fancy free rein—that

331

would lower him in everyone's estimation. Furthermore, when Peyrère published his book, in 1647, he could not possibly have known that the Danish King had only one more year to live. He has been accused of exaggeration, of giving an all too dramatic and romantic account of Munk's death. Is it not more probable that, diplomat as he was, he would try rather to moderate his account as far as possible? He simplified, he linked together two different occurrences; he did not say that the King *struck* the captain—he "prodded him in the chest." And he is content to suggest that Munk afterward died of "grief." It all sounds smoothed over, noncontroversial; there would be no danger of diplomatic complications. Far from exaggerating and dramatizing, Peyrère had every reason to pass lightly over this unfortunate affair. Nevertheless, one might still be inclined to reject his account as the product of a too lively imagination, provided that no factual proof could be found for the rumors Peyrère heard in Copenhagen—for instance, if it could be shown that Jens Munk had not been with the King shortly before his death. But it can be shown that he *had*.

3

Denmark's great misfortunes were long apparent to anyone with eyes to see. They started in 1624. In that year the King was at last to move into his new palace, Rosenborg, but how things had changed in recent years! The skilling had fallen again, for the sixth time during his reign: 100 to the dollar compared with 66 when he came to the throne. Simultaneously the great plague broke out in Copenhagen, lasting for two years and taking 4884 lives. On December 8th instructions were issued for the windows and doors of the houses of the sick to be nailed up; the University was closed; the government fled to Roskilde. Then on February 10th the greatest floods in living memory occurred. St. Peter's Church tower was blown down; there were boats in the streets of the city, large ships stranded in the forest of southern Zealand.

The water subsided, but the plague was not washed away. On July 21st the Court chaplain, Menelaus Povlsen, bemoaned the lawless state of the city following the flight of the authorities. "O Lord, have compassion upon us, for though it is such a time of wretchedness, no sign of penitence is to be observed among our people; instead, new fashions and rich raiment are everywhere, and on Sundays when they should be in church entreating God to turn away this fearful chastisement, by carriage, mounted, and on foot they do take to the woods where they drink, dance, and frisk about till the black night. Our herring fishermen put out to fish tipsy and drunken; our coachmen drink and gamble on Amagertorv; and no maid may fetch a pail of water from the pump without that these bawdy fellows shamelessly take hold of her, so that it is unbecoming to tell of it."

That was the summer when the King marched into Germany. But there was no end to the portents. On November 10th came more floods; on May 11th the victualing house burned down with the fleet's supplies; on August 17th the battle of Lutter am Barenberge took place. Christian IV had catastrophically underestimated the strength of the enemy; that same evening his army was in a state of utter disarray: the foot soldiers were mown down; the cannon, baggage trains, and ammunition were in enemy hands; and the King himself was in headlong flight with his cavalry. Denmark's long period of decline had begun. The money and troops promised by Anstruther did not arrive. The German princes deserted. In the night of July 24-25, 1627, Tilly was able to cross the Elbe, join up with Wallenstein's forces, and advance into Holstein. Panic-stricken, the Council of the Realm decided to arm all men between eighteen and fifty-five fit to bear arms. The King attempted to make a stand near Flensburg, but everything was in chaos. His own mercenaries turned against him and ran amok over the whole of Jutland, robbing nobles, priests, burghers, and farmers of their property, slaying those who did not submit to plunder, ravishing wives and children

333

within sight of husbands and parents. Behind the mercenaries followed Wallenstein's Croats and Cossacks, and in October the whole of Jutland was occupied. Thus ended the campaign, which Christian IV had officially initiated to defend the holy Evangelical Church. *Regna firmat pietas.*

In Copenhagen, the winter of 1627-28 was a hard one. Refugees in hundreds streamed into the capital and terrified the population with their hair-raising stories; the price of foodstuffs rocketed; the citizens were ordered to lay in supplies of powder, shot, and fuses; day and night the peasants labored to improve the neglected defenses. But the wrath of the Lord was not diminished. At one o'clock in the night of January 18th-19th the great steeple of St. Nicholas's was blown down and smashed in the vaulting, so that only the high walls remained standing.

Jens Munk did not see the destruction wrought in the church where he was to be buried a few months later. That year his winter stay in Copenhagen was shorter than ever. He did not return from the Weser as Henrik Vind's second-in-command until November 7th, and by January 5th he was already on board the *Flying Fish*, which lay at anchor together with a large division of the fleet off Nakskov. Three days later he met his superior, Henrik Vind, who went on board the *Lobster*. On March 17th the King arrived at Lolland to take over command of the *Lobster*. As all the other captains of the squadron did, on the following morning Jens Munk on the *Flying Fish* received an order of the day written in the King's own hand: A landing was to be attempted on Fehmern, where the enemy had assembled troops and threatened Lolland. The King would sail in the van with the *Lobster*. When he made sail, the others were to do the same; and when he dropped anchor below Fehmern, the others were to heave to between the royal ship and the coast. Craft which could be beached were to be taken right in; the rest were to move close in to the land, to the point where they had firm ground under their keels.

The operation succeeded. When the squadron sailed in

toward the island, the Imperial troops were drawn up in full battle order on the beach, with muskets and cannon; but the fire from the men-of-war put them to flight, and the following day the island surrendered. Before the departure from Lolland it was decided that the commander of the squadron, Henrik Vind, should be sent north around the Skaw with a handful of ships and sail down to the Elbe, where the fortresses of Glückstadt and Krempe were still holding out. The King cherished the vain hope that Henrik Vind could execute a thrust to the east from these fortresses while he himself landed on the opposite coast, a maneuver by which they might cut off the peninsula of Jutland with Wallenstein and his thirty thousand soldiers. The reconquest of Fehmern gave the King fresh courage, and on March 27th he sent Henrik Vind to the Elbe as squadron admiral aboard the *Dragon*. Up to now this name has misled the historians. However, reliable sources reveal that the ship had two names. The *Dragon* and the *Flying Fish* were one and the same vessel. In other words, Henrik Vind assumed command of the squadron on board the very ship whose captain until that moment had been Jens Munk. At the same time, it is obvious that Munk did not accompany the ship to the Elbe. On March 27th he must therefore have been deprived of his post as captain of the *Flying Fish* for reasons we do not know, and transferred to another of those ships remaining in the Baltic under the King's command. Which?

This question, too, can be answered by a careful study of the events. After Henrik Vind's departure, the King proceeded with the rest of the squadron toward Eckernförde, where again fortune was on his side. The Imperial garrison was defeated and the town taken. The flanks were covered. Now it was the turn of Kiel. This was a case of all or nothing: if the King succeeded in taking this city, he was only sixty miles from Glückstadt. Squeeze hard, and the pincers would close on Wallenstein.

At the beginning of April the royal squadron entered the

fjord at Kiel. Then things began to go wrong. In Kiel the enemy was prepared. The troops which had been set ashore were thrown back to the fjord, and tried to return swimming to the ships, which came under a rain of cannon balls. The *Lobster* suffered worst: the hull was struck by a number of shots between wind and water; musketeers fell dead around the King, and soon there was nothing for it but to sound the retreat. The master plan was shattered. The King left four ships at Fehmern, and on April 9th he himself sailed off to Copenhagen in the flagship *Lobster*.

We know the exact date of his arrival, for another well-known man was on board the ship as it glided into Krabbeløkke Creek. One scholar who has studied the Bremerholm accounts writes that the *Lobster* dropped anchor at Copenhagen on April 16th. *For up to that date maintenance was calculated for Jens Munk, who returned home with this ship, in all likelihood as a sick man.*

Jens Munk may have been wounded during the battle for Fehmern. If this is the case the fact of his being relieved as captain of the *Flying Fish* when that ship was made over to Henrik Vind is justified. Yet it seems hardly likely that they would have sailed for such a long time with a wounded captain. His dismissal at this point in time must surely be seen as a consequence of the King's earlier impatience with him. Munk had already had to make way for Henrik Vind once, and now the same thing was happening again. It may also well be that he had been wounded during the bloody battle at Kiel. This would explain why he was on the *Lobster* directly after the battle. At all events it is certain that during the seven days from April 9th, when the *Lobster* left Kiel Bay, to the 16th, when the frigate reached Copenhagen, Jens Munk and Christian IV were on board the same ship.

And here the story ends. In those early spring days, while the *Lobster* was sailing home across the Baltic, the King and the captain finally stood face to face. They resembled one another: dreamers and men of action combined like so many kings and so many captains. They were of about the same age, and both had passed their prime. On the voyage from Kiel to Copenhagen the King reached the age of fifty-one; in a few months Jens Munk would be fifty. Although the captain was the younger of the two, he was the older in experience. His fate is one which also awaits the King: wounded in war, as the King was to be; cuckolded, as the King was to be; a defeated man, as the King was to be. Had Christian IV no foreboding of this? Did he not detect with an instinctive uneasiness a reflection of his own weakness in this worn-out captain? And did he not have a preference for sleek men around him? After the Weser affair the King surely had no particular sympathy left for Munk. Munk had stooped too low to get those groceries. He is not a sleek man; the King is. There is something about this small captain which he cannot comprehend: his meekness, his mildness. Unlike other normal people, he does not throw his weight about, does not get drunk, does not brag about his exploits. This the King could only put down to arrogance, and it made him uneasy. Christian IV might have his jovial moments, but modesty was not in his style. He believed that history consists of achievements, victories, success. Deep down in his nature was a tendency to feel himself wronged, which easily turned to sudden violence, to brutal callousness. In victory he was like all despots: magnanimous and gracious. In adversity he became vindictive. Sixteen years after these events there was again trouble in Kiel Harbor. The King's squadron commander was now called Peder Galt. Peder Galt had orders to attack the Swedish fleet when it put out of the fjord. This occurred on July 30th, but Peder Galt did not attack. It could not be done, for the wind had changed. On his return, the King had to have a victim for his fury and frustration. He personally assembled a court-martial at Bremerholm. The judgment was a foregone conclusion. On August 31st the seventy-year-old and highly esteemed Captain Galt was dragged into the palace yard and beheaded, while Christian IV stood contentedly watching the scene from a window.

337

This he was capable of in 1644. How much more dangerous he must have been sixteen years earlier, before he had had to accept that honor, power, and grandeur were not to last, and that he too was open to defeat. The spring of 1628 marked the most critical period in his long reign. His allies had hoodwinked him. England, Holland, and the German princes were sniggering behind his back; he had allowed himself to be overrun by Tilly; before the eyes of assembled Europe he had run like a rabbit; his army was scattered and humiliated; half his country was under enemy control. And within his own camp it was no better. The Council of the Realm despised him; the nobility were working to unseat him; his subjects were spreading rumors that he had himself given his mercenaries orders to plunder Jutland. His grandiose plan for cutting off Wallenstein had just foundered at Kiel; and at about this same time he reached his fifty-first birthday. He had to face the fact that he was growing old. Spiteful tongues were whispering about Kirsten Munk and the young Rhinegrave. The sweet young daughters of the burghers no longer brought him the same consolation as before. Hot spiced punch now gave him a pain in the side.

This was the mood in which aboard the *Lobster* he now had to meet that wretched Captain Munk, who had lost him one of his best frigates complete with cannon and crew. And with all that, he had not even found the Anian Strait. How dared he stand there, white-haired, weak-sighted, and toothless, and reminding the King of shipwrecks, lawsuits, and money troubles, all things he particularly wanted to forget! The worst was that he seemed unaffected by all his failures, displaying a placid dignity. But let him not be too sure of himself. The King knew the spot where he was vulnerable. He had put pressure on it before. Peyrère states that Christian IV reproached Munk with having lost the lives of the sailors the King had entrusted to him by his mismanagement of the expedition to Hudson Bay. He is surely right. It was not even necessary to do it in so many words. A mere hint was enough.

It was enough for Munk, too. He was not too happy, either, about having the company of the King during that long journey home to Copenhagen. If the sight of Munk gave the King a sense of future misfortunes, meeting the King must have recalled for Munk those of the past. The thousands of sea miles he had put behind him for this man's sake! He had taken Elfsborg for him; he had captured Mendoza for him; he had put the King's initials on the Northwest Passage and called its straits by his name. He had risked his life to save the King's ships, kept his accounts and inventories, recruited his sailors and shipwrights. Now he had just been wounded for his sake. And for what? The King might have reinstated him in his rights after Elfsborg. The King might have passed over Ove Giedde. And now? Now it was too late. He had no illusions—he had wronged Peiter Isakson, he had gone too far on the Weser. He knew all this, but he also knew that the King's attacks on his leadership in Munk Haven were without foundation. He had done everything possible to save his company. It was not his fault that the *Unicorn* had had to be abandoned. Yet he *was* guilty. He *was* in the wrong. He no longer believed in conquest, power, and glory—that was the trouble. He had seen Man in his infinite weakness; he knew what it was to feel himself "a wild and forsaken bird." He had not recovered from that spring eight years ago when one after another of his men began to decompose while still alive. He could not call them together now to bear witness. Gone, all of them—gone like the *Unicorn*, gone like the *Lamprey*, everything faded away and gone. Except for him. He felt the awful guilt of the man who has survived. And now the King in his ill-temper reproached him with these losses. It was too much. Peyrère states that Munk gave the King a truculent answer. This sounds more than probable. Forgetting himself, the King raised his staff.

The chronicler reaches the end of his account. Peyrère had surely heard correctly. The King cannot be acquitted of the Frenchman's charge. One can convict him only on circum-

339

stantial evidence, but there is much, and it all points in the same direction. And here the story ends. Such was the accolade of knighthood that Jens Munk had dreamed of when he was young.

This was the end. On April 16th he arrived at Copenhagen, "probably as a sick man," and was borne out through the gate of Bremerholm and along the familiar road home to Pilestraede. He did not commit suicide, as his father had done on Dragsholm; but, like him, he died in disgrace.

4

What remained? Kathrine Adriansdatter remained. She married again, her old friend the weaver, and then disappeared into obscurity. Margrethe Tagesdatter remained. She also married again, in 1632, four years after her first husband's death. This time it was no degraded sea captain. Kristoffer Hansen was one of the right kind, "ready and cheerful," as he is called in a contemporary source—in brief, a businessman. He traded with Iceland, had a monopoly of Danish beer imports, became an alderman, burgomaster, member of the law commission, and was finally decorated. Margrethe Tagesdatter bore him three children, but only one survived: a girl called Else. She married the famous professor, Thomas Bartholin, in whose circle she met another gentleman of note, the secretary of the French embassy, Monsieur Isaac de la Peyrère. The professor's wife seems to have known the children of her mother's first husband. When she died in 1675, an elegant funeral service was held for her in St. Nicholas's Church. The sermon was afterward printed and the priest who wrote it was called Jens Jensen Munk. Was this Jens Munk's eldest son, who reached this advanced age as a humble servant of the Lord? If so, this is the only thing we know of him.

What remained? The second in line, Knud, died before the age of twenty and was buried in 1631 by his father's side. The

340

daughter Kathrine was also buried near her father; but that was not until 1686. She was married to the alderman Hans Madsen, and nothing more is known about her. Best known is the fate of the third son, who in 1616 was given the name Erik, because Jens Munk wanted to show the mighty noblemen that he had learned nothing and forgotten nothing. After the death of his cousin and namesake in Munk Haven, he was the only Munk to perpetuate the name. Like Kristoffer Hansen, he was a signatory to the protest of the thirty-two burghers against aristocratic privilege in 1659. He was a more peaceable man than his grandfather; his only weapon was a goose quill. Erik Munk became a brewer.

What remained? Anno Domini 1631: Gustavus Adolphus is triumphant. Christian IV feels old. Denmark goes into decline. In Copenhagen, the new quarter of the city, Christianshavn, which the King had founded in 1619, is being surveyed. The plots had been allocated on condition that the owners should build a "good town house" on their sites; and now, twelve years later, a group of officials was making the rounds to check whether the landlords had complied with the royal ordinance. A clerk compiled a list meticulously describing the various properties. This list has survived until today. Among the Copenhagen citizens who had received a plot in Christianshavn was Jens Munk. That was in 1619, immediately before his departure for Hudson Bay, when he still enjoyed a certain royal esteem; still had hopes of being able to establish himself as a merchant, realize his old dream of being his own master, with his own storerooms and his own cellar. Jens Munk had been given the corner site. His name appears on the clerk's inventory—the last time it appears in contemporary sources. He is entered as No. 19 on the list. In this case the clerk's description was simply: "Jens Munk's plot: waste ground, not built on."

Index

Index

Aalborg 44
Adriansdatter, Kathrine 148 183 313 319
Amundsen, Roald 227
Andersdatter, Karen 154 180
Andersen, Oluf 206 275
Angelibrand 101 102 103 104 105
Archangel 28 98 152-4 310
Arvedsen, Svend 208 231 232 251 273

Baffin, William 224
Bahia 51 56-7
Balfour, David 110 115 155
Bardsøn, Mogens 32
Barents Sea 27 76 77
Bartholomaeidatter, Anna 20 35 36 37 43-4 46
Bentsen, Jørgen 61
Ber, J. 34
Black Dog 126 130 134 137 138
Boshouwer, Marselis de 189 211 212 213 241 242 243 260 287
Bremerholm 108 109-12 148 193
Brockenhaus, Eiler 60
Brok, Hans 102 205 248 251-2 265 269
Button, Thomas 224
Bylot, Robert 224

Cabot, John 221
Cabot, Sebastian 221
Charisius, Jonas 85 86 87 88 102 180-1 187 192 202-3
Christensen, Frederik 43 180
Christian IV, King of Denmark and Norway 63-6 100-10 *passim* 125 130-43 *passim* 152-3 154 172 180 187-91 *passim* 198-206 *passim* 214 216-18 284-5 312-21 323-6 330-41. *See also* Frederiksen, Christian
Copenhagen 62-3 98

Daa, Jørgen 126-36 *passim* 140 144 148 154-78 *passim* 194 198-9 322
Danish Memorial Expedition (1964) 266-7 296 301-3
David 212 213 241
Davis, John 222
Digges Islands 245
Dove 22 39
Dragsholm 57 58
Duez, Duart 48 50
Duez, Miguel 48 50 51

Elfsborg 126-40
Eskimos 234 255

Flekkerø 174 175
Franklin, Sir John 226
Frederick II, King of Denmark
    23-4 40 61
Frederiksen, Christian (King
    Christian IV) 85-93
Fredrikstad 23 36 37 38
Friis, Christian 149
Frobisher Bay 230 247
Frobisher, Martin 221-2 230

Gabriel 177 178
Gerbrantzen, Jacob 46
Giedde, Ove 188-98 203-5 210-
    13 218 240-3 259-62 279-
    82 285-7
Gordon, William 10-11 205 206
    229 230 238 243-4 245 274
Greenland 73 75 92 229 302
Grubbe, Sivert 85 88
Gundersen, Bernt 186 187 192
Gustavus Adolphus, King of Swe-
    den 127 134-5 138 199 203

Hanneberg, Søren 33 34
Haresund 237-8 243
Hector 127 133-4 142 143 149
    154
Hendriksen, Jens 205 208 217
    245 277
Herring Ness 126 127 133 134
    135 152 154 204
Hore, John 221
Hudson, Henry 75 76 77 199 222
Hudson Bay, discovery of 202 222
Hudson Bay, expedition to,
    preparations for 196-210 213-
    17
    starts 217-19 227

reaches   Greenland   229;
    America 230; Hudson Strait
    232-40; Hudson Bay 245
wintering at Munk Haven 9-12
    248-59 262-79
Munk and two other survivors
    287-94
they sail from Munk Haven to
    Norway aboard *Lamprey* 294-
    301 303-8
Hunter 181
Hvid, Jens 75-6 98 261

Iceland 70 75 92
Isakson, Peiter 321-2

Jansen, Albert 48 54
Jensen, Rasmus 206 257 262 263-
    4 268 271
Jørgensen, Jens 208 231 251 277
Jupiter 155 159-68 170 177

Kalmar 12 125 132
Kalmar War 124-43
Karl IX, King of Sweden 127
    132
Kaspersen, Kasper 206 268 269
    270 272
Kildin 86 87 105 152 158 165
    169 175 176
Knaerød, Peace of (1613) 143 145
    149
Kolguev 82-3 96
Krabbeløkke Bay 112 114 124
    151 213

Lamprey
    siege of Elfsborg 128 142
    chosen for Hudson Bay 204
    expedition 217 218 228

missing 245-7
caught in ice 9-11
refloated after winter 291 324 325
La Rochelle 49 74
Leopard 133 177 178
Lindenow, Godske 73 75 93 126 317
Lonighem, Jan 184
Lübeck David 174 177

Madsen, Knud 102
Mansfield Island 245
Mendoza, Jan 149 154 155 158-69 172 173
Migomme, Prince of, *see* Boshouwer
Munk, Erik (Jens' father) 20-36 46 57-61 72
Munk, Erik (Jens' nephew) 206 273
Munk, Erik (Jens' son) 183 341
Munk, Jens
    journal 10-12 14-16 216 268-79
    character 16
    life 16-19 20
    boyhood (1579-88) 37-46; at Aalborg (1588-91) 44-5
    first sea voyage 47-54; his ship sunk (1592) 54-5
    his father's suicide (1594) 60-1
    return to Denmark (1598) 57
    constantly at sea (1600-5) 71-2
    sets up as merchant (1605) 72-3
    buys a share in a ship (1608) 75
    voyage to Novaya Zemlya (1609) 76-84; loss of ship 84; making a boat 93-6; journey to
    Archangel 96-8
    audience with King Christian IV 100-2
    second voyage to northeast (1610) 104-5
    sea captain in war with Sweden (1611) 126-44
    not ennobled 145-8
    married 148
    diplomatic errands (1613-14) 149-54
    pirate-hunting (1615) 155-72; and (1616) 173-8
    interest in whaling 152-3 181 182-7 192-3
    briefly in command of expedition to East Indies 187-8
    voyage in search of Northwest Passage (1619): *see* Hudson Bay, expedition to 196-308
    imprisoned on return to Norway (1620) 311-13
    returns home (1620) 313-14
    King displeased 314-17
    busy in King's service 318-21
    divorces Kathrine Andersdatter (1623) and remarries (1626) 319
    poor 321; out of favour with King 325
    death (1628) 326-40
Munk, Kirsten 90 180
Munk, Niels 20 72 103 152 153 194
Munkenaes 231

Navy, Royal Danish 112-24
Nolk, Anders 102 133

Northeast Passage 77 199
Northwest Passage 194-203 220-27
Novaya Zemlya 28 77 78 80 81 92-3 96 101
Nyborg, Peter 208 231 251 278

Olafsson, Jon 18 115 123 156 167 172-8 207 209
Olluffsen, Jan 205 207-8 217 265 272

Pedersøn, Hans 34 36
Petersen, Jan 133 206 248 251 273
Peyrère, Isaac de la 328-32
Philip II, King of Spain 52
Povlsen, Klavs 155 159 160

Ramel, Henrik 29 66-7 68-71 72
Raphael 135
Red Lion 181
Ribolde, Count 49 51 53 56 74
Rider 101 102 103
Roland of Flushing 48 54
Rut, John 221

San Pedro 171
Santa Maria 39 42
Schoubynacht 48 49 50 51 54 56
Sem, Johan 155
Señora de Rosario 171
Seven Years' War (Scandinavian) 22-3
Sinclair, Daniel 110 112 115 236
Skult, Rasmus 313 319 340

Slange, Niels 199
Spitsbergen 75 77 185 186 187 199
Stenger, Johan 102-3
Stygge, Movritz 9-10 12 207 231 265 274
Svale, Mogens 23-4

Tagesdatter, Margrethe 319 340
Thirty Years' War 323
Tømmerviken 169-71
Trolle, Børge 73-4 85
Trondhjem, Hans 181-2
Tucker, Thomas 156 157

Ulfeldt, Jacob 151
Ulfeldt, Mogens 142 143
Ungava Bay 243-4 245
Unicorn
  launched 73 103 176 177
  chosen for Hudson Bay 204-6
  expedition 9-11 217 218 219
  sunk 14 293

Vaden, James 186
van Bossen, Jan 48 54
Vardø 87 175
Vardøhus 22 77 101 104 152 169
Vibe, Mikkel 167 175 180 181 182 186 187 192
Victor 85-91 104 133 134 135 149 155 157 159-77
Vind, Christen 29 32 34
Vind, Henrik 326 334 335
Volske, David 206 259 262

Watson, John 205